Logic Tools for Programming

Logic Tools for Programming

Philip Pace and Larry Pace

DELMAR PUBLISHERS INC.®

NOTICE TO THE READER

Publisher does not warrant or guarantee any of the products described herein or perform any independent analysis in connection with any of the product information contained herein. Publisher does not assume, and expressly disclaims, any obligation to obtain and include information other than that provided to it by the manufacturer.

The reader is expressly warned to consider and adopt all safety precautions that might be indicated by the activities described herein and to avoid all potential hazards. By following the instructions contained herein, the reader willingly assumes all risks in connection with such instructions.

The publisher makes no representations or warranties of any kind, including but not limited to, the warranties of fitness for particular purpose or merchantability, nor are any such representations implied with respect to the material set forth herein, and the publisher takes no responsibility with respect to such material. The publisher shall not be liable for any special, consequential or exemplary damages resulting, in whole or in part, from the readers' use of, or reliance upon, this material.

Administrative Editor: Christina M. Gallagher
Composition: The Publisher's Network, Morrisville, PA

For more information, address Delmar Publishers Inc.
2 Computer Drive West, Box 15–015
Albany, New York 12212

Printed in the United States of America
Published simultaneously in Canada
by Nelson Canada,
A Division of International Thomson Limited

10 9 8 7 6 5 4

Library of Congress Cataloging-in-Publication Data

Pace, Philip, 1956–
  Logic tools for programming.

  Includes index.
  1. Electronic digital computers--Programming.
I. Pace, Larry, 1948–   . II. Title.
QA76.6.P325   1987   005.1   87–640
ISBN 0-8273-2583-5 (instructor's guide)
ISBN 0-8273-2582-7 (pbk.)

Table of Contents

Preface

As most experienced programmers are acutely aware, the key to good programming is not the language used but rather the elegance and sophistication of the logical structures. Before a good program can be written to accomplish a specific task, that task must be analyzed, and a logical solution to the problem must be developed. This textbook presents and describes the logic tools programmers use in that problem-solving process.

To a certain extent, programming is an art. However, there are specific communication requirements that must be met to convey a message from one person to another in the process of transforming a problem solution into a computer program. It is assumed in the computer industry that an entry-level person will know how a flowchart, or some other logic tool, functions and be able to use such tools to solve day-to-day programming assignments.

The Focus of This Book

The objective of this text is to provide the reader with the proper tools to solve any type of logic problem that he or she might encounter. The book offers detailed explanations of the seven logic tools most commonly used in the computer industry:

1. Flowcharts

2. Pseudocode

3. Hierarchy Charts

4. IPO Charts

5. Nassi-Shneiderman Charts

6. Warnier-Orr Diagrams

7. Structure Charts

A chapter is devoted to each of these tools. The text is language-independent to offer students and professors the utmost flexibility.

Why combine seven different logic tools into one textbook? Most textbooks on programming logic discuss one or two tools in comprehensive detail. The student is not exposed to alternate methods, and thus his or her knowledge of problem-solving techniques is limited. Upon entering the computer industry, the student will likely be exposed to one or more of these seven commonly used tools and should be familiar with each one.

Similarly, programming texts often discuss problem solving using one logic tool in the introductory chapters. The focus of the rest of the text is on learning a specific programming language. If the student does not fully understand the logic tool and problem-solving techniques from the beginning, he or she could have difficulty understanding the thought processes involved in designing computer programs. Not only does this make learning a programming language more difficult, it also creates problems as the student encounters one or more logic tools later in his or her programming career and is expected to be familiar with them.

In *LOGIC TOOLS FOR PROGRAMMING,* we have presented each of the seven logic tools in a comprehensive manner so that the student acquires sufficient knowledge to use whatever logic tool he or she encounters or finds most comfortable to use. This text is ideal for two types of readers. First, for students who have had no exposure to computers and the problem-solving process involved in programming, the book may be used separately or in conjunction with a programming language text. Second, for more experienced computing students or programmers who want exposure to alternative logic tools, this material is ideal for independent learning and reference.

Unique Features

The book was specifically designed for maximum flexibility. Chapter 1 presents data processing and programming fundamentals. The rest of the chapters are independent and may be studied in any order. If the instructor wishes to concentrate on three or four tools, the balance of the material may be covered in less depth or left for independent study or reference.

In Chapter 1, six problems are introduced which are revisited in each of the succeeding chapters. The problems are representative of the variety of tasks a student may encounter in his or her first job assignment in the computer industry. In each chapter detailed solutions to each of the problems are presented and discussed using that chapter's logic tool. These six problems allow the students to "learn by example" how a tool is implemented using realistic problems. They can concentrate on learning the tool without being required to learn new problems. They can also readily compare the various logic tools and draw upon their experience with one tool to learn another. The six problems cover the following concepts:

Leaves Versus Buy Option	Introduces the tool, covers decisions
Payroll	Calculations, repetitions
Health and Diet	Controlled repetition, interdependent calculations
Daily Sales	Control breaks, accumulators, repetition
House Construction	Nested repetition, calculations, multiple decisions
Personnel Statistics	Counters, multiple decisions, repetition

The amount of time spent on these six problems in each chapter may vary. The problems are intended to be used as a reference to emphasize the concepts introduced for each logic tool.

In addition to the "Big Six" problems, there are five to ten problems at the end of each chapter for students to solve. These problems are challenging and provide students with the chance to "test drive" the logic tool. After all, the only way a student can verify his or her understanding is to attempt some "hands-on" experience. We tried to make the problems as realistic as possible, and occasionally make an attempt at humor. Hopefully, our goal was achieved.

In addition to the seven logic tools discussed, there are three advanced topics presented in separate appendices at the end of the text. These topics are arrays (or tables), file updating, and sorting. Each of these appendices may be integrated into the textbook material at any time. Additional logic problems incorporating the new topic are included at the end of each appendix.

An instructor's guide is available to adopters and includes the following components for each chapter:

1. Solutions to multiple-choice questions

2. Solutions to fill-in-the-blank questions

3. Solutions to short-answer questions

4. Solutions to additional logic problems

5. Examination questions

In closing, we would like to take this opportunity to thank our reviewers: Beverly Bishausen, College of Du Page; Peter Irwin, Richland College; Gilbert Noble, Southwestern Community College; E. Gladys Norman, Linn-Benton Community College; Roger Kenneth Walter, Weber State College; Margaret Heard, East Central College; Jim Phillips, University of Kentucky; and Seth Hock, Columbus Technical Institute. The insightful and useful suggestions helped transform a rough and primitive manuscript into a not-so-primitive textbook.

Philip Pace and Larry Pace

Programming Logic

OBJECTIVES

After reading this chapter you should be familiar with:

- The concept of data processing

- Different types of computer programs

- The program development process

- The purpose and reasons for using a logic development tool

- Three program logic structures

- Concepts and philosophies to consider for program design

- The hierarchy of data and related data structures manipulated by computer programs

- Rules followed by computer programming languages while performing arithmetic operations

- Five general activities that occur in the majority of computer programs

- Verification of logic tool solution

- Seven logic tools discussed in this textbook and a general comparison of all seven

- The six problems that are solved in each succeeding chapter with a different logic tool

Introduction

In this modern society the computer has an impact on some aspect of everyone's daily life. Whether it involves depositing your paycheck through electronic funds transfer or flagging your tax return for audit by some vigilant computer, the computer will continue to be an integral part of your life. Some individuals view this as an unnecessary intrusion, and others have made a small fortune from their computer expertise. The objective of this book is not to make the reader wealthy, but to provide an education in computer programming logic.

Before we can discuss logic, we need to define some computer terminology and other technical jargon. Don't get the wrong impression; everything you need to know about computers and computer programs will not be covered in this short chapter. This chapter's purpose is to provide a general background for the reader who is not familiar with computers. If you have had experience with programming and how computers operate in general, you may wish to advance to the section entitled "Logic Tools" near the end of the chapter; if not, proceed with the general discussion of computer concepts.

What is Data Processing?

To define the term *data processing* (without the smug definition of "the processing of data"), two terms must be examined and explained: data and information. *Data* is raw facts or events that occur independently. Data by itself is not of much value. Its value is realized when the data has been collected and organized in a manner that is understandable or can be used to make decisions. The definition of *information* is data that has been processed. Using these definitions of data and information, let's define data processing. *Data processing* is the manipulation of data to provide information using a computer. With this definition in mind, the next few sections discuss computer programs and logic tools.

Computer Programs

The emphasis of this text is on how to use a computer to produce information. To tame and control this electronic wonder requires the use of a computer program. A computer program consists of a set of instructions given to a computer to perform some function.

Computer programs, also known as software, consist of two general types: system and application. System programs manage and control the actual hardware activities of the computer and the administration of other programs, such as communications between a terminal and the computer, or the translation of a program from human-readable form to machine-readable form. Applications programs are more concerned with the human inter-face to the computer. A computer user is an individual who requests computer resources for some purpose. The user may request that the current manual payroll system or inventory system be automated via computer. Most applications programmers view the user as a necessary evil, but without the user's requests for programs, a programmer would not have a job. An applications programmer writes the software needed to provide the information requested by the original end user.

Application programs are written for two types of data-processing environments: on-line and batch. On-line programs allow the computer user to retrieve or update data through a computer terminal. The biggest advantage of on-line processing is that the user can achieve results instantaneously. With batch processing this is not the case. A batch program runs periodically, which could be daily, weekly, monthly, or some other time frame. Data is collected (batched) and is run on user request. Its biggest disadvantage is that the user must wait for some time period for the desired information.

Program Development Process

When writing a computer program, the following series of steps must be followed:

1. **Problem Definition** This step normally identifies the general input and output desired (the reason for the program) and an idea of the processing steps required. Often this information is provided in what is referred to as a *program specification* or *narrative*.

2. **Identification of Desired Output** The output is the end result of the program. Generally, if a report is to be produced, a report layout is designed that identifies all the heading and field information to be printed. Refer to Figure 1.1 for a sample report layout.

3. **Inspection of Desired Input** Input items are usually the easiest to identify. These are the items that produce the output. This input can reside on several types of media such as tape, disk, and punched cards. The user is aware of the existing information and it then becomes the programmer's job to generate the requested output from this input.

4. **Develop an Algorithm or Method of Solution** This step is the one in which logic tools play a part. The programmer must map out the sequence of steps necessary to convert the input to the requested output. A good analogy is the concept of writing an English composition. Before actually writing the composition, a student will organize ideas using an outline. From this outline the student will expand statements to form sentences, paragraphs, and ultimately the completed composition. The same concept applies when writing a computer program. The programmer must identify and organize the processes needed to produce the desired results.

5. **Convert the Algorithm to a Computer Program** Once the programmer has developed an algorithm using some type of logic tool, this solution is then used to write a computer program in some specific language (BASIC, COBOL, FORTRAN, etc.). This process is known as *coding*.

6. **Test and Debug the Program** To determine if the program conforms to program specifications, sample data must be prepared and executed. Corrections can then be made where necessary.

```
              CHEAPO MANUFACTURING COMPANY
                  WEEKLY PAYROLL REPORT
                     APRIL 15, 19XX


EMPLOYEE NAME            HOURS      PAY       GROSS       FICA        NET
                        WORKED     RATE        PAY      WITHHELD     PAY

JIM JONES                 40        10       400.00      24.00      376.00
BONZO MARELLI             35        20       700.00      42.00      658.00
SANDY SMITH               20        15       300.00      18.00      282.00
```

Figure 1.1 Sample Report Layout

What is a Logic Tool?

So far you may be asking yourself, "Am I reading the wrong book? I thought this was a logic textbook." To answer your question, yes, this is a logic textbook and we are ready to define the term *logic tool*. Programming logic involves the detailed instructions needed to develop a computer program. A logic tool groups and represents these instructions by using symbols and/or other naming conventions. These symbols are meant to be programming language independent. This means that if you can write programs in one language and you want to learn another, the program development process outlined above is the same. Once you have learned a logic tool and are comfortable with that tool, there will be no need to change when you use a different programming language.

Program Logic Structures

A computer program may use any one or all three of the program logic structures: sequence, selection, and repetition. The normal execution of any high-level computer programming language is to proceed in order from the first instruction to the last until the program terminates (see Figure 1.2).

The logic structure represented by this program pattern is known as *sequence*. For the first computer programs written, this logic pattern was fine because those programs were not very sophisticated.

As the activities that a program was designed to perform became more complex, other conventions had to be incorporated into programs. This incorporation called for the development of more complex logic structures called *selection* and *repetition*. Under certain program conditions, other instructions in the program may need to be executed. Making this decision is known as selection and is concerned with evaluating a condition and determining if it is true or false. Look at Figure 1.3. If condition-1 is TRUE, Instruction 4 is executed; otherwise, Instruction 4 will never be executed.

As an example of selection, assume that you want to know how many people in your class are older than 21, you would ask each person in the class that question, and based on their response (yes or no) you accumulate statistics recording the number of students in the class over 21 and 21 or younger. Different programming languages utilize varying techniques to

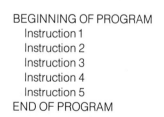

```
BEGINNING OF PROGRAM
   Instruction 1
   Instruction 2
   Instruction 3
   Instruction 4
   Instruction 5
END OF PROGRAM
```

Figure 1.2 Sequence Logic Structure

allow selection; some use line numbers, others use paragraph names or procedure names to segment program instructions and allow conditional branching to other instructions. Figure 1.4(a) illustrates branching. If condition-1 is TRUE, program control branches to the instructions after Paragraph-2.

Figure 1.4(b) accomplishes a similar goal as Figure 1.4(a) but in a different manner. The negative (NOT) side of condition-1 is tested. If TRUE, Instructions 3–5 are executed; if FALSE, program control proceeds to Instructions 6–8.

The ability to conditionally select which instructions to execute was a powerful program development, but it was not enough. Computers are incredibly fast and with this speed they can do repetitive functions flawlessly. The true power of a computer cannot be tapped unless a program has the ability to "loop back" or repeat sections of the program. This process is known as *iteration*. Figure 1.5 shows an example of this concept.

```
BEGINNING OF PROGRAM
    Instruction 1
    Instruction 2
    Instruction 3
    IF condition-1 THEN Instruction 4
    Instruction 5
    Instruction 6
END OF PROGRAM
```

Figure 1.3 Selection Logic Structure

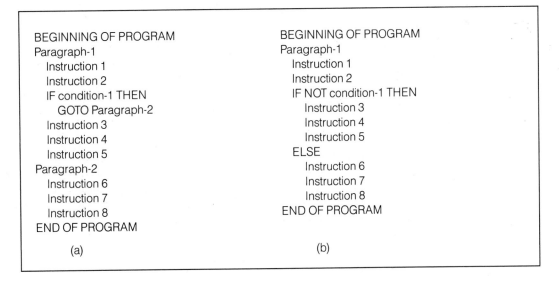

```
BEGINNING OF PROGRAM                BEGINNING OF PROGRAM
Paragraph-1                         Paragraph-1
    Instruction 1                       Instruction 1
    Instruction 2                       Instruction 2
    IF condition-1 THEN                  IF NOT condition-1 THEN
        GOTO Paragraph-2                    Instruction 3
    Instruction 3                           Instruction 4
    Instruction 4                           Instruction 5
    Instruction 5                       ELSE
Paragraph-2                                 Instruction 6
    Instruction 6                           Instruction 7
    Instruction 7                           Instruction 8
    Instruction 8                   END OF PROGRAM
END OF PROGRAM
        (a)                                     (b)
```

Figure 1.4 Two Alternate Selection Logic Structures

```
BEGINNING OF PROGRAM
   Instruction 1
   Instruction 2
   Instruction 3
   Instruction 4
   Instruction 5
   GOTO Instruction 1
END OF PROGRAM
```

Figure 1.5 An Endless Loop Repetition Structure

```
BEGINNING OF PROGRAM
   Instruction 1
   IF condition-1 THEN GOTO END OF PROGRAM
   Instruction 2
   Instruction 3
   Instruction 4
   Instruction 5
   GOTO Instruction 1
END OF PROGRAM
```

Figure 1.6 Using the Selection Logic Structure to Avoid Endless Repetition

Figure 1.5 is the same as Figure 1.2 except a new instruction has been added after instruction 5, GOTO Instruction 1. This is an unconditional instruction that instructs program control to branch back to Instruction 1 and start the entire process all over again. But now we have another problem: the program represented in Figure 1.5 is an endless program; there are no conditions set up to indicate when the program should stop running. This is where the selection logic pattern comes to our assistance. Figure 1.6 demonstrates the solution to this problem. If condition-1 is TRUE, then program control branches to END OF PROGRAM and program execution ceases.

A preferred way to represent repetitive functions is with a WHILE or REPEAT loop (see Figure 1.7). With the WHILE iteration control structure, Instructions 1–4 will be repeatedly executed while condition-1 is TRUE. With the REPEAT loop structure, Instructions 1–6 will be continually executed while condition-1 is FALSE.

```
BEGINNING OF PROGRAM              BEGINNING OF PROGRAM
  WHILE condition-1                 REPEAT
    Instruction 1                     Instruction 1
    Instruction 2                     Instruction 2
    Instruction 3                     Instruction 3
    Instruction 4                     Instruction 4
  END OF WHILE LOOP                   Instruction 5
END OF PROGRAM                        Instruction 6
                                    UNTIL condition-1
```

Figure 1.7 Preferred Repetition Structure that Avoids Use of GOTO

Program Design

We have discussed some of the activities performed in computer programs, and now let's consider the factors that should be included in program design. Computer programs can become quite large and complex, but the human mind more often works with relatively small pieces of information. Because of the limitations of the human mind and to alleviate the possibility of error, problems should be divided into smaller, more manageable units.

In computer programs the separate units or activities into which the problem is segmented are referred to as *modules*. The reasoning is sound: develop a program one module at a time, test each module for functional accuracy and validity, and then develop the next module. With this building-block approach, each module should perform correctly and the problem is solved one step at a time. Modules may need to be changed during the development of the program. A complex module is rarely 100% correct the first time it is written. The process of enhancing and changing the activities within a module before the finished module is complete is known as *stepwise refinement*. This modular design concept is discussed in detail in Chapters 4 and 8. The structured or modular program design approach makes the programming task an easier and more flexible process for the programmer.

Now that the individual pieces have been separated into correctly performing modules, these modules must be integrated. One module must be identified as the "boss" module that will command all of the previously developed modules. This program design technique is called *top-down design* or *structured programming*. The concept is relatively simple: separate a program into single-entry, single-exit modules that perform one general function. These subordinate modules are called by a "boss" module that orchestrates all activities within the program.

Data Structures

As discussed earlier, one of the main objectives of a computer program is to convert input data into some sort of output. Most often this output is incorporated into a report for user reference. A program temporarily places this data into storage locations referred to as *variables*. Variables are defined by the programmer and must follow the rules of the particular language used. A programmer tries to give meaningful names to variables. An example of a variable name to store the hourly pay rate of an employee would be PAY.RATE (in BASIC), PAY-RATE (in COBOL), and PAY__RATE (in Pascal).

In addition to naming a variable, the programmer specifies the type of data that variable can store. Data types are of two main categories: alphanumeric (or character) and numeric. A data variable that is defined to store character information can accept and manipulate any character represented on the keyboard. A variable named STREET.ADDRESS can store values such as 311 CARR AVENUE or 152 NORMAN DRIVE, APT. #393. Calculations (multiplication, division, subtraction, addition) cannot be performed on character-type variables. Numeric-type variables can store integer (whole number) or real-number (fractional) values. The PAY.RATE variable previously discussed can store values such as 10 or 12.56.

A technique to define the type and length of data variables used by a logic tool is known as a *data dictionary*. The data dictionary contains a list of variables and their characteristics used within the logic tool solution. The following is a sample data dictionary listing:

```
NAME            C(20)
STREET          CCCCCCCCCCCCCCC or C(15)
CITY            C(15)
STATE           CC
ZIP.CODE        NNNNN
PAY.RATE        NN.NN
```

There are separate variable names, such as NAME and STREET, followed by the type of variable (C for character, N for numeric). Notice how NAME is defined as C(20). When a type character is followed by a number in parentheses, that number specifies how often the character is repeated. The maximum length of a value stored in the NAME variable is 20 characters. With numeric variables such as PAY.RATE, the type of symbol used is N. Observe how the decimal capability is shown with a decimal point in the appropriate place. The maximum value that can be stored in PAY.RATE is 99.99. The data dictionary keeps all variable definitions in one place to allow for convenient review when referenced in the logic tool solution.

Hierarchy of Data

To be meaningful and to facilitate input/output operations in a program, data is grouped into four different categories. These categories are presented from the least inclusive to the most inclusive:

1. **Character or byte**—any key represented on a computer keyboard: A–Z, 0–9, and special symbol keys, i.e. #, $, !, etc.

2. **Field or variable**—a group or collection of logically related characters

3. **Record**—a group or collection of logically related fields

4. **File**—a group or collection of logically related records

Figure 1.8 illustrates all of the terms defined above. This figure shows sample data that could be collected to maintain a mailing list. A character is information in any one of the fields, whether it is the J in Joseph in the first record or the 1 in the 123 Apple Lane field. A field (or variable) is the collection of characters used to store data values. Any of the individual columns, such as NAME, ADDRESS, or CITY, are field names that can store only one value at a time. A record groups fields together; NAME, ADDRESS, CITY, STATE, ZIP CODE are all part of a record. It is easy for programs to deal with records, because all the variables in that record can be referred to collectively. A file consists of all the records. In our example, there are six records in the file.

NAME	ADDRESS	CITY	STATE	ZIP CODE
Joseph Smith	123 Apple Lane	Riverside	CA	23412
Larry Boscoe	9045 Pecan Street	Paris	TX	73458
Shirley Colson	541 Beach Street	Gaithersburg	MD	20760
Maria Landers	15701 Norman Drive	Rockville	FL	63097
Jason Fielding	545 Jasper Lane	New York	NY	76109
Donald Duckling	7632 Disney Lane	Orlando	FL	65789

Figure 1.8 Illustration of the Hierarchy of Data

Arithmetic Operations

There are five arithmetic functions that can be performed on a computer system: addition, subtraction, multiplication, division, and exponentiation (raising a number to a power). Because of this mathematical capability, many people refer to a computer as a giant calculator, which is not a bad description. One of the computer's greatest attributes is its ability to calculate rapidly. For a programmer to gain access to this remarkable ability, he or she must be aware of the order in which the computer performs arithmetic operations. Most computers evaluate mathematical operations in the following order of precedence (the symbol that this text uses to represent an operation appears to the right of the operation):

1. Parentheses ( )

2. Exponentiation   ^

3. Multiplication/Division   * /

4. Addition/Subtraction   + −

The computer begins the evaluation of a mathematical equation at the right of the equal sign, scanning the symbols and calculating intermediate results in left-to-right order. The final result on the right-hand side of the equal sign will replace the previous value stored in the variable named on the left-hand side of the equal sign. The arithmetic operators that are on the same level (such as multiplication and division) are calculated on the basis of which is encountered first. Let's look at an example: Assume that there are three variables named A, B, and C which have the following values:

$$A = 10; B = 5; C = 15$$

They are inserted into this equation:

$$G = (A + B) / C * 2 \wedge 2 / 4$$

The first step is to plug the values into the variables and rewrite the equation.

$$G = (10 + 5) / 15 * 2 \wedge 2 / 4$$

Beginning at the equal sign and scanning from left to right, the equation is evaluated in this order:

1. $(10 + 5) = 15$ New equation: $G = 15 / 15 * 2 \wedge 2 / 4$
2. $2 \wedge 2 = 4$ New equation: $G = 15 / 15 * 4 / 4$
3. $15 / 15 = 1$ New equation: $G = 1 * 4 / 4$
4. $1 * 4 = 4$ New equation: $G = 4 / 4$
5. $G = 1$

Program Activities

A program is written with some particular purpose or goal in mind. This section discusses some of the activities that could occur in a program, such as:

1. Accept and edit input from a computer screen or other device

2. Generate a simple report

3. Summation through counters and accumulators

4. Generate a report with control breaks

5. Update a file or database

Accept and Edit Input

For a program to function it needs to receive data from some external source. In most cases, program input is keyed in directly from the computer keyboard in response to screen prompts. Examine Figure 1.9. This is an input screen for Cheapo Manufacturing Company.

Notice the three fields EMPLOYEE NAME, PAY RATE, and HOURS WORKED. The program will accept direct input from the user as responses are typed into each of the underscored fields. The user has direct interaction with the program; that is, the program cannot proceed until the user types in the appropriate information.

Input data can also be captured through a data entry or keypunch operator. The data entry operator works with a screen similar to the one shown in Figure 1.9, but the input is written via machine directly to magnetic disk or magnetic tape in a prescribed record format. A

```
             CHEAPO MANUFACTURING COMPANY
                PAYROLL INPUT SCREEN


    EMPLOYEE NAME:  _____


    PAY RATE:  __.__


    HOURS WORKED:  __._
```

Figure 1.9 Sample Input Screen

record with three fields would be created in our example. A program will read the data from this disk or tape storage and no other interaction occurs. For some businesses this method may be more practical because data entry operators' typing skills are usually better than those of the average user. Therefore, a program, which can execute at faster speeds than a human can type, is used in a more efficient manner.

There is one major problem with input captured from humans: there is a good chance that the data could be keyed in error. For this reason, a program must perform what is referred to as the *editing process*. A program can ensure that the data entered adheres to the data type definition for each variable. For example, if a variable such as HOURS WORKED is defined as a numeric type, the program should only allow the characters 0–9 to reside in that variable. Each numeric input field must be edited to ensure that characters such as A–Z or other special characters are not stored in that field. If that situation occurs, the data value should be flagged as an error. Character variables are harder to edit because by definition they are designed to store any character. The editing process cannot ensure that the value entered in the variable is correct, such as misspelling a name or address. The editing process can only check to see if the values entered for a variable are valid in a limited way: if a variable is set up to store only numeric data then that is all the program will permit to be stored there.

Generate a Simple Report

To understand the meaning of a simple report, let's examine the principal activities of a program. Basically, a program can be broken down into three main activities: input, process, and output. The input activity involves reading or accepting data and then editing that data. The process activity takes the input data and massages it through calculations or transformation of the input variables.

The main function of this activity is to ready the input or transformed variables for the output activity. Whether that involves creating a report, a new file, or updating an existing file. The last activity, output, will receive the variables from the process activity and generate records for reports or files. A simple report program reads input data, performs a few calculations or other rudimentary activities, and lists most of the input variables with the other new variables created during the process section of the program. An example of a program to generate a simple report is a program that takes the data entered from the screen in Figure 1.9 and produces the report shown in Figure 1.1.

Summation Through Counters or Accumulators

Since a computer can perform repetitive functions so quickly, a program activity that occurs often is the process of counting or accumulating some type of information. This requirement has identified the need for two functions to be conducted by a numeric variable: counting and accumulating.

A counter variable will be incremented by a constant value through the looping process of the program. For example, assume that you want to count the number of records your program has read. The program instructions to do this would be:

```
WHILE condition-1 THEN
    READ INPUT.RECORD
    RECORDS.READ = RECORDS.READ + 1
    .
    .
    .
END OF WHILE LOOP
```

The above program instructions add 1 to a variable named RECORDS.READ and set that result equal to the same variable name RECORDS.READ. You are thinking algebraically that does not compute, but remember, the result to the right of the equal sign replaces the previous value stored in the variable to the left of the equal sign. What is actually being done to the variable RECORDS.READ is that it is being incremented by a constant value of 1. So when condition-1 is FALSE and the WHILE loop stops executing, the variable RECORDS.READ will contain the number of records that were read.

An accumulator variable works similarly to a counter variable. The only difference is that an accumulator variable is incremented during the looping process by a variable containing different values. To provide an example of an accumulator requires a slight modification to the earlier example. Assume that you want to accumulate the total gross payroll figure for all of the employees read and processed. This example would contain:

```
WHILE condition-1 DO
    READ NAME, HOURS.WORKED, PAY.RATE
    GROSS.PAY = HOURS.WORKED * PAY.RATE
    TOTAL.GROSS.PAY = TOTAL.GROSS.PAY + GROSS.PAY
    .
    .
    .
END OF WHILE LOOP
```

The program is reading in a record that consists of three fields: NAME, HOURS.WORKED, and PAY.RATE. The next instruction calculates the GROSS.PAY by multiplying HOURS.WORKED by PAY.RATE. TOTAL.GROSS.PAY is an accumulator variable that sums all of the individual GROSS.PAY amounts calculated for each record. This illustrates the main difference between accumulators and counters: the accumulator increases by a variable amount and the counter increases by a constant amount.

Generate a Report with Control Breaks

This function is very similar to generating a simple report. In this case, data is also being processed in a specific order so that report pages can be produced based on a specific grouping of a major data item; that is, when a major data item changes, such as department code, a new page of the report is started and a *control break* has occurred. The program logic is set up to check the major data item, or controlling field, to determine when a change in that field has occurred. This is done by comparing the item to the previous control field value. A sample of a report which has been generated using control breaks is shown in Figure 1.10. In this case, the control field is the department number. A change in the department number read causes the control break shown.

There is always a requirement that must be satisfied before control breaks can be used in report generation. The file or input data used to generate report information must be sorted (i.e., put in order) in a sequence, using the appropriate control field or fields. This sorted order is the mechanism which permits program logic to test for a control break condition and begin a new page or skip a few lines to separate control break information.

```
                 CHEAPO MANUFACTURING COMPANY
                    WEEKLY PAYROLL REPORT
                     FOR DEPARTMENT 10
                      APRIL 15, 19XX


  EMPLOYEE NAME     HOURS      PAY      GROSS        FICA        NET
                    WORKED     RATE      PAY       WITHHELD      PAY

   MEGAN PACER        40        10      400.00      24.00      376.00
   JEFF PACEO         35        20      700.00      42.00      658.00
   LAURA PACESTEIN    20        15      300.00      18.00      282.00



                 CHEAPO MANUFACTURING COMPANY
                    WEEKLY PAYROLL REPORT
                     FOR DEPARTMENT 20
                      APRIL 15, 19XX


  EMPLOYEE NAME     HOURS      PAY      GROSS        FICA        NET
                    WORKED     RATE      PAY       WITHHELD      PAY

   ZACHARY PACER      40        20      800.00      48.00      752.00
   JIM PACEWAX        30        20      600.00      36.00      564.00
   KAREN PACEOLLI     25        20      500.00      30.00      470.00
```

Figure 1.10 Example of Report with a Control Break

Update a File or Database

Updating is the computer process for *maintaining* a file or a database. Maintaining is the term for adding, changing, or deleting data items from a file or database. Updating is a process that is performed by a specific type of program designed just for maintaining databases. Update programs can be very complex and are usually written by applications programmers with several years of experience. The three types of maintenance activities (adding, changing, and deleting data) should be explained so the update process can be more easily understood.

Adding data items to a file is one of the three types of maintenance activities in the update process. This activity allows the user to put new items in a file or database when these items become available or known to the user. Adding data to a file may require a complete rewrite, sorting, or reindexing of a file. An example of the adding function is the process that occurs when a new employee is added to a company payroll master file. All required data items related to that employee's payroll record are added to the file or database so the employee will be paid during the next payroll-processing period. Without this add capability, no new employee records could be placed on the payroll master file. Changing existing data items on a file or a database is another one of the maintenance activities in the update process. As the word "changing" implies, this activity permits the user to change items in a file or a database once they have been added. Using the payroll master file example, one can understand what the change function really means. Without the ability to change fields such as hourly pay rate or job title, employee records on the master file could not reflect actions such as promotions.

Deleting existing data items from a file or a database is the third of the maintenance activities in the update process. This activity is the opposite of the adding function because it removes data items from the file or database when these items are no longer needed or current. Again using the payroll master file example, this function would be performed when it became necessary to remove an employee's pay record from the payroll master file. Without this capability, unwanted or unused data items would remain in a file or database forever.

> **NOTE:**   Some important advanced topics are not discussed in this chapter but have been incorporated into three appendices at the end of this book: file processing, arrays or table handling, and sorting.

Verification of Logic Tool Solution

In the previous section the general activities found in a computer program were outlined. As mentioned earlier the emphasis of this textbook is to provide the reader with the fundamentals of seven different logic tools. This should be the starting point for all computer programs. Use one of these logic techniques to solve the problem and then convert it into a computer program. But how will you know if your logic solution functions correctly? The ultimate verification of any logic tool occurs when it is converted to a computer program and executed on a computer, but there are steps to test a logic solution before that stage. This process is known as *logic tool walkthrough*. (There are also program walkthroughs, but that is not the concern of this text.) After you have completed your logic tool solution you must verify it for accuracy. On a separate piece of paper, list all variables identified in your solution. Leave room to write under each variable name. Begin with the first symbol in your solution and "walk through" all instructions. If a symbol asks for variables to be read, plug in some actual values for the variables and write them under the listed variable names. Remember, each variable can only store one value at a time. Proceed through the actual logic of the program, changing the contents of the variables as instructed by the logic tool. If the solution uses the repetitive logic structure, repeat the process using different data values.

A question that is often asked is, "How do I know what values to plug in when I'm walking through my logic solution?" Try expected and extreme values; your objective is to attempt to make your solution function incorrectly. If your program is testing for specific values or ranges of values, try values within that range and those falling outside the range and determine how the solution functions. The more thorough your testing for errors in logic solutions at the beginning stages, the easier the testing of your actual program will be in later stages.

Logic Tools

The authors have identified the prevailing logic tools used in the academic and business communities. This textbook is divided into individual chapters devoted to each logic tool.

The logic tools are:

Flowchart—Chapter 2

Pseudocode—Chapter 3

Hierarchy Chart—Chapter 4

IPO Chart—Chapter 5

Nassi-Shneiderman Chart—Chapter 6

Warnier-Orr Diagram—Chapter 7

Structure Chart—Chapter 8

Each chapter discusses in detail the rules and guidelines associated with that particular logic tool. The chapters are designed to be totally independent; you can choose the tool of interest and read only that chapter without reading the other chapters first.

Comparison of the Seven Logic Tools

Six general categories have been identified to use as a basis of comparison for the seven logic tools. The ratings are based on a scale of 1 (poor) to 5 (excellent). The following is a brief description of each category:

Ease of use This is the general complexity of the logic tool: the amount of time required to learn the rules and requirements of the particular tool and the degree of flexibility available when modifying the tool.

Conciseness This is the degree to which the components of the tool stand alone. If the tool combines facets of other logic tools to provide a complete problem solution, then the tool is less concise. For example, the Nassi-Shneiderman logic tool uses pseudocode and some features of flowcharting.

Structure This is the number of symbols used by a particular logic tool and the complexity of relating these symbols in a solution.

Documentation To decide the merits of a logic tool as support for program documentation, ask this question: When a program needs to be modified, would the details of the solution be easier to comprehend by reading the logic tool or the actual program?

Readability For moderately complex problems the solution should fit on one or two pages and not extend over three or more pages. If the solution requires several pages, it becomes difficult for the reader to follow the logic.

Modularity This is the level to which the solution is divided into succinct, clear modules. Some logic tools are too detail-oriented to segment different problem activities into related modules.

Figure 1.11 provides a general comparison of the seven logic tools.

	Flowchart	Pseudocode	IPO Chart	Hierarchy Chart	Nassi-Shneiderman Chart	Warnier-Orr Diagram	Structure Chart
Ease of Use	3	5	5	4	4	4	4
Conciseness	5	5	5	3	4	4	3
Structure	3	5	4	4	4	3	4
Documentation	3	3	4	5	4	4	5
Readability	3	4	4	4	3	3	4
Modularity	2	3	3	5	4	5	5

Rating Scale: 5 —Excellent
4 —Good
3 —Average
2 —Fair
1 —Poor

Figure 1.11 Comparison of Seven Logic Tools

The "Big Six" Problems

In support of chapter independence, six problems have been selected to assist you in the learning process. These problems are designed to put into practice the concepts discussed earlier in this chapter. A detailed solution to all six problems is presented in each of the following chapters. This facilitates learning the logic tool in each chapter and saves you from being required to learn a new set of problems with each tool. These problems can be used as a frame of reference. If you are familiar with another logic tool, you can briefly review the "big six" solutions for that tool, learn a new logic tool, and drawing from previous experience with the first logic tool, compare the differences between the techniques. Conversely, if you have no experience with any logic tool, these six problems will facilitate the learning process as you can readily compare the solutions between different logic tools as you learn a new tool.

The "big six" problems are not designed as required reading for each chapter. They are there as a reference and an instrument for learning reinforcement. If you understand the explanation presented in the chapter and are ready to solve additional problems at the end of the chapter for that new logic tool, it may not be necessary for you to read through each one of the "big six" solutions.

What are the "big six" problems? Here is a list of the problems and the concepts presented within each:

Problem 1—Lease Versus Buy	Introduction to tool, decisions
Problem 2—Payroll	Calculations, repetition
Problem 3—Health and Diet	Controlled repetition, interdependent calculations
Problem 4—Daily Sales	Control breaks, accumulators, and repetition
Problem 5—House Construction	Nested repetition, calculations, and multiple decisions
Problem 6—Personnel Statistics	Counters, multiple decisions, and repetition

The next few pages present a problem description and sample report format for each of the six problems. They are presented at this time for convenience. In each individual chapter the problem description is restated but the sample report format is not. If you need to refer back to the sample report formats, they can be easily located in one place.

▶ Problem 1—Lease Versus Buy ◀

Ajax Manufacturing Company has the option to purchase outright or lease (with an option to buy at lease-end) a computer system to aid in its business operations. If Ajax purchases the system for $10,000, it will finance the full amount for four years at a 10% interest rate.

> **NOTE:**   Simple Interest (I) = Principal (P) × Rate (R) × Time Period (T).

If Ajax leases the equipment for four years and decides to purchase at lease-end, the monthly cost will be $250 with a final payment of $3000. Which option should Ajax choose in order to minimize the total cost of the computer system? The problem solution should satisfy varying lease versus buy input information.

SAMPLE REPORT FORMAT:

```
            LEASE VERSUS BUY ANALYSIS
         FOR AJAX MANUFACTURING COMPANY
                COMPUTER SYSTEM


   TOTAL COST FOR THE PURCHASE OPTION    = $NNN,NNN.NN

   TOTAL COST FOR THE LEASE-BUY OPTION   = $NNN,NNN.NN

   THE RECOMMENDED OPTION IS _____ OPTION
```

► Problem 2—Payroll ◄

Easymoney Inc. desires to generate their current manual payroll via computer. The information collected every payroll period includes the employee social security number, pay rate, hours worked, and total other deductions. The payroll department would like a report listing these items: employee social security number, hours worked, pay rate, gross pay, FICA withheld (6.13% of gross pay), federal tax withheld (20% of gross pay), total other deductions, and net pay.

SAMPLE REPORT FORMAT:

```
                        EASYMONEY INC.
                        PAYROLL REPORT
```

SOC SEC NUMBER	HOURS WORKED	PAY RATE	GROSS PAY	FICA WITH	FED TAX WITH	OTHER DEDUCT	NET PAY
CCC-CC-CCCC	NN.N	NN.NN	NNNN.NN	NNN.NN	NNN.NN	NNN.NN	NNNN.NN
CCC-CC-CCCC	NN.N	NN.NN	NNNN.NN	NNN.NN	NNN.NN	NNN.NN	NNNN.NN
CCC-CC-CCCC	NN.N	NN.NN	NNNN.NN	NNN.NN	NNN.NN	NNN.NN	NNNN.NN

▶ Problem 3—Health and Diet ◀

Bedford Waistwatchers Association requests that a program be written to motivate members to stay on their diet and show the cost savings that can result from a change in diet. One of the staple diet items recommended is yogurt. If a member follows the Association diet strictly, a large amount of yogurt can be consumed over a short period of time. The cost effectiveness of buying yogurt or making yogurt at home should be evaluated. If a monetary savings can be realized by making yogurt at home versus buying it at the store, how many cups of yogurt must be produced to achieve this savings? The data needed to provide an analysis is store cost of yogurt per cup, cost of yogurt maker if made at home, cost of home ingredients per cup, and number of cups. An analysis should show the home cost, store cost, and savings or loss per cup.

```
SAMPLE REPORT FORMAT:


              BEDFORD WAISTWATCHERS ASSOCIATION
                   DIET BREAKEVEN ANALYSIS

STORE COST OF YOGURT PER CUP:       $N.NN
HOME COST OF INGREDIENTS PER CUP:   $N.NN
COST OF YOGURT MAKER:               $NN.NN
NUMBER OF CUPS:                     NNN


CUP          HOME COST        STORE COST        SAVINGS/LOSS

NNN          $NNN.NN          $NNN.NN           $NNN.NN

NNN          $NNN.NN          $NNN.NN           $NNN.NN

NNN          $NNN.NN          $NNN.NN           $NNN.NN

  .              .                .                 .

  .              .                .                 .

  .              .                .                 .

NNN          $NNN.NN          $NNN.NN           $NNN.NN
```

▶ Problem 4—Daily Sales ◀

Vidal Blass is the owner of Obnoxious Telephone Sales. Vidal has had up to 20 employees solicit sales via telephone on a specific day. Vidal would like to produce a sales summary report at the end of each business day to determine which salespeople generate the most revenue. Employees make a phone sale, write the sales information down on a receipt with their name and the total sale, and place the receipt in a bin shared by all of the employees. At the end of the day, all of the receipts are gathered and the summary report produced by entering the name and sales amount from each receipt. The first activity the computer will perform is to sort all input records in name order. (Assume that no two salespeople have the same name.) The sales summary will list the total sales by each name and the grand total sales for the day's business activities.

SAMPLE REPORT FORMAT:

```
                    OBNOXIOUS TELEPHONE SALES
                      SALES SUMMARY REPORT

            SALESPERSON NAME                 TOTAL SALES

            CCCCCCCCCCCCCCCCCCCC             $NNNN.NN

            CCCCCCCCCCCCCCCCCCCC             $NNNN.NN

                      .                          .

                      .                          .

                      .                          .

            CCCCCCCCCCCCCCCCCCCC             $NNNN.NN


            GRAND TOTAL SALES:    $NNNNN.NN
```

▶ Problem 5—House Construction ◀

Well-Bilt Homes Inc. would like you to design a program which enables builders to calculate home building costs based on prospective room sizes. This program is interactive; it allows the user to input the number of rooms desired and the individual room dimensions (length and width only). The building cost per square foot is based on the following:

1000 square feet or less	$60 per square foot
1001–2000 square feet	$50 per square foot
More than 2000 square feet	$40 per square foot

Develop the logic to compute the building cost of the house.

SAMPLE REPORT FORMAT:


```
                    WELL-BILT HOMES INC.
                    BUILDING COST REPORT

            NUMBER OF ROOMS   -- NN

            ROOM              ROOM              ROOM SQUARE
            LENGTH            WIDTH             FOOTAGE

              NN                NN                  NNNN
              NN                NN                  NNNN
              NN                NN                  NNNN
              NN                NN                  NNNN


            TOTAL SQUARE FOOTAGE OF HOUSE:    NNNNN

            COST PER SQUARE FOOT:             $NNN.NN

            TOTAL COST OF HOUSE:              $NNNNNNN.NN
```

► Problem 6—Personnel Statistics ◄

The chairman of the board of Eldorado Enterprises Inc. has requested a report from the Personnel Department that will show various types of information about the company's work force. This report should provide the following:

1. The total number of males and females (SEX CODE = M for males, F for females)

2. The total number of employees by the following age categories (BIRTHDAY YEAR)
   a. less than 21
   b. 21–30
   c. 31–40
   d. 41–50
   e. 51–60
   f. 61–70
   g. over 70

3. The total number of people who have been with the company for 10 years or more (SENIORITY CODE = 3, 4, or 5)

4. The total number of engineers (OCCUPATION CODE = 7) in the company

SAMPLE REPORT FORMAT:

```
                      ELDORADO ENTERPRISES INC.
               STATISTICAL WORKFORCE ANALYSIS REPORT

TOTAL NUMBER OF MALES:           NNNNN

TOTAL NUMBER OF FEMALES:         NNNNN

TOTALS BY AGE CLASSIFICATIONS:
      LESS THAN 21     --   NNNN
      21-30            --   NNNN
      31-40            --   NNNN
      41-50            --   NNNN
      51-60            --   NNNN
      61-70            --   NNNN
      OVER 70          --   NNNN

TOTAL NUMBER OF EMPLOYEES WITH COMPANY OVER 10 YEARS   --   NNNN

TOTAL NUMBER OF ENGINEERS   --   NNNN
```

The "big six" problems are solved for the logic tool discussed in each of the succeeding chapters. After being introduced to a new logic tool in the first part of each chapter, the solved problems allow you to "learn by example" how the concepts are implemented with actual problems. Since you are familiar with the problems, concentrate on learning the logic tool. The authors hope this approach will benefit you in understanding the logic tools presented in future chapters.

SUMMARY

You have just completed the chapter that sets the stage for the rest of this textbook. It is time well spent to briefly review key chapter topics.

Data processing is the manipulation of data to provide information using a computer. A computer program consists of a set of instructions given to a computer to perform some function. There are two types of computer programs: application and system. When writing a computer program there are six steps to follow:

1. Problem definition

2. Identification of desired output

3. Inspection of desired input

4. Developing an algorithm or method of solution

5. Converting the algorithm to a computer program

6. Testing and debugging the program

Programming logic involves the detailed instructions needed to develop a computer program. A logic tool groups and represents these instructions by using symbols and/or other naming conventions which are programming language independent. Once you have learned and are comfortable with a logic tool, there is no need to change tools when you use a new programming language. There are three program logic structures: sequence, selection, and repetition. When designing a program it is important to divide the program into manageable units that perform a specific function. For computer programs the separate units or activities of a problem are referred to as modules. Segmenting programs into independent units (or modules) is referred to as structured or modular programming.

One of the main objectives of a computer program is to convert input data into some sort of output. Most often this output is incorporated into a report for user reference. A program temporarily places this data into storage locations referred to as variables. Variables are defined by the programmer and must follow the rules of the particular language used. Data is classified and divided into four categories: character or byte, field or variable, record, and file. There are five main activities that could occur in a computer program:

1. Accept and edit input

2. Generate a simple report

3. Sum through counters or accumulators

4. Generate a report with control breaks

5. Update a file or database

The logic tool is the building block for the program development process. A problem should be initially solved using a logic tool which is ultimately converted into a computer program. The scope of this textbook concentrates on seven logic tools. The seven logic tools are:

1. Flowchart

2. Pseudocode

3. Hierarchy Chart

4. IPO Chart

5. Nassi-Shneiderman Chart

6. Warnier-Orr Diagram

7. Structure Chart

These logic tools have been selected because they are the predominant techniques used throughout the computer industry. Some of these logic tools have been available for over twenty-five years (the flowchart) and others are fairly recent, such as the structure chart which is approximately eight years old.

This chapter has exposed you to a large number of concepts about the data processing industry in general and program/logic tools specifically. Don't be alarmed if you are confused at this time; the concepts will sink in as you proceed to other chapters. This chapter has presented a foundation to assist you through the rest of this textbook. From this point, advance through the following chapters in any order (they are independent) and refer back to Chapter 1 for clarification as needed.

REVIEW QUESTIONS

MULTIPLE CHOICE
1. Data processing is the
   a. collection and processing of data
   b. organization and dissemination of data
   c. manipulation of data to produce information using a computer
   d. none of the above

2. The two types of data processing environments are
   a. on-line and real-time
   b. batch and on-line
   c. transaction and on-line
   d. real-time and batch

3. Which one of the following is not a category within the hierarchy of data?
   a. field
   b. character
   c. database
   d. record

4. The only activities that can occur when updating a file or database are
   a. adding data items to a file
   b. deleting data items from a file
   c. changing existing data items on a file
   d. all of the above

5. A report control break
   a. must have the input data sorted by control field
   b. checks the control field value for changes
   c. groups information by a major item or control field
   d. all of the above
   e. none of the above

FILL IN THE BLANK

1.   The two types of computer programs are _____ and _____.

2.   The three program logic structures are _____, _____, and _____.

3.   The _____ logic structure evaluates a condition and determines if it is TRUE or FALSE.

4.   The two main data types are _____ and _____.

5.   The two summation functions performed by a numeric variable are _____ and _____.

SHORT ANSWER

1. Define data processing in terms of data and information.

2. Briefly describe the six steps in the program development process.

3. Describe the relationship between a logic tool and a computer program.

4. Explain the concept of structured programming and top-down design.

5. What is a data variable?

6. What is meant by data type?

7. Explain the evaluation order of arithmetic operations within a computer program.

8. Briefly describe the five general activities found in computer programs.

9. Explain the rationale of logic tool solution verification.

10. What is the reasoning behind the concept of the "big six" problems?

11. Why is a data dictionary used within a logic tool solution?

The Flowchart

OBJECTIVES

Upon completion of this chapter, you should be able to:

- Define the term flowchart

- List and discuss the advantages and disadvantages of the flowchart as a logic development tool

- Identify and use the rules and constraints associated with the flowchart

- Solve word problems using the flowchart as a logic development tool

Introduction

The flowchart is probably the most basic logic development tool and the one most commonly used in beginning programming courses. What exactly is a flowchart? Many authors have used many different definitions for this tool. Let's try to present one that's not too "textbookish" but good enough to convey what a flowchart really is. A *flowchart* is a pictorial representation of the processes, in the correct sequence, required to solve a specific problem.

Pretty simple definition. But, how do you draw one? Where do you start and how do you know you're finished? These are very logical questions and by the time you've reached the end of this chapter, you'll know the answers to these and many other questions.

Flowcharting uses special symbols to represent different activities and processes. You must learn what each of these symbols means so that you will know how to apply flowcharting methodology to actual problem solving.

Components

There are several different symbols used in flowcharting. These symbols are contained on an instrument called a *flowcharting template*. Many programmers own and use the template on a daily basis. Templates are used primarily for flowcharting the logic steps involved in writing a computer program, or for documenting these same steps as part of the formal documentation for a completed program. A flowcharting template is shown in Figure 2.1.

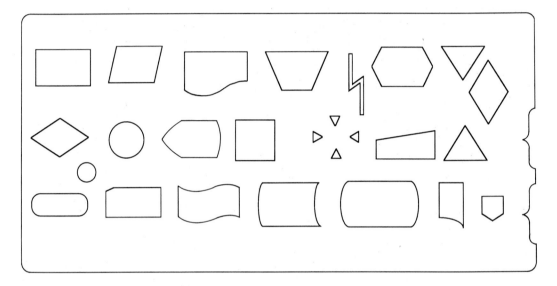

Figure 2.1 Flowcharting Template

As you can see, there are many symbols on a template. However, there are only a few that are usually required to depict the logic necessary to solve a computer programming problem. The most commonly used symbols are shown in Figure 2.2.

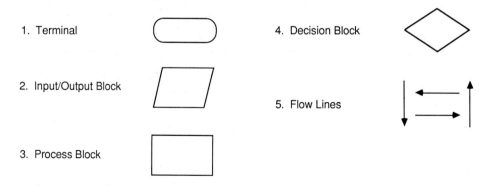

1. Terminal

2. Input/Output Block

3. Process Block

4. Decision Block

5. Flow Lines

Figure 2.2 Five Basic Flowcharting Symbols

One question that you may be asking yourself at this point is, "Do I need to buy a template in order to do flowcharting?" The answer to this question is no. However, your instructor may require one for any flowcharts that you submit for problems that you do for this course. Each of the five basic flowchart symbols are defined in the following paragraphs.

Terminal

The terminal is a symbol shaped like an ellipse that denotes the physical beginning and ending of a flowchart. What this means is that in any flowchart, the first and last symbols used are terminal symbols. The beginning terminal symbol usually has the word START written inside the symbol as shown in Figure 2.3. The ending terminal symbol normally has the word STOP written inside the symbol as shown in Figure 2.4.

Figure 2.3 Input Terminal   **Figure 2.4** Output Terminal

Input/Output Block

The input/output block is a symbol shaped like a parallelogram that denotes an input or output (read or write) operation at a particular point in a flowchart. This block tells the reader that data is being input (a READ operation) to the program or data is being output (a WRITE operation) to a physical device such as a terminal, printer, tape, or disk. The input block is shown in Figure 2.5. This figure says to write or output a data value as input and store the value in a variable called X. The output block is shown in Figure 2.6. This figure says to write or output a data value contained in the variable called Y.

Figure 2.5 Input Block   **Figure 2.6** Output Block

Process Block

The process block is a symbol shaped like a rectangle that exhibits a process or activity other than an input/output operation. This block tells the reader that the process denoted inside the symbol is being performed at this particular point in the flowchart. A typical process might be a calculation, or an assignment of a value to a particular variable. The process block shown in Figure 2.7 depicts the process of calculating gross pay based on multiplying hours worked by the hourly pay rate.

```
Gross Pay =
Hours Worked
x Hourly
Pay Rate
```

Figure 2.7 Process Block

Decision Block

The decision block is a symbol shaped like a diamond that signifies a decision-making action that will cause a transfer of processing control in the flow of operations being displayed by the flowchart. This block tells the reader that:

1. A condition is being tested at this point in the flowchart to see if it is true or false.

2. Based on the tested outcome of the condition, processing control will transfer at this point to the location in the flowchart specified by the TRUE path if the condition is TRUE, or control will transfer to the location specified by the FALSE path if the condition is FALSE.

The decision block is shown in Figure 2.8.

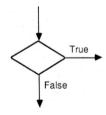

Figure 2.8 Decision Block

Flow Lines

Flow lines are not really symbols, but as the name implies, are lines with arrowheads attached to one end to show the logical flow or sequence of steps shown in a flowchart. Flow lines are the "linking pins" of a flowchart in that they are the mechanism for connecting all the symbols contained in the flowchart. Examples of flow lines are shown in Figure 2.9.

Figure 2.9 Flow Lines

Rules and Constraints

The rules for drawing flowcharts are very straightforward. All flowcharts must begin and end with a terminal symbol. By convention, flowchart blocks or symbols are usually drawn in columns. Starting at the top of the column, the blocks or symbols physically appear one below the other in the column. Flow lines connect the blocks or symbols in the sequence in which the processes are to be performed.

Flow lines also have a set of rules defining how they are to be used in flowcharts. First, a line can connect two and only two flowchart symbols. Second, a line may have only one arrowhead appearing at the end of the line connecting to the symbol to which processing control is being passed. The example shown in Figure 2.10 illustrates this key point.

In Figure 2.10, processing control is being transferred from Block A to Block B. This can be ascertained because the arrowhead at the end of the flow line connecting Block A and Block B is physically in contact with Block B, the process to which control is being passed.

Understanding the relationship of flow lines to processing control between flowchart symbols is the key to developing logic steps for problem solving using flowcharts. Flow lines show the order in which the processes depicted by flowcharting symbols will be performed.

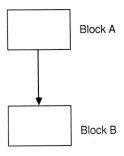

Figure 2.10 Processing Flow Between Symbols

Now that we've talked about the five basic flowcharting symbols, let's look at an example of a very simple flowchart. Figure 2.11 illustrates the processing requirements for computing and printing out the gross pay for one employee for one pay period.

First, note that the flowchart begins with the standard terminal symbol with the word START printed inside. This, of course, identifies the beginning of the flowchart. The next symbol is the input/output block which says that two values are being inputted and stored in the variables called HOURS WORKED and HOURLY PAY RATE. Next, we see a process block which depicts the gross pay calculation that is being performed; that is, GROSS PAY = HOURS WORKED × HOURLY PAY RATE. Processing flow is then transferred to the next symbol which is an input/output block that contains the instruction to print out the GROSS PAY for this employee. The last symbol, as always, is the terminal symbol with the word STOP to indicate the end of the flowchart.

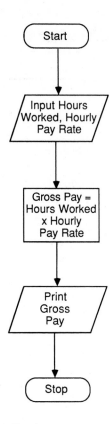

Figure 2.11 Gross Pay Calculation—One Employee

Sample Problem

Assume that you have been given the following problem to solve:

> A student's grade is based on the average of four test scores that he or she has received during the semester. Compute and print out the student's course grade based on the average of the four test scores.

The first thing you should do in attempting to solve this problem is to analyze what you are being asked to provide as output for this problem. Go back and look the problem over again. What are you being asked to deliver? The result is an average grade which will be the course grade earned by the student.

Next you have to identify the specific processes required to enable you to provide the course grade. You must also identify the specific order in which these processes must occur to arrive at the correct solution. This is where the fun really begins, so follow along and go through this flowchart one step at a time. What's the first thing that you should do in drawing your flowchart? You're correct—the START terminal symbol as shown in Figure 2.12.

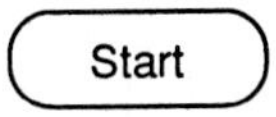

Start

Figure 2.12 START Terminal Symbol

The next process is inputting the four test grades as part of the processing logic depicted by the flowchart. Now is the time to use the input/output block in the flowchart. Logic should tell you that the first process which should be performed is to obtain the four test grades via the input process. The flowchart at this point is shown in Figure 2.13.

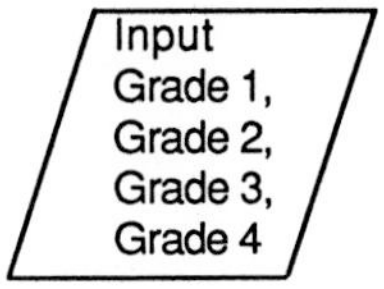

Input
Grade 1,
Grade 2,
Grade 3,
Grade 4

Figure 2.13 Input Symbol for Test Grades

The next process should also be fairly obvious: now that you have obtained the four test scores, what do you have to do in order to determine the student's average grade? Right! You must calculate the average grade by adding the four test scores and dividing by four. This is shown in the flowchart shown in Figure 2.14.

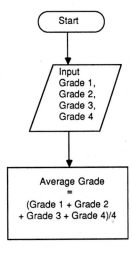

Figure 2.14 Average Grade Calculation

One final process now remains before the flowchart is complete. You must print out the average score so you can see the student's final grade. This process is represented by using another input/output block. In this instance, the block depicts an output operation, namely the printing of the final course grade. The completed flowchart is shown in Figure 2.15.

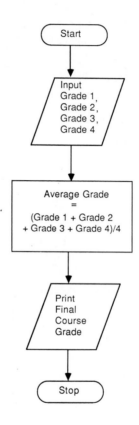

Figure 2.15 Flowchart Solution for Sample Problem

Program Logic Structures

Sequence

The sequence control structure is the default control structure used in any flowchart. Figure 2.10 represents the sequence control structure under structured programming methodology. What this means is that the sequence control structure is represented by two symbols connected by a flow line which shows processing control flowing in sequence from one symbol to the next.

Selection

The selection control structure is depicted in flowcharting as the decision symbol. The decision symbol (Figure 2.8) signifies that a condition is being tested for a TRUE or FALSE result. The outcome of this test will control the processing flow at that point in the flowchart. This symbol represents the selection control structure required by structured programming methodology.

Iteration

The iteration control structure required by structured programming methodology is shown in Figure 2.16.

This hexagon-shaped symbol depicts processing control that is going to pass through a certain set of processes in the flowchart on a repetitive basis for some specified number of times. This symbol is covered in more detail later in this chapter. What is important to note at this point is that the iteration control structure is contained in flowcharting methodology and is available for use in solving logic problems.

Figure 2.16 Iteration Control Flowchart Symbol

Advantages and Disadvantages of Flowcharts

Some of the advantages of flowcharting are:

- It is pictorial in nature

- Specific symbols represent specific processes being performed

- Processes inside symbols can generally be translated on a one-for-one basis to a high-level language program statement

- It is relatively easy to use

Some of the disadvantages include:

- Symbols used have special meanings which must be memorized

- Diagrams can become quite lengthy for complex problems

- Changes to a flowchart can be difficult, especially for long logic solutions

Summary of Flowcharting Procedures

The following list is a summary of the steps to be followed in using flowcharting procedures to solve a logic problem.

1. Begin the flowchart in the upper left-hand corner of the page with a terminal symbol labeled as START.

2. Determine what the output requirements of the problem are: a report, the result of a calculation, a message, a file, for example.

3. Determine what input data has been provided by the problem.

4. List, either mentally or on a piece of paper, each of the processes that must be performed in order to take the input data, process it, and provide the desired output.

5. Determine the proper sequence in which the processes identified in step 4 must be performed. This is not an easy task to accomplish, especially for beginners.

6. Start with the first process identified in step 5 and draw the appropriate flowchart symbol depicting this process under the terminal symbol that you drew for step 1. Write the process being performed inside the symbol just drawn. Then connect the two symbols with a flow line and arrow.

7. Continue the same way as you did in step 6: determine the next process in sequence to be performed, draw the appropriate flowchart symbol for this process, and connect the two symbols with a flow line and arrow.

8. When you have finished the last process, draw another terminal symbol, label it with a STOP, and connect it to the previous symbol with a flow line and arrow.

Now, using this list, let's tackle the standard set of problems appearing in each of the remaining chapters of the textbook. Hopefully, solving this problem set will provide you with the necessary experience to become a good novice "flowcharter."

PROBLEM SOLUTIONS

▶ Problem 1—Lease Versus Buy ◀

Ajax Manufacturing Company has the option to purchase outright or lease (with an option to buy at lease-end) a computer system to aid in its business operations. If Ajax purchases the system for $10,000, it will finance the full amount for four years at a 10% interest rate.

NOTE: Simple Interest (I) = Principal (P) × Rate (R) × Time Period (T).

If Ajax leases the equipment for four years and decides to purchase at lease-end, the monthly cost will be $250 with a final payment of $3000. Which option should Ajax choose in order to minimize the total cost of the computer system? The problem solution should satisfy varying lease versus buy input information.

Where do you begin? As always, draw a terminal symbol with the word START written inside. Next analyze what the output requirements are as stated in the problem. What you are being asked to solve for specifically is the recommended option for procuring the computer system. What this means is that you have to compute and compare the total cost of each option to determine which is least expensive.

What data has been provided? You have been given all of the necessary data to compute the total cost of each option for the four-year period. All that you need to do is to determine the calculations necessary to compute the costs. Let's work through the problem, developing the logic and calculations as they are required.

At this point, let's compute the cost of the purchase option. Before you can do any computations, you must input the data related to the purchase option. You do this with an input/output (parallelogram) symbol. Draw a parallelogram under the terminal symbol and connect both symbols with a flow line and arrow. Inside the input/output symbol, write "Input Purchase Price, Interest Rate, Time Period." Please refer to Figure 2.17.

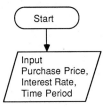

Figure 2.17 Input Statement—Standard Problem 1

Now draw a process (rectangle) symbol under the input/output symbol. Inside the process symbol, write "Finance Cost (FC) = Purchase Price (PP) × Interest Rate (IR) × Time Period (TP)." Refer to Figure 2.18.

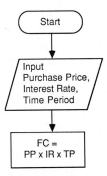

Figure 2.18 Finance Cost Calculation—Standard Problem 1

As you noticed in the process symbol in Figure 2.18, FC is used to represent finance cost, PP to represent purchase price, and IR to represent interest rate. These abbreviations make it easier to label what's inside flowchart symbols and they also represent, in data processing parlance, things called variables.

A variable is a term used to describe the data items that you're working with when solving a problem. They are called variables because the data values contained in the items can change, or vary, at different points in time during the processing being performed in a flowchart.

The next calculation determines total cost for this option. Draw another process symbol and connect it to the previous process symbol. Label this symbol "Total Purchase Cost (TPC) = Purchase Price (PP) + Finance Cost (FC)." Refer to Figure 2.19.

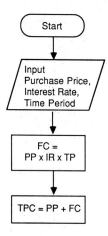

Figure 2.19 Total Cost Calculation—Purchase Option—Standard Problem 1

You have now completed almost half of the problem, namely the total cost associated with the purchase option. Continuing the flowchart, you must now input the data for the lease-purchase option. Draw another input/output symbol and label it with "Input Monthly Lease Cost (MLC), Number of Payments (NP), Lump Sum Cost (LSC)." At this point, it will be assumed that you know to connect the flowchart symbols with flow lines.

Next you need to compute the Lease Cost (LC) for this option. Since this is a process, draw a process block and label it with "LC = MLC × NP." The next action required in the flowchart is to compute the total cost for this option. Draw another process block and label it "TLC = LC + LSC." As you probably suspect, TLC stands for Total Lease Cost. Please refer to Figure 2.20.

Now pause and consider just where you are in solving this problem. You're almost finished because you have computed the cost of both options. All that is left for you to do is to compare the cost of the two. How do you show this on a flowchart? Right, the decision symbol! Figure 2.21 shows the decision symbol for this cost comparison.

Notice the TRUE and FALSE branches associated with this decision. If the total cost of the purchase option is greater than the total cost of the lease-purchase option, then the message THE RECOMMENDED OPTION IS THE LEASE-PURCHASE OPTION is printed. Notice this message is shown inside the input/output block shown in the TRUE branch of the decision.

Look at the FALSE branch of the decision. How does processing control flow to the FALSE branch? If the condition being tested is not TRUE, then control passes to the FALSE branch. In this case, if control passes to the FALSE branch, then the message THE RECOMMENDED OPTION IS THE PURCHASE OPTION is printed. Again, notice that this message is shown inside the input/output block shown in the FALSE branch of the decision.

Is there anything else required to solve this problem? No, because you have solved for the requested result: you have identified which option Ajax should select and the flowchart for this problem is complete.

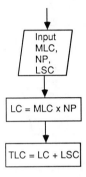

Figure 2.20 Total Cost Calculation—Lease-Purchase Option—Standard Problem 1

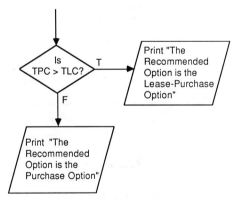

Figure 2.21 Cost Comparison of the Two Options—Standard Problem 1

Now look at the whole flowchart in Figure 2.22.

Now let's solve this problem by plugging in the numbers given in the problem statement.

As you can see from Figure 2.23, the recommended option for Ajax Manufacturing Company is the purchase option.

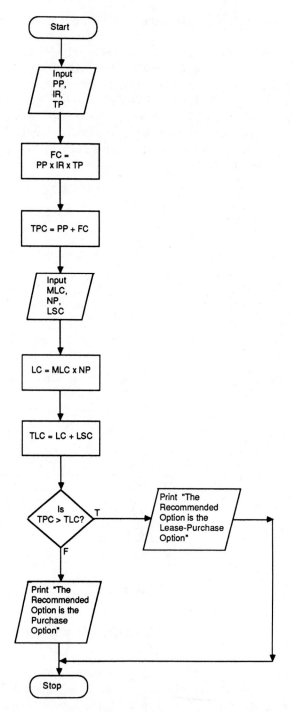

Figure 2.22 Flowchart Solution for Standard Problem 1

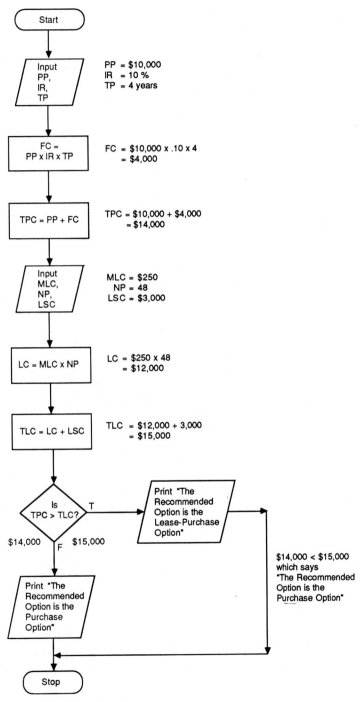

Figure 2.23 Solution for Standard Problem 1

► Problem 2—Payroll ◄

Easymoney Inc. desires to generate their current manual payroll via computer. The information collected every payroll period includes the employee social security number, pay rate, hours worked, and total other deductions. The payroll department would like a report listing these items: employee social security number, hours worked, pay rate, gross pay, FICA withheld (6.13% of gross pay), federal tax withheld (20% of gross pay), total other deductions, and net pay.

Let's go ahead and label the data items given to us in this problem with variable names as follows:

SSN   =   employee social security number
PR   =   pay rate
HW   =   hours worked
GP   =   gross pay
OT   =   overtime pay
FICA =   FICA withheld
FT   =   federal tax withheld
TOD   =   total other deductions
NP   =   net pay

This approach will make the flowcharting process easier by using these variable names inside the flowchart symbols. Now, let's get started with this problem solution.

As always, start with a terminal symbol labeled START. The output required by this problem is a report showing the requested payroll information as stated in the problem. You have been given a set of input data to work with so the next logical process to be shown on the flowchart would be an input/output block labeled with INPUT SSN, HW, PR, TOD. These are all of the input data items that you have to work with in this problem. The flowchart as it appears so far is shown in Figure 2.24.

Notice the new flowchart symbol in Figure 2.24. It is a circle with a number inside. This circle is called a *connector* and it transfers control at this point to the connector labeled with this number. There are two kinds of connectors in flowcharting. This one is called an *on-page connector*. The other one is called on *off-page connector* and is drawn like this:

The off-page connector works exactly like the on-page connector except that processing control is transferred to another page containing the off-page connector labeled with the same number or letter as the transferring off-page connector. You'll see exactly how connectors work when you see the final flowchart solution to this problem. Now back to the problem. The next step is to figure out how to use these data items to derive the other necessary information for our desired report.

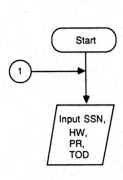

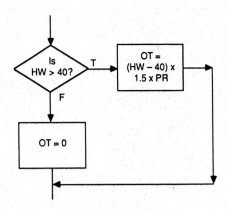

Figure 2.24 Input Statement—
Standard Problem 2

Figure 2.25 Overtime Hours Computation—
Standard Problem 2

At this point, you are interested in computing gross pay (GP) because GP is used to calculate FICA and federal tax. In order to compute GP, you must check to see if the employee has worked any overtime during the pay period. This requires a decision symbol and a TRUE and FALSE branch as shown in Figure 2.25.

Notice how the overtime pay (OT) is computed in the process symbol for the TRUE branch of the decision evaluation. Also notice that if the hours worked is less than or equal to 40, the OT is set equal to zero. For the gross pay calculation, a process block is drawn and the GP calculation is labeled inside the block as follows:

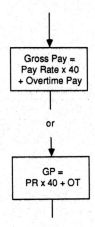

Now that you have computed GP, the next step is to compute FICA. This requires another process block labeled as follows:

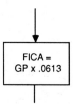

The next step in the flowchart is also a process block showing the federal tax (FT) calculation. The process block is labeled as follows:

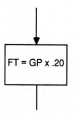

Go back and review the problem statement. Have you computed all the necessary items in order to perform the net pay (NP) calculation? Yes! So the next symbol in the flowchart is another process block labeled with the following NP calculation.

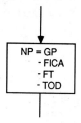

Now you are ready to write a line on the report for this employee. Depict this with the following input/ouput symbol.

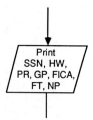

This essentially completes the flowchart as far as the processing required to do the necessary calculations and produce the line items on the requested report. The only function left to perform is to check to see if all employees have been processed. This check is depicted on the flowchart with the following decision symbol.

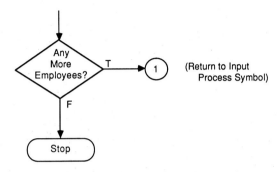

As you can see, the condition that you are checking for is, "Are there any more employees to be processed?" If there are (a TRUE condition), then return to the input/output symbol in the flowchart where data is input for each employee. If there are no more employees to be processed, then follow the FALSE branch which takes you to the flowchart's final terminal symbol labeled with a STOP. The entire flowchart depicting the solution for this problem is shown in Figure 2.26.

▶ Problem 3—Health and Diet ◀

Bedford Waistwatchers Association requests that a program be written to motivate members to stay on their diet and show the cost savings that can result from a change in diet. One of the staple diet items recommended is yogurt. If a member follows the Association diet strictly, a large amount of yogurt can be consumed over a short period of time. The cost effectiveness of buying yogurt or making yogurt at home should be evaluated. If a monetary savings can be realized by making yogurt at home versus buying it at the store, how many cups of yogurt must be produced to achieve this savings? The data needed to provide an analysis is store cost of yogurt per cup, cost of yogurt maker if made at home, cost of home ingredients per cup, and number of cups. An analysis should show the home cost, store cost, and savings or loss per cup.

Begin the same way as you did in the previous problem. Label the data items with variable names to aid in developing the flowchart.

SC = store cost of yogurt per cup
HC = home cost of ingredients per cup
MC = cost of yogurt maker if made at home
NC = number of cups

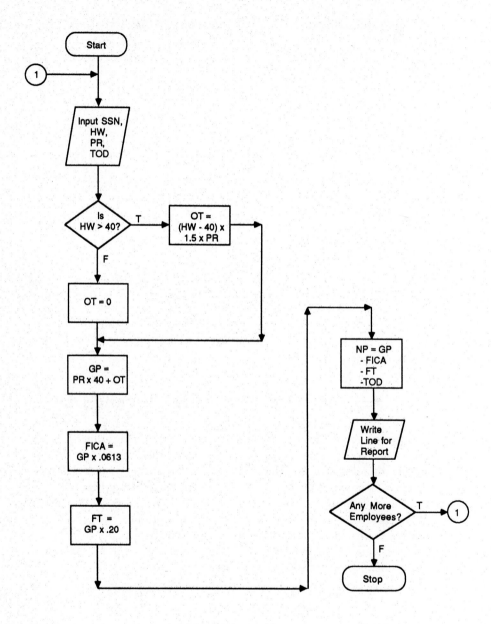

Figure 2.26 Flowchart Solution for Standard Problem 2

As always, start with a terminal symbol labeled START. Next label an input/output block as follows:

Now a counter must be established to indicate the number of cups for which the cost comparison has been made. This is shown in the following figure. Since this is the first cup, the counter is set to one.

Now you are ready to compute the cost of either buying the yogurt from the store or making it at home. Compute the home cost first as shown in the following process block.

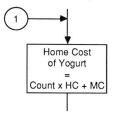

Next, compute the store cost of the yogurt, again using a process block.

What's the next thing that you need to do in the flowchart? You need to compare the two costs to see which is least expensive. There are really three conditions that can occur as the result of our cost comparison. They are as follows:

1. Both costs can be equal

2. The home cost is less than the store cost

3. The store cost is less than the home cost

You need to test for these three conditions in the flowchart. Of course, you must use a decision symbol to make the test. In fact, you must use two decision symbols. Let's test for the equal condition first as shown by the following:

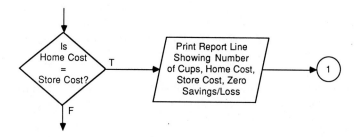

Notice what happens in this test. If the condition is TRUE, the desired report line is produced showing zero savings/loss. However, if the condition is FALSE, you proceed to the following decision symbol.

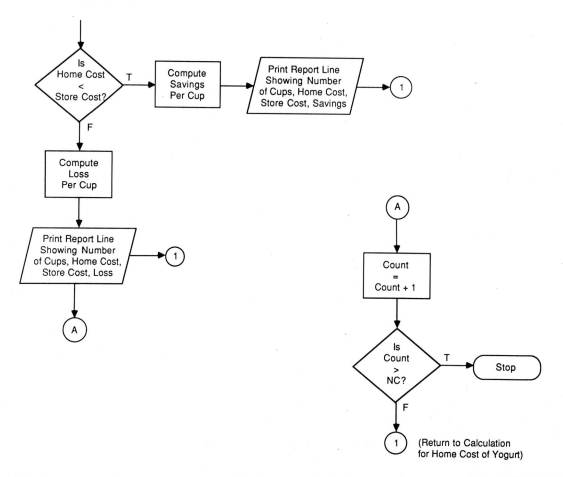

In this test, if the condition is TRUE, you compute the savings per cup, produce the desired report line showing the savings and proceed to check if processing should be stopped. If the tested condition is FALSE; that is, the store cost is less than the home cost, you proceed to the next flowchart symbol, a process block, where the loss per cup is computed. After this computation, you proceed to an input/output block showing that the desired report line is produced showing the loss. You now check to see if processing should be stopped; that is, if you have computed costs for each number of cups specified. The entire flowchart is shown in Figure 2.27.

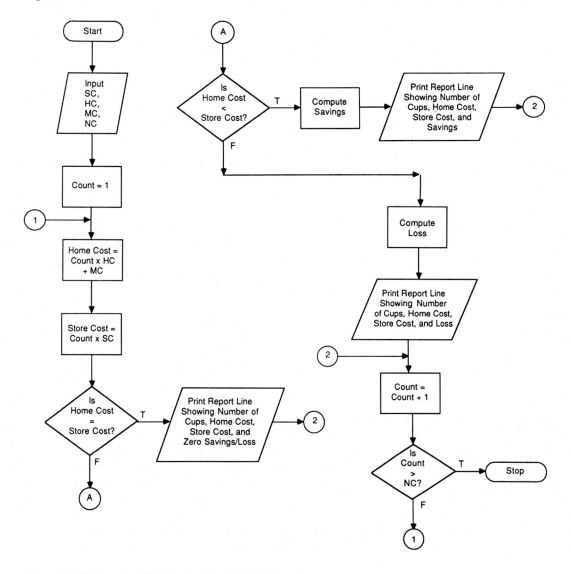

Figure 2.27 Flowchart Solution for Standard Problem 3

► **Problem 4—Daily Sales** ◄

Vidal Blass is the owner of Obnoxious Telephone Sales. Vidal has had up to 20 employees solicit sales via telephone on a specific day. Vidal would like to produce a sales summary report at the end of each business day to determine which salespeople generate the most revenue. Employees make a phone sale, write the sales information down on a receipt with their name and the total sale, and place the receipt in a bin shared by all of the employees. At the end of the day, all of the receipts are gathered and the summary report produced by entering the name and sales amount from each receipt. The first activity the computer will perform is to sort all input records in name order. (Assume that no two salespeople have the same name.) The sales summary will list the total sales by each name and the grand total sales for the day's business activities.

Develop the logic to provide this summary report. Here's a list of the data items and variable names that you'll be working with in this problem:

SN = salesperson name
SA = sales amount from individual sales receipt
ST = daily sales total accumulator—each salesperson
DS = daily sales accumulator—all names

After the START terminal symbol, you need an input/output block showing the inputting of the salesperson's name and sales amount.

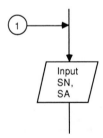

Now you are confronted with a data processing concept called a control break. A control break is a test (decision) in a flowchart (or program) to see if a sequenced data item (or variable name) has changed its value since the last time it was processed.

This type of activity is known as *subgrouping* or *subtotaling* within a reporting operation. Remember the part of the problem statement that said that the input was sorted by salesperson's name (SN)? This has been done because you are going to subtotal daily sales by salesperson to determine what amounts have been sold by each individual. Sorting means that all sales receipts will be grouped by name. Your logic will have to check and see when a change in name occurs so that you can keep track of (subtotal) sales for each salesperson.

Test to see if the salesperson's name has changed. Do this with the following decision block.

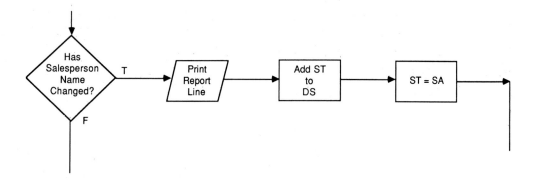

The TRUE branch of this decision means that a new salesperson's sales receipt has been encountered. This means that:

1. It is time to print a report line for the previous salesperson because you have totaled all of his or her daily sales receipts.

2. You need to add the current salesperson's first daily sales amount to the daily sales (DS) accumulator.

3. You must move the current salesperson's first daily sales amount to the daily sales total accumulator (ST).

The three symbols appearing in the TRUE branch of this decision represent respectively the three actions mentioned above. If the TRUE branch is followed, then this means a control break has occurred; that is, a saleperson's name has changed.

If the FALSE branch is followed, then a control break has not occurred and you are simply adding to the daily sales subtotal for the same salesperson. This is shown in the following process block.

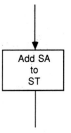

Next you want to test to see if there are any more daily sales receipts to be processed. If there are, you need to return to the point in the flowchart where you input the salesperson name and sales amount for the receipt. If there are no more receipts, then continue on to the next process in the flowchart. This logic is represented in the following decision symbol.

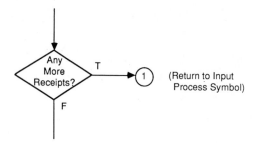

The next process to be performed if the previous test proves to be FALSE is to add the last salesperson's sales amount (SA) to the daily sales (DS) accumulator. You must also print a report line showing this last sales receipt processed. These two actions are shown in the following process and input/output blocks.

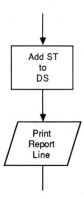

You're almost finished. The only remaining item is to print the daily sales total for all salespeople. After you do this, your required processing is complete. These actions are depicted with the following input/output block and terminal symbol.

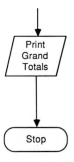

The entire solution to this problem is shown in Figure 2-28.

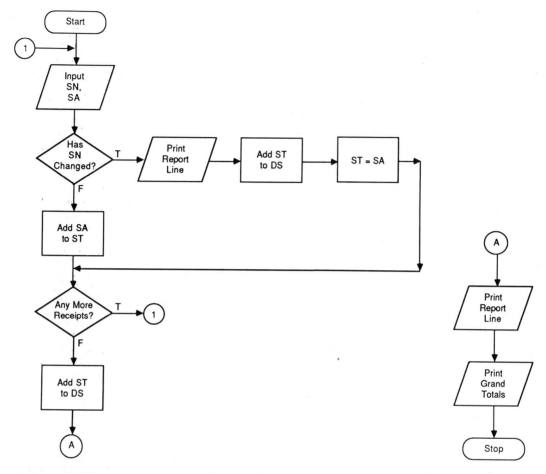

Figure 2.28 Flowchart Solution for Standard Problem 4

► Problem 5—House Construction ◄

Well-Bilt Homes Inc. would like you to design a program which enables builders to calculate home building costs based on prospective room sizes. This program is interactive; it allows the user to input the number of rooms desired and the individual room dimensions (length and width only). The building cost per square foot is based on the following:

1000 square feet or less	$60 per square foot
1001–2000 square feet or less	$50 per square foot
More than 2000 square feet	$40 per square foot

Develop the logic to compute the building cost of the house.

Let's define the variable names to be used in solving this problem.

NR   =   number of rooms
L   =   length in feet of the room
W   =   width in feet of the room
RSF =   room square footage
TSF =   total square footage of the house (accumulator)
BC   =   building cost per square foot

As with the last problem, begin the flowchart with a START terminal symbol and input/output symbols as follows:

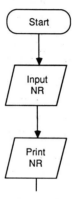

The first input/output symbol shows that you are inputting the total number of rooms to be included in this house. The second input/output symbol depicts the printing of a report line that shows the total number of rooms in the house.

The next process is to check and see if the room dimensions for all desired rooms in the house have been entered. This process is a test to see if the number of rooms that was entered for the variable NR are given dimensions. This checking is shown with the following iteration or looping symbol mentioned earlier in the chapter.

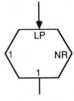

The LP inside the symbol is called the *loop counter*. It controls the number of times that the processes inside the loop are performed. The leftmost number in the symbol says that LP is initially set at 1. The bottom number says that LP is incremented by 1 each time the loop is performed. Finally, the variable on the right, NR, denotes how many times the loop will be performed.

One other symbol, a large connector, is used in conjunction with the looping symbol. This connector represents the physical end of the loop and also contains the loop counter variable. This means that all processes physically located between the looping symbol and the connector are performed on each pass through the loop. When the loop has been performed the maximum number of times, control is passed to the next flowchart symbol after the large connector symbol.

The following processes are occurring each time through the loop.

1. Input the length (L) and width (W) dimensions for the room.

2. Compute the room square footage by multiplying length by width.

3. Add this room's square footage to the accumulator for the total square footage for the house.

4. Print a report line showing the room dimensions and room square footage for this individual room.

These four activities are depicted in the following four symbols.

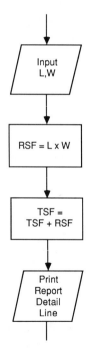

The loop is terminated with the large connector symbol.

Control is passed at the appropriate time to the next process. This process checks the total square footage for the house (TSF) and determines what cost-per-square-foot factor should be used in computing the building cost for the house. This processing logic is shown in the next set of decision symbols.

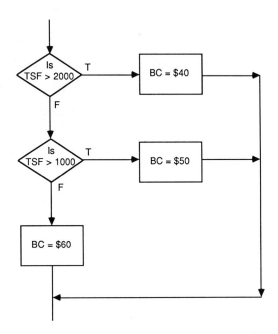

After the building cost factor is determined, the cost to build the house can be calculated. This calculation is shown in the following process block.

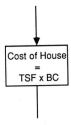

Now all that remains to do is to print out:

1.   The total square footage in the house

2.   The building cost per square foot to build the house

3.   The total building cost of the house

These three processes are depicted by the three following input/output blocks.

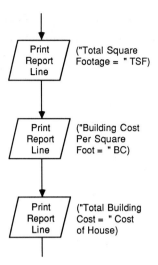

After you draw the STOP terminal symbol, you are finished! The complete solution for this problem is shown in Figure 2.29.

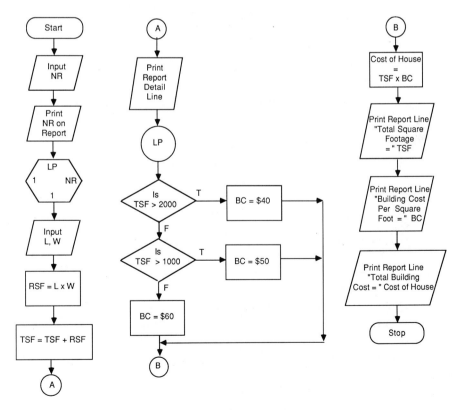

Figure 2.29 Flowchart Solution for Standard Problem 5

▶ **Problem 6—Personnel Statistics** ◀

The chairman of the board of Eldorado Enterprises Inc. has requested a report from the Personnel Department that will show various types of information about the company's work force. This report should provide the following:

1. The total number of males and females (SEX CODE = M for males, F for females)

2. The total number of employees by the following age categories (BIRTHDAY YEAR)
   a. less than 21
   b. 21–30
   c. 31–40
   d. 41–50
   e. 51–60
   f. 61–70
   g. over 70

3. The total number of people who have been with the company for 10 years or more (SENIORITY CODE = 3, 4, or 5)

4. The total number of engineers (OCCUPATION CODE = 7) in the company

The variables used in this problem are accumulators or counters to show the number of employees who fall into each of the requested categories. These variables (counters) are:

TY	=	today's year
BY	=	birthday year
AGE	=	employee age in years
SEX	=	sex code
SC	=	seniority code
OC	=	occupation code
MALE-COUNT	=	number of males
FEMALE-COUNT	=	number of females
OVER 70	=	over 70 counter
61–70 CT	=	between 61–70 counter
51–60 CT	=	between 51–60 counter
41–50 CT	=	between 41–50 counter
31–40 CT	=	between 31–40 counter
21–30 CT	=	between 21–30 counter
UNDER 21	=	under 21 counter
10-YR	=	10-year counter
EC	=	engineer counter

As usual, begin with the START terminal symbol and an input/output block as follows:

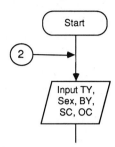

The previous input/output block shows that you are inputting today's year, sex code, birthday year, seniority code, and occupation code for this employee. Next check the sex code (SEX) to see if the employee is a male or female. This is shown in the following decision symbol.

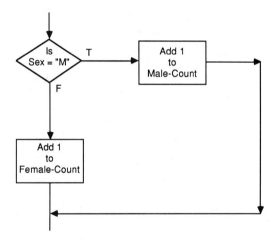

If the employee is a male, then one is added to the male counter variable MALE-COUNT. If the employee is a female, then one is added to the female counter variable, FEMALE-COUNT.

The next process to be performed in the flowchart is the year calculation to determine the employee's age. This is depicted in the following process block.

In this block, the age (AGE) is calculated in years by subtracting the birthday year (BY) from today's year (TY). The result of this calculation is then tested to determine which counter you update to reflect this employee's age category. The following decision symbols illustrate the logic necessary to accomplish this task.

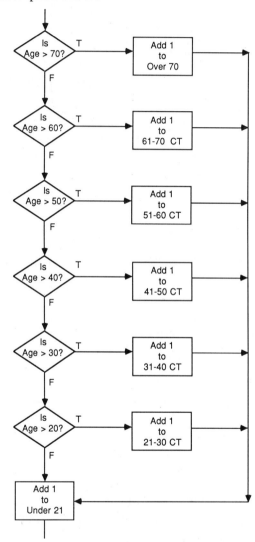

As you can see from the previous set of decision symbols, testing is being done to determine the appropriate age category for the respective employee. When the correct age category is found (a TRUE condition), the counter for that category is updated by one. Processing flow then bypasses the other age tests and continues on to the next process to be performed in the flowchart. If a FALSE condition is encountered, processing flow continues to the next age category test in sequence.

The next condition to be tested in the flowchart is the seniority code check.

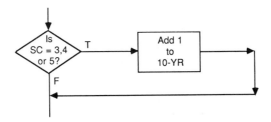

As you can see, this test is checking for a match to one of three possible values. If one of these values is found, then the 10-year counter (10-YR) is increased by one and processing flow continues to the next flowchart symbol. If one of these values is not found, then the 10-year counter is not incremented by one and processing flow continues to the next flowchart symbol.

The next testing process is very similar to the previous one. It appears with a decision symbol.

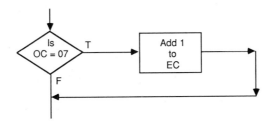

This test is checking the occupation code to determine if the employee is an engineer. If the code is equal to 07, the engineer counter is incremented by one; otherwise, the counter is not incremented.

At this point, you need to make one more test to complete the logic for this problem. The decision symbol for this test is:

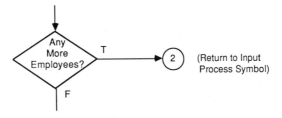

This is the final check to see if all employees have been processed. If this test is TRUE, then you return to the input process block in the flowchart. If this test is FALSE, then you print out a report showing all of the employee statistics that you have accumulated in the respective counters that you have been using.

You need to add one final symbol—the STOP terminal symbol—and then you will be finished. The entire flowchart solution for this problem is shown in Figure 2.30.

This completes the standard problem set for this chapter.

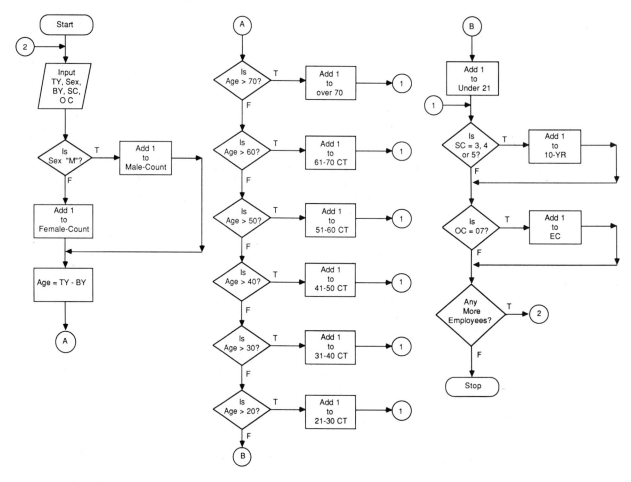

Figure 2.30 Flowchart Solution for Standard Problem 6

Flowcharting Walk-Through

This section of the chapter shows solutions to two problems from the standard problem set using sample data values for the variables.

► Problem 2—Payroll ◄

The following data is provided for two typical employees of Easymoney Inc.

Employee Number	Social Security Number	Hours Worked	Hourly Pay Rate	Other Deductions
1	234-56-7890	70	$10.00	$100.00
2	123-45-6789	40	10.00	50.00

Employee #1:
The following processing occurs for this employee.

1. Input SSN = 234-56-7890, HW = 70, PR = $10.00, TOD = $100.00

2. Since Hours Worked (HW) is greater than 40
    Overtime Pay (OT) = (HW − 40) × 1.5 × PR
                        = (70 − 40) × 1.5 × 10.00
                        = $450.00

3. Gross Pay (GP) = Pay Rate times 40 plus Overtime Pay
                   = $10.00 × 40 + $450.00
                   = $850.00

4. FICA = Gross Pay times 0.0613
         = $850.00 × 0.0613
         = $52.11

5. Federal Tax (FT) = Gross Pay times 0.20
                     = $850 × 0.20
                     = $170.00

6. Net Pay (NP) = Gross Pay − FICA − Federal Tax
                    − Total Other Deductions (TOD)
                 = $850.00 − $52.11 − $170.00 − $100.00
                 = $527.89

7. Write a Report Line.

Social Security Number	Hours Worked	Hourly Pay Rate	Gross Pay	FICA Tax	FED Tax	Total Other Deductions	Net Pay
234-56-7890	70	10.00	850.00	52.11	170.00	100.00	527.89

Refer to Figure 2.31 to trace the flowchart logic for Employee #1.

Employee #2:
The following processing occurs for this employee.

1. Input SSN = 123-45-6789, HW = 40, PR = $10.00, TOD = $50.00

2. Since HW is not greater than 40, Overtime Pay (OT) = $0

3. GP = PR times 40 + OT
       = $10.00 × 40 + 0
       = $400.00

4. FICA = GP times 0.0613
         = $400.00 × 0.0613
         = $24.52

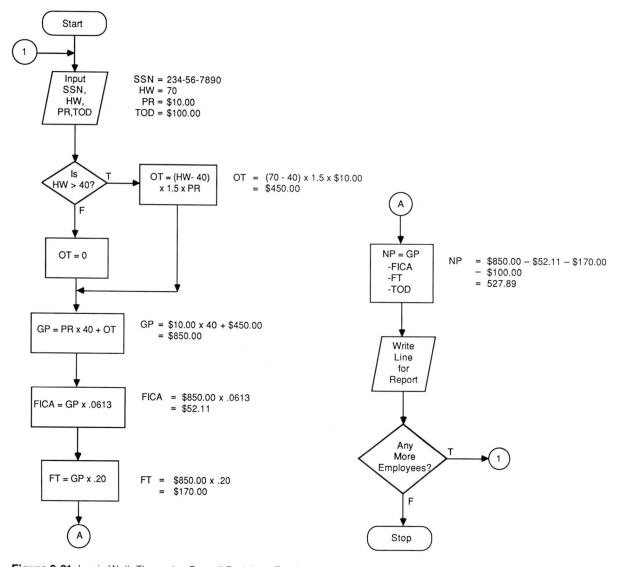

Figure 2.31 Logic Walk-Through—Payroll Problem, Employee #1

5. FT = GP times 0.20
   = \$400.00 × 0.20
   = \$80.00

6. NP = GP − FICA − FT − Total Other Deductions (TOD)
   = \$400.00 − \$24.52 − \$80.00 − \$50.00
   = \$245.48

7. Write a Report Line.

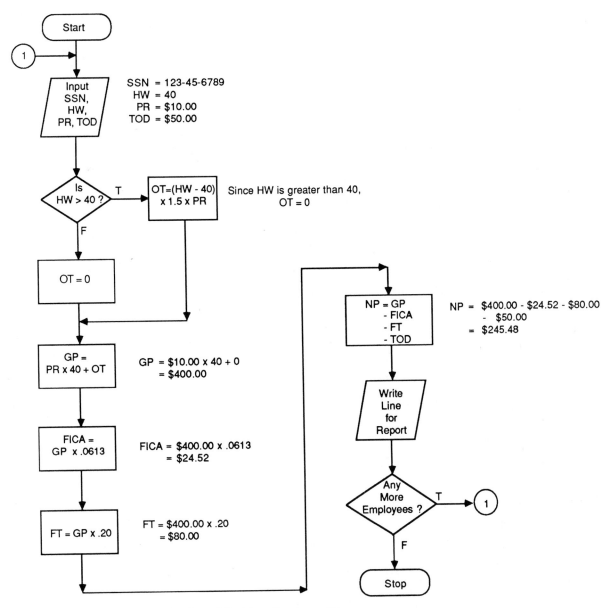

Figure 2.32 Logic Walk-Through—Payroll Problem, Employee #2

Social Security Number	Hours Worked	Hourly Pay Rate	Gross Pay	FICA Tax	FED Tax	Total Other Deductions	Net Pay
123-45-6789	40	10.00	400.00	24.52	80.00	50.00	245.58

Refer to Figure 2.32 to trace the flowchart logic for Employee #2.

► **Problem 3—Health and Diet** ◄

The following data is provided for determining whether or not to purchase yogurt from a store or make it at home.

Store cost per cup of yogurt $= \$1.00$

Home cost of ingredients per cup $= \$.50$

Cost of yogurt maker $= \$12.00$

Number of cups of yogurt required $= 40$

The following processing occurs.

1. Input Store Cost (SC) = $1.00, Home Cost of Ingredients (HC) = $.50, Yogurt Maker Cost (MC) = $12.00, and Number of Cups of Yogurt Required (NC) = 40

Case 1: Count = 1

2. Home Cost of Yogurt $=$ Count times HC plus MC
   $= 1 \times \$.50 + \$12.00$
   $= \$12.50$

3. Store Cost of Yogurt $=$ Count times SC
   $= 1 \times \$1.00$
   $= \$1.00$

4. Since the Home Cost ($12.50) is greater than the Store Cost ($1.00), our output for this problem would appear as follows:

CUP	HOME COST	STORE COST	SAVINGS/LOSS
1	$12.50	$1.00	−$11.50

Case 2: Count = 24

2. Home Cost of Yogurt $=$ Count times HC plus MC
   $= 24 \times \$.50 + \$12.00$
   $= \$12.00 + \$12.00$
   $= \$24.00$

3. Store Cost of Yogurt $=$ Count times SC
   $= 24 \times \$1.00$
   $= \$24.00$

4. Since the Home Cost ($24.00) equals the Store Cost ($24.00), our output for this problem would appear as follows:

CUP	HOME COST	STORE COST	SAVINGS/LOSS
24	$24.00	$24.00	$.00

Case 3: Count = 40

2. Home Cost of Yogurt = Count times HC plus MC
   $$= 40 \times \$.50 + \$12.00$$
   $$= \$20.00 + \$12.00$$
   $$= \$32.00$$

3. Store Cost of Yogurt = Count times SC
   $$= 40 \times \$1.00$$
   $$= \$40.00$$

4. Since the Store Cost ($40.00) is greater than the Home Cost ($32.00), our output for this problem would appear as follows:

CUP	HOME COST	STORE COST	SAVINGS/LOSS
40	$32.00	$40.00	$8.00

Thus, our analysis for this set of problem data has shown that one should purchase yogurt from the store for quantities up to 24 cups; for quantities greater than 24 cups, it is more cost beneficial to make the yogurt at home.

Please refer to Figure 2.33 on the next page to follow the flowchart logic for Case 2 of this problem.

SUMMARY

In this chapter, you saw that the flowchart is a pictorial representation of the processes, in the correct sequence, required to solve a specific problem. The components of flowcharting are a group of special symbols that represent different activities and processes. These special symbols can be found on an instrument called a template which is used to aid in flowcharting the logic steps required to solve problems.

You also studied the following rules of flowcharting.

■ All flowcharts must begin and end with a terminal symbol.

■ By convention, flowchart blocks or symbols are usually drawn in columns.

■ Starting at the top of a column, the blocks or symbols physically appear one below the other in the column.

■ Flow lines connect the blocks or symbols in the sequence in which the processes are to be performed.

■ A flow line can connect two and only two flowchart symbols.

■ A flow line may have only one arrowhead appearing at the end of the line connecting to the symbol to which processing control is being passed.

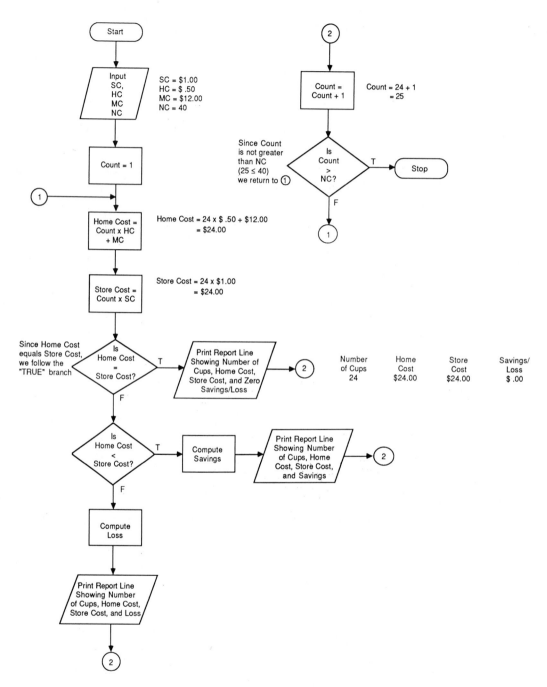

Figure 2.33 Logic Walk-Through—Health and Diet Problem

The advantages of the flowchart as a logic development tool are:

- They are pictorial in nature.
- They use specific symbols to represent specific processes that are being performed.
- The processes inside symbols can generally be translated on a one-for-one basis to a high-level language program statement.
- They are relatively easy to use.

The disadvantages are:

- The symbols used in flowcharts have special meanings which must be memorized.
- The diagrams can become quite lengthy for complex problem solutions.
- Required changes to a flowchart can be difficult, especially for long logic solutions.

The flowchart is probably the most basic logic development tool and the one most commonly used in beginning programming courses. It is a popular logic development tool for both beginning and experienced programmers.

REVIEW QUESTIONS

MULTIPLE CHOICE

1. Input and output operations in a flowchart are depicted by the use of which one of the following symbols?
   a. parallelogram
   b. circle
   c. rectangle
   d. terminal

2. Which of the following control structures cannot be shown by using a flowchart?
   a. iteration
   b. sequence
   c. selection
   d. performance

3. Which of the following is not used in flowcharting?
   a. flow lines
   b. step numbers
   c. blocks
   d. decision symbols
   e. terminal symbols

4. A process block in a flowchart typically denotes which of the following functions is being performed?
    a. calculation or assignment
    b. decision
    c. branching
    d. looping

5. A flowchart always begins with which one of the following symbols?
    a. decision
    b. block
    c. terminal
    d. parallelogram

FILL IN THE BLANK

1. A decision symbol in a flowchart has _____ branches representing _____ possible outcomes from a condition test.

2. A flowcharting _____ is an instrument often used by programmers in the drawing of flowcharts.

3. The _____ control structure is the default logic control structure used in flowcharting.

4. In flowcharting, processing control proceeds in the direction of the _____ shown as part of the flow line.

5. The diamond-shaped symbol in a flowchart says that a _____ is being made at this point in the processing logic of the problem solution.

SHORT ANSWER

1. Define the term *flowchart*.

2. Why is the flowchart a popular logic development tool for both beginning and experienced programmers?

3. Describe how program logic control structures are implemented in flowcharting.

4. What are the advantages of the flowchart as a logic development tool?

5. What are the disadvantages of the flowchart as a logic development tool?

EXERCISES

1. Draw a flowchart to compute the sum of the first *I* even integers.

2. Draw a flowchart to show the logic required to read five numbers, sort the numbers in ascending sequence (smallest to largest), and print out the sorted numbers.

3. Joe's Bar and Grill wants you to develop a program that will generate customer checks. Draw a flowchart that will depict the necessary logic to print out a customer check showing a description of the meal and its cost. Input items will be the meal description and its costs. Also, provide the capability to include a local sales tax percentage in the meal cost calculation.

4. Harvey's Discount Warehouse would like for you to write a program that will generate customer billings. The program should compute a discount based on the total sales amounts for all items purchased. The discount should be computed as follows:

   More than $2000—25%

   $1000–$2000—15%

   Less than $1000—10%

   Develop the logic to print customer billings based on the following input data record.

   1. Customer account number

   2. Item number

   3. Item description

   4. Item price

5. Smallville Library needs a system to keep track of overdue books. A daily report is needed that shows book number, book title, name of borrower, borrower's address, and due date for each overdue book. Develop the logic required to provide this report.

6. Acme Industries needs a personnel report that shows the ethnic distribution of its workforce. Draw a flowchart to produce a report that shows ethnic category, the total number of employees in each category, and the overall percentage in each category. Use the following codes to generate categories:

   1—White

   2—Black

   3—Oriental

   4—American Indian

   5—Other

7. Draw a flowchart to depict the logic required to show transactions entered against a checking account. Output requirements are a printed transaction log showing the date of activity, transaction type (W = withdrawal, D = deposit), amount of transaction, and current account balance. Assume a beginning balance of $1000.

8. Bonzo's Bargain Store would like a report showing its busiest day each week for in-store customers. Mr. Bonzo has accumulated records which show the total number of customers in the store on a daily basis (Monday through Friday). Draw a flowchart showing the logic required to determine the busiest day each week and print out the name of the day and the total number of customers on that day.

9. Each day the sales manager for A-OK Used Cars prepares a sales record showing that day's sales volume for all vehicles sold. Draw a flowchart to show the total number of days during the month when sales were greater than $1000. Assume the month had 30 days.

10. Draw a flowchart showing the logic required to print out a person's age in years based on the following input.

    1. Today's date (MM/DD/YY)

    2. The person's birthday (MM/DD/YY)

Pseudocode

OBJECTIVES

Upon completion of this chapter, you should be able to:

- Define the term pseudocode
- List and discuss the advantages and disadvantages of pseudocode as a logic tool
- Identify and use the rules and constraints associated with pseudocode
- Solve word problems using pseudocode as a logic development tool

Introduction

Pseudocode is a logic development tool that uses English-like statements or clauses to present the logical steps or activities necessary to solve a specific problem. What exactly does the term *pseudocode* mean? "Pseudo" technically means "false," so pseudocode, taken literally, means "false code." As used in logic development, the term is somewhat of a misnomer because pseudocode is really statements or clauses written in abbreviated form to depict the steps, in the correct sequence, required to solve a specific problem. These statements, or "code," can then be directly translated into computer programming language instructions. Pseudocode is "false code" only in the sense that it is not the programming language statements or "code" that is used to direct the action of the computer.

There are no special symbols required with pseudocode, but there are certain guidelines and elements of structure associated with using this methodology. Pseudocoding is a relatively easy technique to master and is a very common logic development tool in the commercial business environment.

Components

The best way to illustrate the components of pseudocode is to provide a sample. Figure 3.1 lists the pseudocode statements that depict the logic to compute the net pay for an employee for a given pay period.

As you can see from Figure 3.1, pseudocode is nothing more than short statements or clauses that convey the specific actions required in performing a particular process. Therefore, the only components of pseudocode are:

1. Words

2. Clauses

3. Sentences

These components and their ease of use are what make pseudocode such an attractive logic development tool to both beginning students and seasoned professional programmers. There are no special symbols with special meanings (such as flowcharting) that have to be memorized, and the rules and constraints are few, easy to understand, and highly flexible depending on an individual's personal writing style.

```
1. If hours worked is greater than 40,
      calculate overtime hours = hours worked minus 40
      calculate overtime pay rate = hourly pay rate times 1.5
      calculate overtime pay = overtime hours times overtime pay rate
      calculate regular pay = hourly pay rate times 40
      calculate gross pay = overtime pay plus regular pay
      calculate net pay = gross pay minus tax amounts minus other deductions.
2. If hours worked is less than or equal to 40,
      calculate gross pay = hours worked times hourly pay rate
      calculate net pay = gross pay minus tax amounts minus other deductions.
```

Figure 3.1 Sample Pseudocode Showing Net Pay Calculation

Rules and Constraints

The following rules for pseudocoding are easy to learn and use.

1. All statements should be presented in enough detail so the reader can clearly understand the activity or action being described in each individual statement.

2. The data names of variables being used to solve the problem should be totally descriptive of what the variable is or represents.

3. Each activity or action being depicted should be presented on a single line. Appropriate indentation should be used if the activity or action being described cannot fit on one line.

4. Indentation should be used where appropriate when coding statements to show the logical grouping of related activities or actions.

5. Statements should be numbered and presented in the required sequence to correctly solve the problem. These numbers are usually called *step numbers* because they represent logical steps in the solution to a problem.

Some of these rules may not seem too clear at this point. Let's work through a sample problem and illustrate how the rules are used in solving the problem.

Sample Problem

Assume that you have been asked to solve the following problem.

A salesperson's monthly commission is based on the total gross sales made during the month. The company records sales on a weekly basis and pays its commissions at the end of the month. The commission amount is 5% of total sales. Develop the pseudocode required to compute the monthly commission for a salesperson.

The first thing to do is determine what you are being asked to provide. In this problem, you are being asked to compute a monthly commission, so the output required to solve this problem will be some dollar amount.

Next you need to determine what data will be provided to work with in making the sales commission computation. As stated in the problem, you are provided weekly sales amounts. This means that you will have to sum all of the weekly amounts to arrive at a monthly sales total in order to compute the monthly commission.

Now you are ready to identify the specific processes required to solve this problem; that is, to provide a monthly commission amount. The first process involved in solving this problem is the matter of inputting the data, namely the weekly sales totals. A pseudocode statement to depict the process of data input is shown in Figure 3.2.

---

1. Input all weekly sales totals for the salesperson.

Figure 3.2 Pseudocode Statement Depicting Data Input

The next process with which you must be concerned is a calculation. This calculation is the adding or summing of all weekly sales totals for the salesperson. A pseudocode statement for this summation is shown in Figure 3.3.

The third process required to solve this problem is also a calculation, the computation of the monthly sales commission. Since you were given the factor (5%) for computing the sales commission and you have just completed the calculation of total monthly sales, you are now ready to compute the monthly sales commission. The pseudocode statement for this is shown in Figure 3.4.

You have now completed the sample problem using pseudocode. The complete set of pseudocode for this problem is contained in Figure 3.5.

Now, please refer back to the "Rules and Constraints" portion of this chapter. Let's compare these rules to the pseudocode shown in Figure 3.5.

The pseudocode in Figure 3.5 follows the guidelines of rule 1 in that each statement is presented in sufficient detail that the reader is able to understand the activities being presented.

The data names (weekly sales totals, monthly salesperson sales, and monthly sales commission) in Figure 3.5 are totally descriptive for the reader (rule 2).

---

2. Calculate monthly salesperson sales = the sum of the weekly sales totals

---

Figure 3.3 Pseudocode Statement for Monthly Sales Calculation

---

3. Calculate monthly sales commission = monthly salesperson sales times .05

Figure 3.4 Pseudocode Statement for Calculation of Monthly Sales Commission

---

```
SOLUTION TO SALESPERSON COMMISSION PROBLEM USING PSEUDOCODE
1. Input all weekly sales totals for the salesperson.
2. Calculate monthly salesperson sales  =  the sum of the
                                            weekly sales totals
3. Calculate monthly sales commission  =  monthly salesperson sales
                                            times .05
4. Stop processing.
```

Figure 3.5 Pseudocode Solution for Sample Problem

Each activity is presented on a single line when possible (rule 3).

Indentation is used in statements 2 and 3 to easily identify the processing activities involved (rule 4).

Each statement in Figure 3.5 is numbered and presented in the exact sequence in which the activity must be performed (rule 5).

Now that you have seen how the rules for this methodology work, let's discuss how pseudocode relates to structured programming methodology.

Program Logic Structures

Sequence

The sequence control structure is the default control structure used in pseudocoding. Notice that the statements (Figure 3.5) are each preceded by a step number which identifies the order in which the processes are being performed. In pseudocoding, statements are done in sequential fashion unless one of the pseudocode statements contains an instruction that interrupts the normal sequential flow from one step number to the next.

Selection

The pseudocode presented in Figure 3.1 represents how one would code the selection control structure under pseudocoding. Notice that when a decision is being represented with pseudocode, an IF statement is presented. There can only be two logical outcomes as a result of an IF statement being processed: the condition being tested is either TRUE or FALSE. In pseudocoding, an IF statement is usually presented as shown in Figure 3.6.

Many programmers and systems analysts do not use the more formal version of the selection control structure as depicted in Figure 3.6. Instead, they use the format shown in Figure 3.1 because it is somewhat less lengthy than the formal format, but it is just as valid in terms of the logic-processing activities being shown.

```
IF condition being tested is TRUE
  THEN
   - do all statements that are listed here
  ELSE the condition being tested is FALSE
   - do all statements that are listed here
```

Figure 3.6 IF-THEN-ELSE Control Structure Under Pseudocoding

Iteration

The iteration control structure in pseudocoding is usually implemented as shown in Figure 3.7. This statement implies that the activity or action stated in step 3 will be performed repetitively until the condition that all employee records have been processed is TRUE. Thus, pseudocode has the capability of providing the iteration control structure required by structured programming methodology.

```
6.  Perform step 3 until all employee records are processed.
```

Figure 3.7 Iteration Control Structure Under Pseudocode

Advantages and Disadvantages of Pseudocode

Some of the advantages of pseudocode are:

- It is easy to use because it uses English-like statements

- No special symbols are used to represent specific functions

- No specific syntax is required

- Statements can generally be translated on a one-for-one basis to high-level language program statements

Some of the disadvantages are:

- Diagrams can become quite lengthy for complex problems

- To present top-down design concepts, pseudocode must usually be used in conjunction with another logic development tool

Summary of Pseudocoding Procedures

The following list is a summary of the steps to be followed in using pseudocode procedures to solve a logic problem.

1. Determine what is the required output of the problem: a report, the result of a calculation, a message, or a file, for example.

2. Determine what input data has been provided by the problem.

3. List, either mentally or on a piece of paper, each of the processes that must be performed in order to take the input data, process it, and provide the desired output.

4. Next determine the proper sequence in which the processes identified in step 3 must be performed.

5. Start with the first process identified in step 4 and label it as step 1 using the appropriate words, clauses and/or sentences to communicate the activity or action that must be accomplished at this point in the logic.

6. Repeat step 5 for as many processes as are required to solve the problem. Number each successive process with the next step number in the sequence.

Now let's solve the standard set of six problems. After completing this problem set, you should be well qualified as a beginning pseudocoder.

PROBLEM SOLUTIONS

▶ Problem 1—Lease Versus Buy ◀

Ajax Manufacturing Company has the option to purchase outright or lease (with an option to buy at lease-end) a computer system to aid in its business operations. If Ajax purchases the system for $10,000, it will finance the full amount for four years at a 10% interest rate.

> **NOTE:** Simple Interest (I) = Principal (P) × Rate (R) × Time Period (T).

If Ajax leases the equipment for four years and decides to purchase at lease-end, the monthly cost will be $250 with a final payment of $3000. Which option should Ajax choose in order to minimize the total cost of the computer system? The problem solution should satisfy varying lease versus buy input information.

As always in solving any word problem, you need to determine what the output requirements are. In this problem, you are being asked to identify the recommended option for procuring the computer system. This means that you have to calculate and compare the total cost of each option in order to make a recommendation.

All of the cost data associated with each option has been given as the input for solving this problem. You need to determine what calculations must be done on this data in order to provide a total cost for each option.

To compute the cost of the purchase option, the first step that you must provide for in your pseudocode is inputting the data for this option. Refer back to Figure 3.5, the sample problem solution. Step 1 for this problem (Figure 3.8) is very similar to step 1 in Figure 3.5.

1. Input all data for the purchase option:
   - purchase price
   - interest rate
   - time period

Figure 3.8 Input Statement—Purchase Option—Standard Problem 1

There are two costs associated with the purchase option: one is the purchase price of the computer system and the other is the finance cost. You are given the purchase price as part of the problem statement. However, you must compute the finance cost, so the next process that must be shown in the pseudocode is shown in Figure 3.9. You now have all the data you need to compute the total cost of the purchase option as shown in Figure 3.10.

2. Calculate the finance cost of the purchase option:
Finance cost = purchase price times interest rate times time period

Figure 3.9 Finance Cost Calculation—Standard Problem 1

3. Calculate the total cost of the purchase option:
Total purchase cost = purchase price plus finance cost

Figure 3.10 Total Cost Calculation—Purchase Option—Standard Problem 1

The next process for solving this problem is similar to step 1, the inputting of data for the lease-purchase option. Refer to Figure 3.11.

4. Input all data for the lease-purchase option:
- monthly lease cost
- number of payments
- lump sum cost

Figure 3.11 Input Statement—Lease-Purchase Option—Standard Problem 1

Now that you have all of the input data for this option, you need to consider what costs make up the total cost of the option. As you can see from the problem statement, there are two costs: the total cost for the lease and the lump sum cost. You are given the lump sum cost in the problem statement, but you must calculate the total lease cost. This is step 5 as shown in Figure 3.12.

```
5. Calculate the total lease cost of the lease-purchase option:
   Total lease cost = monthly lease cost times number of payments
```

Figure 3.12 Lease Cost Calculation—Standard Problem 1

The next step is just like step 3, but step 6 represents the total cost of the lease-purchase option as shown in Figure 3.13.

```
6. Calculate the total cost of the lease-purchase option:
   Total lease-purchase = total lease cost plus
        option cost            lump sum cost
```

Figure 3.13 Total Cost Calculation—Lease-Purchase Option—Standard Problem 1

Now that you have determined the cost of each option, you need only to compare the two costs. Refer to Figure 3.14. This step completes the requested action of the problem statement because it identifies which option should be selected by Ajax. All of the pseudocode for the solution of this problem is shown in Figure 3.15.

```
7. If the total cost of the purchase option is greater than the total cost of the lease-purchase option
      then
          print  "THE RECOMMENDED OPTION IS THE LEASE-PURCHASE OPTION"
          stop processing
      else
          print  "THE RECOMMENDED OPTION IS THE PURCHASE OPTION"
          stop processing
```

Figure 3.14 Cost Comparison of the Two Options—Standard Problem 1

---

1. Input all data for the purchase option:
   - purchase price
   - interest rate
   - time period
2. Calculate the finance cost of the purchase option:
   Finance cost = purchase price times interest rate
                                       times time period
3. Calculate the total cost of the purchase option:
   Total purchase cost = purchase price plus finance cost
4. Input all data for the lease-purchase option:
   - monthly lease cost
   - number of payments
   - lump sum cost
5. Calculate the total lease cost of the lease-purchase option:
   Total lease cost = monthly lease cost times
                               number of payments
6. Calculate the total cost of the lease-purchase option:
   Total lease-purchase option cost = total lease cost
                                              plus
                                     lump sum cost
7. If the total cost of the purchase option is greater
   than the total cost of the lease-purchase option
       then
           print "THE RECOMMENDED OPTION IS THE LEASE-PURCHASE
                  OPTION"
           stop processing
       else
           print "THE RECOMMENDED OPTION IS THE PURCHASE
                  OPTION"
           stop processing

Figure 3.15 Pseudocode Solution for Standard Problem 1

Now you can solve the problem with the actual data provided by the problem. Refer to Figure 3.16.

1. Input all data for the purchase option:
   - purchase price = $10,000
   - interest rate   = 10%
   - time period   = 4 years
2. Calculate the finance cost of the purchase option:
   Finance cost = purchase price times interest rate times time period
   $$= \$10,000 \times 0.10 \times 4$$
   $$= \$4000$$
3. Calculate the total cost of the purchase option:
   Total purchase cost = purchase price plus
                         finance cost
   $$= \$10,000 + \$4000$$
   $$= \$14,000$$
4. Input all data for the lease-purchase option:
   - monthly lease cost   = $250
   - number of payments = 48
   - lump sum cost   = $3000
5. Calculate the total lease cost of the lease-purchase option:
   Total lease cost = monthly lease cost times number of payments
   $$= \$250 \times 48$$
   $$= \$12,000$$
6. Calculate the total cost of the lease-purchase option:
   Total lease-purchase option cost = total lease cost plus lump sum cost
   $$= \$12,000 + \$3000$$
   $$= \$15,000$$
7. If the total cost of the purchase option is greater than the total cost of the lease-purchase option
        then
            print "THE RECOMMENDED OPTION IS THE LEASE-PURCHASE OPTION"
            stop processing
        else
            print "THE RECOMMENDED OPTION IS THE PURCHASE OPTION"
            stop processing
   The total cost of the purchase option is $14,000 and the total cost of the lease-purchase option is
   $15,000. Since $14,000 is less than $15,000, the recommended option is the PURCHASE option.

Figure 3.16 Solution for Standard Problem 1

► Problem 2—Payroll ◄

Easymoney Inc. desires to generate their current manual payroll via computer. The information collected every payroll period includes the employee social security number, pay rate, hours worked, and total other deductions. The payroll department would like a report listing these items: employee social security number, hours worked, pay rate, gross pay, FICA withheld (6.13% of gross pay), federal tax withheld (20% of gross pay), total other deductions, and net pay.

As always, first determine what your output requirements are. In this problem, you have been requested to provide a report showing the payroll information as stated in the problem. You have also been provided with a set of the input data required for processing, so the first statement of pseudocode would look like Figure 3.17.

---

1. Input the employee's payroll data:
   - social security number
   - hours worked
   - hourly pay rate
   - total other deductions

Figure 3.17 Input Pseudocode Statement—Standard Problem 2

After these data items have been input, you are ready to do the first calculation: figure gross pay for the employee. In order to compute gross pay, you must test hours worked to see if the number of hours exceeds 40 so overtime pay can be included in the gross pay figure if appropriate. Do this test with the pseudocode statement shown in Figure 3.18.

---

2. If hours worked is greater than 40
      then
         overtime pay = (hours worked minus 40) times 1.5 times hourly pay rate
      else
         overtime pay = 0

Figure 3.18 Overtime Hours Computation—Pseudocode Statement—Standard Problem 2

Now you can compute gross pay for the employee as shown in Figure 3.19. Next you can calculate the net pay for the employee using the three pseudocode statements shown in Figure 3.20.

3. Calculate gross pay for the employee:
   Gross pay = hourly pay rate times 40 plus overtime pay

Figure 3.19 Gross Pay Calculation—Pseudocode Statement—Standard Problem 2

4. Calculate FICA tax for the employee:
   FICA tax = gross pay times 0.613
5. Calculate federal tax for the employee:
   Federal tax = gross pay times 0.20
6. Calculate net pay for the employee:
   Net pay = gross pay minus FICA tax
               minus federal tax
               minus total other deductions

Figure 3.20 Net Pay Calculation—Pseudocode Statement—Standard Problem 2

Now you have finished all of the required calculations for the employee and are ready to write a line on the requested report showing all of the payroll items for the employee. Depict the writing of this line with the pseudocode statement shown in Figure 3.21.

7. Write report line for the employee including the following items:
   - social security number
   - hours worked
   - hourly pay rate
   - gross pay
   - FICA tax
   - federal tax
   - total other deductions
   - net pay

Figure 3.21 Report Line Output—Pseudocode Statement—Standard Problem 2

There is only one more process to perform to complete this problem. You must check to ensure that you have processed all employees for this report. This is a pseudocode statement that uses an iterative process to perform a range of steps until the last employee has been processed. This statement is illustrated in Figure 3.22.

The complete set of pseudocode for the problem is shown in Figure 3.23.

8. Perform steps 1 through 7 until all employees have been processed.

Figure 3.22 Iterative Pseudocode Statement to Process All Employees—Standard Problem 2

1. Input the employee's payroll data:
   - social security number
   - hours worked
   - hourly pay rate
   - total other deductions
2. If hours worked is greater than 40
   then
      overtime pay = (hours worked minus 40) times 1.5 times hourly pay rates
   else
      overtime pay = 0.
3. Calculate gross pay for the employee:
   Gross pay = hourly pay rate times 40 plus overtime pay
4. Calculate FICA tax for the employee:
   FICA tax = gross pay times 0.0613
5. Calculate federal tax for the employee:
   Federal tax = gross pay times 0.20
6. Calculate net pay for the employee:
   Net pay = gross pay minus FICA tax minus federal tax minus total other deductions
7. Write report line for the employee including the following items:
   - social security number
   - hours worked
   - hourly pay rate
   - gross pay
   - FICA tax
   - federal tax
   - total other deductions
   - net pay
8. Perform steps 1 through 7 until all employees have been processed.
9. Stop processing.

Figure 3.23 Pseudocode Solution for Standard Problem 2

► **Problem 3—Health and Diet** ◄

Bedford Waistwatchers Association requests that a program be written to motivate members to stay on their diet and show the cost savings that can result from a change in diet. One of the staple diet items recommended is yogurt. If a member follows the Association diet strictly, a large amount of yogurt can be consumed over a short period of time. The cost effectiveness of buying yogurt or making yogurt at home should be evaluated. If a monetary savings can be realized by making yogurt at home versus buying it at the store, how many cups of yogurt must be produced to achieve this savings? The data needed to provide an analysis is store cost of yogurt per cup, cost of yogurt maker if made at home, cost of home ingredients per cup, and number of cups. An analysis should show the home cost, store cost, and savings or loss per cup.

What are you being asked to solve for in this problem? You are being asked to compare the cost of either making yogurt or buying it at the store for a range of cups from 1 to the number of cups specified. The first process involved in making this comparison is to input the data that you will be working with. Refer to Figure 3.24.

---

1. Input all data for the yogurt cost comparison:
   - store cost of yogurt per cup
   - home cost of ingredients per cup
   - cost of yogurt maker if made at home
   - number of cups

Figure 3.24 Input Pseudocode Statement—Standard Problem 3

The next process that you are concerned with are the calculations of the two costs for the yogurt. The pseudocode for these calculations is shown in Figure 3.25. Now you are ready to compare the home cost of yogurt versus the store cost. Do this with the two pseudocode decision statements shown in Figure 3.26.

---

2. Calculate the home cost of yogurt:
   Home cost = current number of cups times the home cost of ingredients per cup plus the cost of the yogurt maker
3. Calculate the store cost of yogurt:
   Store cost = current number of cups times the store cost of yogurt per cup

---

Figure 3.25 Yogurt Cost Calculations—Standard Problem 3

4. If the home cost of yogurt is equal to the store cost
    then
            print a report line showing current number of cups, home cost, store cost, and zero
                savings/loss
    else
            continue to step 5.
5. If the home cost of yogurt is less than the store cost
    then
            compute the savings,
            print a report line showing current number of cups, home cost, store cost,
                and savings
    else
            compute the loss,
            print a report line showing current number of cups, home cost, store cost,
                and loss.

Figure 3.26 Yogurt Cost Comparisons—Standard Problem 3

All that remains to solve this problem is to repeat steps 2 through 5 for the number of cups specified; that is, from 1 to whatever number of cups are desired as part of the analysis. This iteration process is shown as step 6 in Figure 3.27.

This completes the pseudocoding for this problem. The entire set of pseudocode is shown in Figure 3.27.

▶ Problem 4—Daily Sales ◀

Vidal Blass is the owner of Obnoxious Telephone Sales. Vidal has had up to 20 employees solicit sales via telephone on a specific day. Vidal would like to produce a sales summary report at the end of each business day to determine which salespeople generate the most revenue. Employees make a phone sale, write the sales information down on a receipt with their name and the total sale, and place the receipt in a bin shared by all of the employees. At the end of the day, all of the receipts are gathered and the summary report produced by entering the name and sales amount from each receipt. The first activity the computer will perform is to sort all input records in name order. (Assume that no two salespeople have the same name.) The sales summary will list the total sales by each name and the grand total sales for the day's business activities.

It's relatively easy to see what the output requirements of this problem are—a report showing daily sales for each salesperson and a grand total for all daily sales. Input data will be processed by the pseudocode statement shown in Figure 3.28.

1. Input all data for the yogurt cost comparison.
   - store cost of yogurt per cup
   - home cost of ingredients per cup
   - cost of yogurt maker if made at home
   - number of cups
2. Calculate the home cost of yogurt:
   Home cost = current number of cups times the home cost of ingredients per cup plus the cost of the yogurt maker
3. Calculate the store cost of yogurt:
   Store cost = current number of cups times the store cost of yogurt per cup
4. If the home cost of yogurt is equal to the store cost
      then
              print a report line showing current number of cups, home cost, store cost, and zero
                 savings/loss
      else
              continue to step 5.
5. If the home cost of yogurt is less than the store cost
      then
              compute the savings,
              print a report line showing current number of cups, home cost, store cost,
                 and savings
      else
              compute the loss,
              print a report line showing current number of cups, home cost, store cost,
                 and loss.
6. Perform steps 2 through 5 for the range 1 to the number of cups specified.
7. Stop processing.

Figure 3.27 Pseudocode Solution for Standard Problem 3

1. Input sales data for each salesperson:
   - salesperson name
   - sales amount from each individual sales receipt

Figure 3.28 Input Pseudocode Statement—Standard Problem 4

You must now test for what is called a control break; that is, a change in the salesperson name. If you don't remember what a control break is, please take a few moments and refer back to the flowchart solution for this problem in Chapter 2. Perform the test for a name change as shown in Figure 3.29.

2. If the salesperson name has changed
      then
            print a report line showing total daily sales for the current salesperson,
            add the current salesperson's daily sales total to grand total sales for all sales-
                  people,
            set the individual salesperson daily sales total equal to the sales amount from the first daily
                  sales receipt for the new salesperson just processed
      else
            add the current salesperson's sales amount from the current sales receipt to the individual
                  salesperson daily sales total.

Figure 3.29 Salesperson Name Change Test—Standard Problem 4

The next five pseudocode statements are related to the repetitive processing of all salespeople in the company, processing the data for the last set of daily sales receipts for the last salesperson, printing a grand total for all daily sales and the termination of processing. These statements are shown in Figure 3.30.

3. Perform step 1 and step 2 until all daily sales receipts have been processed.
4. Add the last salesperson's daily sales total to grand total sales for all salespeople.
5. Print a report line showing the total daily sales for the last salesperson processed.
6. Print a grand total line on the report showing grand total sales for the company.
7. Stop processing.

Figure 3.30 Repetitive and Termination Processing—Standard Problem 4

This completes the solution for this problem. The complete set of pseudocode is shown in Figure 3.31.

1. Input sales data for each salesperson:
   - salesperson name
   - sales amount from each individual sales receipt
2. If the salesperson name has changed

   then

   print a report line showing total daily sales for the current salesperson,
   add the current salesperson's daily sales total to grand total sales for all salespeople,
   set the individual salesperson daily sales total equal to the sales amount from the first daily
   sales receipt for the new salesperson just processed

   else

   add the current salesperson's sales amount from the current sales receipt to the individual
   salesperson daily sales total.
3. Perform step 1 and step 2 until all daily sales receipts have been processed.
4. Add the last salesperson's daily sales total to grand total sales for all salespeople.
5. Print a report line showing the total daily sales for the last salesperson processed.
6. Print a grand total line on the report showing grand total sales for the company.
7. Stop processing.

Figure 3.31 Pseudocode Solution for Standard Problem 4

► Problem 5—House Construction ◄

Well-Bilt Homes Inc. would like you to design a program which enables builders to calculate home building costs based on prospective room sizes. This program is interactive; it allows the user to input the number of rooms desired and the individual room dimensions (length and width only). The building cost per square foot is based on the following:

1000 square feet or less	$60 per square foot
1001–2000 square feet	$50 per square foot
More than 2000 square feet	$40 per square foot

Develop the logic to compute the building cost of the house.

In reviewing the problem, you can see that the output requirements are to provide the following for the user of this program:

■ The number of rooms in the house

■ The dimension (length and width) in feet of each room

■ The square footage for each room

■ The total square footage of the house

■ The total building cost for the house

Begin the solution for this problem with the two processes shown in Figure 3.32. Now that you know the number of rooms in the house, perform the actions shown in Figure 3.33 for the number of rooms specified.

---

1. Input the number of rooms desired for the house.
2. Output (or print) the number of rooms.

Figure 3.32 Inputting and Printing the Number of Rooms Desired—Standard Problem 5

---

3. Input the length and width dimensions for the current room being processed.
4. Calculate the square footage for the room dimensions specified in step 3.
5. Add the square footage computed in step 4 to the total square footage (accumulator) for the entire house.
6. Print an output (report) line showing the room dimensions and room square footage for the current room being processed.
7. Perform steps 3 through 6 for the number of rooms specified in step 1.

Figure 3.33 Processes for Each Desired Room—Standard Problem 5

The next process is the calculation of building costs. You must test the total square footage amount contained in the accumulator identified in step 5 so you can determine the appropriate building cost to use in the computation of the total cost of the house. Please refer to Figure 3.34.

8. If the total square footage of the house is greater than 2000 square feet, then use a building cost factor of $40 per square foot.
9. If the total square footage of the house is greater than 1000 square feet, but less than 2001 square feet, then use a building cost factor of $50 per square foot.
10. If the total square footage of the house is less than 1001 square feet, then use a building cost factor of $60 per square foot.

Figure 3.34 Building Cost Factor Determination—Standard Problem 5

All that remains for you to do to solve this problem is to calculate the cost of the house and output (print out) the total square footage, the building cost per square foot, the total cost of the house, and then stop processing. These processes are shown in Figure 3.35.

11. Calculate total cost of the house:
    Cost = total square footage times building cost factor per square foot
12. Print an output line showing the total square footage for the house.
13. Print an output line showing the building cost per square foot.
14. Print an output line showing the total building cost of the home.
15. Stop processing.

Figure 3.35 Cost Calculation and Final Output Items—Standard Problem 5

This completes Standard Problem 5. The entire set of pseudocode for this problem is contained in Figure 3.36.

1. Input the number of rooms desired for the house.
2. Output (or print) the number of rooms.
3. Input the length and width dimensions for the current room being processed.
4. Calculate the square footage for the room dimensions specified in step 3.
5. Add the square footage computed in step 4 to the total square footage (accumulator) for the entire house.
6. Print an output (report) line showing the room dimensions and room square footage for the current room being processed.
7. Perform steps 3 through 6 for the number of rooms specified in step 1.
8. If the total square footage of the house is greater than 2000 square feet, then use a building cost factor of $40 per square foot.
9. If the total square footage of the house is greater than 1000 square feet, but less than 2001 square feet, then use a building cost factor of $50 per square foot.
10. If the total square footage of the house is less than 1001 square feet, then use a building cost factor of $60 per square foot.
11. Calculate total cost of the house:
    Cost = total square footage times building cost factor per square foot
12. Print an output line showing the total square footage for the house.
13. Print an output line showing the building cost per square foot.
14. Print an output line showing the total building cost of the home.
15. Stop processing.

Figure 3.36 Pseudocode Solution for Standard Problem 5

▶ Problem 6—Personnel Statistics ◀

The chairman of the board of Eldorado Enterprises Inc. has requested a report from the Personnel Department that will show various types of information about the company's work force. This report should provide the following:

1. The total number of males and females (SEX CODE = M for males, F for females)

2. The total number of employees by the following age categories (BIRTHDAY YEAR)
   a. less than 21
   b. 21–30
   c. 31–40
   d. 41–50
   e. 51–60
   f. 61–70
   g. over 70

3. The total number of people who have been with the company for 10 years or more (SENIORITY CODE = 3, 4, or 5)

4. The total number of engineers (OCCUPATION CODE = 7) in the company

In reviewing this problem, notice that it is requesting a wide variety of information related to company personnel. You will need to make several decisions or tests and add to accumulators to derive the number of employees who meet any of the requested criteria. Begin pseudocoding with two input statements: one for inputting today's year and the other for inputting data about an individual employee. Refer to Figure 3.37.

```
1. Input today's year.
2. Input all data for the individual employee:
   - sex code
   - birthday year
   - seniority code
   - occupation code
```

Figure 3.37 Input Pseudocode Statements—Standard Problem 6

Next check to see if the employee is a male or female so that you may increment the accumulators for male or female, respectively. Refer to Figure 3.38. Next, calculate the employee's age in years in order to perform the age grouping counts that are requested by the problem. This is shown in Figure 3.39. Now you are ready to perform the series of tests to determine the age category for the employee. These tests are shown in Figure 3.40. The final two decisions related to accumulation are for seniority code and occupation code. These two statements are contained in Figure 3.41. There are only three more processes required to solve this problem. The final three are shown in Figure 3.42.

```
3. If sex code is equal to "M"
      then
            add 1 to male accumulator
      else
            add 1 to female accumulator.
```

Figure 3.38 Sex Code Test and Accumulate—Standard Problem 6

4. Calculate employee's age in years:
    Age = today's year minus birthday year

Figure 3.39 Employee Age Calculation—Standard Problem 6

5. If employee age is greater than 70 add 1 to over-70 accumulator.
6. If employee age is greater than 60 add 1 to 61-70 accumulator.
7. If employee age is greater than 50 add 1 to 51-60 accumulator.
8. If employee age is greater than 40 add 1 to 41-50 accumulator.
9. If employee age is greater than 30 add 1 to 31-40 accumulator.
10. If employee age is greater than 20 add 1 to 21-30 accumulator.
11. If employee age is less than 21 add 1 to under-21 accumulator.

Figure 3.40 Age Category Accumulations—Standard Problem 6

12. If seniority code is equal to 3 or 4 or 5 add 1 to 10-year seniority accumulator.
13. If occupation code is equal to 07 add 1 to engineer-count accumulator.

Figure 3.41 Seniority Code and Occupation Code Tests—Standard Problem 6

14. Perform step 2 through step 13 until all employees have been processed.
15. Print a report showing all of the employee statistics that have been accumulated in the respective accumulators used in the previous processing steps.
16. Stop processing.

Figure 3.42 Iterative Processing and Output Statements—Standard Problem 6

This completes Standard Problem 6. The complete set of pseudocode statements depicting the solution for this problem is shown in Figure 3.43. At this point you should be relatively comfortable with pseudocode as a logic development tool for problem solving. Now, let's work through a few of the standard problems using some typical data values.

1. Input today's year.
2. Input all data for the individual employee:
   - sex code
   - birthday year
   - seniority code
   - occupation code
3. If sex code is equal to "M"
       then
               add 1 to male accumulator
       else
               add 1 to female accumulator.
4. Calculate employee's age in years:
   Age = today's year minus birthday year
5. If employee age is greater than 70 add 1 to over-70 accumulator.
6. If employee age is greater than 60 add 1 to 61-70 accumulator.
7. If employee age is greater than 50 add 1 to 51-60 accumulator.
8. If employee age is greater than 40 add 1 to 41-50 accumulator.
9. If employee age is greater than 30 add 1 to 31-40 accumulator.
10. If employee age is greater than 20 add 1 to 21-30 accumulator.
11. If employee age is less than 21 add 1 to under-21 accumulator.
12. If seniority code is equal to 3 or 4 or 5 add 1 to 10-year seniority accumulator.
13. If occupation code is equal to 07 add 1 to engineer-count accumulator.
14. Perform step 2 through step 13 until all employees have been processed.
15. Print a report showing all of the employee statistics that have been accumulated in the respective accumulators used in the previous processing steps.
16. Stop processing.

Figure 3.43 Pseudocode Solution for Standard Problem 6

Pseudocode Walk-Through

This section of the chapter shows solutions to two problems from the standard problem set using sample data values for the variables.

▶ Problem 2—Payroll ◀

The following data is provided for two typical employees of Easymoney Inc.:

Employee Number	Social Security Number	Hours Worked	Hourly Pay Rate	Total Other Deductions
1	123-45-7898	40	$5.00	$50.00
2	222-01-1234	50	6.00	75.00

Please refer to Figure 3.23 for the logic used to compute the employee's individual pay.

Employee #1:

1. Input 123-45-7898, 40, $5.00, $50.00

2. Since Hours Worked is not greater than 40, Overtime Pay = 0.

3. Gross Pay = Hourly Pay Rate times 40 plus Overtime Pay
   = $5.00 × 40 + 0
   = $200.00

4. FICA Tax = Gross Pay times 0.0613
   = $200.00 × 0.0613
   = $12.26

5. Federal Tax = Gross Pay times 0.20
   = $200.00 × 0.20
   = $40.00

6. Net Pay = Gross Pay − FICA Tax − Federal Tax − Total Other Deductions
   = $200.00 − $12.26 − $40.00 − $50.00
   = $97.74

7. Write a Report Line.

Social Security Number	Hours Worked	Hourly Pay Rate	Gross Pay	FICA Tax	FED Tax	Total Other Deductions	Net Pay
123-45-7898	40	5.00	200.00	12.26	40.00	50.00	97.74

Employee #2:

1. Input 222-01-1234, 50, $6.00, $75.00

2. Since Hours Worked is greater than 40,
   Overtime Pay = (Hours Worked − 40) times 1.5 times Hourly Pay Rate
   = (50 − 40) × 1.5 × $6.00
   = $90.00

3. Gross Pay = Hourly Pay Rate times 40 plus Overtime Pay
   = $6.00 × 40 + 90.00
   = $330.00

4. FICA Tax = Gross Pay times 0.0613
   = $330.00 × 0.0613
   = $20.23

5. Federal Tax = Gross Pay times 0.20
    = $330.00 × 0.20
    = $66.00

6. Net Pay = Gross Pay − FICA Tax − Federal Tax − Total Other Deductions
    = $330.00 − $20.23 − $66.00 − $75.00
    = $168.77

7. Write a Report Line.

Social Security Number	Hours Worked	Hourly Pay Rate	Gross Pay	FICA Tax	FED Tax	Total Other Deductions	Net Pay
222-01-1234	50	6.00	330.00	20.23	66.00	75.00	168.77

► Problem 4—Daily Sales ◄

The following sales data is provided for salespeople of the Obnoxious Telephone Sales Company:

Salesperson Name	Sales Amount
Jones	$50.00
Jones	60.00
Jones	100.00
Smith	30.00
Smith	150.00
Turner	200.00
Turner	70.00

Please refer to Figure 3.31 for the logic used in solving this problem.

Jones, First Sales Receipt

1. Input Jones, $50.00

2. Since the name has not changed, add the current daily sales (SA) to the individual salesperson accumulator (ST):
    compute ST = ST + SA
      = 0 + $50.00
      = $50.00

Jones, Second Sales Receipt

1. Input Jones, $60.00

2. Since the name has not changed,
   compute ST $=$ ST + SA
   $=$ \$50.00 + \$60.00
   $=$ \$110.00

Jones, Third Sales Receipt

1. Input Jones, $100.00

2. Since the name has not changed,
   compute ST $=$ ST + SA
   $=$ \$110.00 + \$100.00
   $=$ \$210.00

Smith, First Sales Receipt

1. Input Smith, $30.00

2. Since the name has changed, print a report line showing total daily sales for the current salesperson.

SALESPERSON NAME	DAILY SALES
JONES	$210.00

Add the current salesperson's daily sales total (ST) to the daily sales accumulator (DS) for all salespeople.
   compute DS $=$ DS + ST
   $=$ 0 + \$210.00
   $=$ \$210.00

Set ST $=$ \$30.00, the first daily sales amount for the just processed salesperson, Smith.

Smith, Second Sales Receipt

1. Input Smith, $150.00

2. Since the name has not changed,
   compute ST $=$ ST + SA
   $=$ \$30.00 + \$150.00
   $=$ \$180.00

Turner, First Sales Receipt

1. Input Turner, $200.00

2. Since the name has changed,print a report line showing total daily sales for the current salesperson.

SALESPERSON NAME	DAILY SALES
SMITH	$180.00

Add the current salesperson's daily sales total to the daily sales accumulator for all salespeople.

$$\text{compute DS} = \text{DS} + \text{ST}$$
$$= \$210.00 + \$180.00$$
$$= \$390.00$$

Set ST = $200.00, the first daily sales amount for the just processed salesperson, Turner.

Turner, Second Sales Receipt

1. Input Turner, $70.00

2. Since the name has not changed,

$$\text{compute ST} = \text{ST} + \text{SA}$$
$$= \$200.00 + \$70.00$$
$$= \$270.00$$

Since there are no more sales receipts to be processed, proceed as directed in step 4 of Figure 3.31.

$$\text{compute DS} = \text{DS} + \text{ST}$$
$$= \$390.00 + \$270.00$$
$$= \$660.00$$

Then print a line for the last salesperson processed (step 5, Figure 3.31):

SALESPERSON NAME	DAILY SALES
TURNER	$270.00

Finally, print a grand total line showing total daily sales for the company (step 6, Figure 3.31).

TOTAL DAILY SALES FOR THE OBNOXIOUS TELEPHONE SALES COMPANY = $660.00

This completes the logic walk-through using pseudocode.

SUMMARY

In this chapter, you learned that pseudocode is a logic development tool that uses English-like statements or clauses to present the steps or activities that are necessary to solve a specific problem. The components that make up pseudocode are words, clauses, and sentences. These components are used in conjunction with the following rules.

- All statements should be presented in sufficient detail to convey a clear meaning to the reader.

- The data names of variables being used to solve the problem should be totally descriptive of what the variable represents.

- Each activity being depicted should be presented on a single line whenever possible.

- Indentation should be used where appropriate when coding statements to show the logical grouping of related activities.

- Statements should be numbered and presented in the required sequence to correctly solve the problem.

The advantages of pseudocode as a logic development tool are:

- It is easy to use because it uses English-like statements.

- It uses no special symbols to represent specific functions.

- It does not require a special syntax.

- Statements can generally be translated on a one-for-one basis to a high-level language program statement.

The disadvantages are:

- It requires lengthy diagrams to depict complex problem solutions.

- It must usually be presented in conjunction with another logic development tool in order to depict top-down design concepts.

Since pseudocode is easy to learn and use, it is a popular logic development tool for both beginning and experienced programmers.

REVIEW QUESTIONS

MULTIPLE CHOICE

1. Which of the following special symbols are used in pseudocode?
    a. blocks
    b. flow lines
    c. decision symbols
    d. uses no special symbols

2. Which of the following is not a component of pseudocode?
    a. flow lines
    b. words
    c. clauses
    d. sentences

3. Which of the following is not a rule for pseudocoding?
    a. Indentation should be used where appropriate in the coding.
    b. Data names of variables should be meaningful and descriptive.
    c. Statements can be listed in any desired order.
    d. Each activity being described should be presented on a single line whenever possible.

4. Which of the following control structures cannot be shown in pseudocode?
    a. iteration
    b. sequence
    c. transfer
    d. selection

5. Pseudocode statements are listed in the required order for processing. The numbers used to show the order of sequence are called one of the following:
    a. label numbers
    b. step numbers
    c. identifier numbers
    d. help numbers

FILL IN THE BLANK

1. Pseudocode uses _English like_ statements or clauses to present the steps necessary to solve a problem.

2. The _data names_ of variables used in pseudocode statements should be descriptive of what the variable represents.

3. _Steps_ should be used where appropriate when coding pseudocode statements to show the logical grouping of related activities.

4. The _sequential_ control structure is the default logic control structure in pseudocoding.

5. Pseudocode statements can usually be translated on a one-for-one basis into high-level program _code_ statements.

SHORT ANSWER

1. Define the term *pseudocode*. _English statements in steps._

2. Pseudocode is an attractive logic development tool for beginning and experienced programmers. Why? _Its easy to use,_

3. Briefly describe how program logic control structures are implemented in pseudocode.

4. What are the advantages of pseudocode as a logic development tool?

5. What are the disadvantages of pseudocode as a logic development tool?

EXERCISES

1. The Bozo Transfer and Storage Company would like you to write a computer program to compute the cost to ship items from one location to another. Your input data for each shipment will be a shipment number, zone number, cost per unit of weight, and item weight. Develop the logic to calculate and print out the total cost for each shipment that Bozo processes.

2. Tippy's Taco House desires a computer program that will itemize and summarize its monthly operating expenses. Tippy's keeps records showing the following:

   1. Expense item description

   2. Date incurred

   3. Amount of expense

   4. To whom paid

   5. Date paid

Develop the logic required to produce a report that will list each of Tippy's monthly expenses in detail and will calculate and print out Tippy's total monthly expenses.

3. Dirty Harry's Office Supply Company needs to know when the quantity on hand for any of its items is less than or equal to the desired safety stock level so that Dirty Harry can reorder these items. Show the logic required to produce a report that will list any items that Harry needs to reorder. Data items that should appear on the report are item number and reorder quantity.

4. The State Board of Labor is investigating Mary's Fly-By-Night Office Cleaning Company for unfair labor practices. Mary's payroll records show the following data:

     1. Employee name

     2. Employee social security number

     3. Hourly pay rate

     4. Hours worked

   The State Board would like you to develop a program which will list the above data on all employees who are paid at an hourly pay rate of less than $3.35 and/or have worked in excess of 100 hours during the pay period. Show the logic required for this program.

5. The State Department of Motor Vehicles is compiling a statistical report on the relationship between auto colors and traffic accidents. This agency would like you to provide a report which shows, by year, the total number of auto accidents for each auto color category. Your input data records will contain the accident year and auto color code for all accident reports filed. Develop the logic to produce this report. (Assume that your input file will be sorted by accident year and color code within year.)

Hierarchy Charts

OBJECTIVES

Upon completion of this chapter, you should be able to:

- Define the term hierarchy chart
- List and discuss the advantages and disadvantages of the hierarchy chart as a logic development tool
- Identify and use the rules and constraints associated with hierarchy charts
- Solve word problems using the hierarchy chart as a logic development tool

Introduction

The *hierarchy chart* is a logic development tool that uses boxes and connecting lines to depict program structure and the flow of program logic processes or activities. It is very similar to a structure chart which is another logic development tool discussed in a later chapter. A hierarchy chart is a pictorial representation of the structural relationships between the logical processes or activities that must be performed to solve a problem. The structural relationships are depicted as flow lines connecting each major process or activity. These lines show the controlling order in which the processes or activities are carried out as the problem is being solved.

There are special symbols required by the hierarchy chart logic development methodology. However, these will not be strangers to you if you have been through the flowcharting chapter of this textbook.

Components

The only two symbols used by hierarchy charts are shown in Figure 4.1. Figure 4.1(a) shows a "box" or rectangle which is used in a hierarchy chart to depict a process or activity that is being performed by the logic. You will notice that this is the same symbol used in flowcharting, also to show a process or activity.

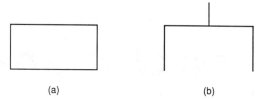

(a)   (b)

Figure 4.1 Symbols Used in Hierarchy Charts

However, there is a major difference as to how this symbol is used in a hierarchy chart versus how it is used in a flowchart. In a flowchart, the rectangle typically represents a single process or activity. In a hierarchy chart, the rectangle usually represents a group of processes or activities that are being performed at a particular point in the program. This group is logically related to a major function that is being shown as a single box to depict its overall relationship to all other major functions that are being performed in the program. These groups are usually referred to as *modules* and, as such, represent the major processes of the program. The pictorial depiction of these modules connected with flow lines represents the structure characteristic of the hierarchy chart methodology.

Figure 4.1(b) is a flow line much like the one used in flowcharting. However, there again is a difference as to how it is used in a hierarchy chart. Flow lines in a hierarchy chart move only in two directions, from top to bottom (or up to down) and from left to right. They do not use an arrow to depict the direction of the processing flow.

One other characteristic of hierarchy charts is the labeling of the boxes or rectangles with the name or description of the major function being shown by the box. This label identifies what set of activities or processes are occurring at this point in the logic.

Now let's illustrate a hierarchy chart with a sample problem. The hierarchy chart in Figure 4.2 represents the logic required to determine what items in a store's inventory are out of stock and print a report showing these items.

In reviewing Figure 4.2, you can see the basic format for hierarchy charts. Notice that the first box or block is on a level by itself. This level is called Level 1. By convention, this block is called the *driver* (or *main control*) module. As its name implies, this module controls directly or indirectly the processing of all other modules within the hierarchy chart.

Under the driver module are three other blocks, each labeled with a statement or phrase that is descriptive of the process that is represented by the respective block. Notice that two of these blocks are side by side and are on one level, labeled as Level 2. Processing control starts with the first block on the left for a given level of blocks and proceeds to each successive block, moving from left to right, unless there are other blocks directly underneath a particular block. When this occurs, processing control transfers directly to the block immediately underneath the higher level block. Please note in this example that the flow of control from block to block is controlled by statements contained in the driver module at the highest level.

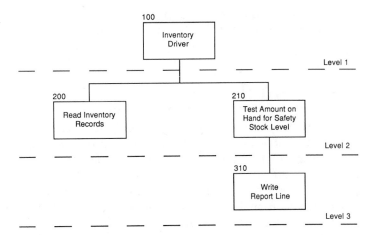

Figure 4.2 Sample Hierarchy Chart Inventory Problem

Rules and Constraints

The rules for using hierarchy charts are stated from the standpoint that this methodology will not stand alone as a logic development tool for developing detailed logic statements that can be easily transformed to specific programming code. For this reason, the following rules incorporate an additional component into this technique—pseudocode (Chapter 3).

1. Rectangles (blocks) must be used to represent the major processes to be performed in the hierarchy chart. These blocks are called "modules."

2. Modules should be labeled with an appropriate description of the exact function of the module. They should also be labeled with a number immediately above the upper left corner of the module (refer to Figure 4.2). The first number of the module label number should be the same as the level number on which the module occurs.

3. A module in a hierarchy chart must be connected to another module or modules using a flow line.

4. A hierarchy chart must begin with a main control (driver) module as the only module on the first logical level (Level 1) in the chart.

5. Each processing level within a hierarchy chart must be subordinate to the processing level above it.

6. Logical processing flow proceeds in a top-down, left-to-right fashion starting with the driver module. This means that processing control proceeds from an upper level module to a module occurring immediately underneath the upper one whenever the modules are so arranged. If there are no modules directly underneath a module, then processing control proceeds to the next module occurring on the right on the same processing level.

7. Use pseudocode statements as appropriate to define the specific processes that are being performed by each module in the hierarchy chart.

At this point, let's illustrate how these rules are applied by doing a sample problem.

Sample Problem

You have been given the following problem to solve.

Applegate Public Library needs a computer program to aid in keeping track of its overdue books. The library maintains a file of the following information about each of its books: book number, book title, author, borrower's name, borrower's address, and overdue status (Y if overdue, N if not overdue). Applegate would like you to generate a report that will show the following information: borrower's name, borrower's address, book number, book title, and author for any book whose overdue status is equal to a Y. Develop the logic to produce the requested report.

From the problem statement it is easy to determine that the output requirement of this problem is a report. You can also see from looking at the information requested on the report that you have all the necessary input data available. Processing to produce this report will consist of reading a file and checking a status field to see if you have encountered an overdue book.

Now identify the modules you will use in the problem solution. First, you will have a driver module with the functions listed as pseudocode statements. Refer to Figure 4.3. By looking at the driver module in Figure 4.3, you see that you will need two other modules to complete the problem solution. The module necessary for step 2 in the driver module is shown in Figure 4.4.

Please note that step 2 is calling a lower-level module to perform a major processing function; that is, inputting a book record for processing. This illustrates an important point concerning hierarchy charts: most statements contained in the various modules of a chart are invoking or "calling" lower-level (subordinate) modules to perform certain functions at a particular point in the problem-solving logic being depicted. These statements should not be construed to be "plain" logic instructions, but should be recognized as calling mechanisms for performing the various modules shown in the hierarchy chart.

LIBRARY REPORT DRIVER
1. Set END-OF-FILE indicator = 'NO'.
2. Input all data for this book (i.e., a BOOK RECORD).
3. If overdue status = 'Y'
    write a report line for this book.
4. Perform step 2 and step 3 until all books have been processed, i.e. END-OF-FILE indicator = 'YES'.
5. Stop processing.

Figure 4.3 Driver Module for Sample Hierarchy Chart Problem

INPUT BOOK RECORD
1. Read BOOK RECORD
2. If last record has been read
      then
            set END-OF FILE indicator = 'YES'.

Figure 4.4 Input Module for Sample Hierarchy Chart Problem

The modules necessary to do step 3 in the driver module are presented in Figures 4.5 and 4.6. These three modules represent the major processing functions required to solve the problem. The hierarchy chart representing the three modules is shown in Figure 4.7.

1. If overdue status = 'Y'
      then
            write a report line for this book.

Figure 4.5 Overdue Status Test Module for Sample Hierarchy Chart Problem

WRITE REPORT LINE
1. If the line-count for this page has been exceeded,
      then write new page heading information.
2. Write a report line showing the required data items.

Figure 4.6 Output Module for Sample Hierarchy Chart Problem

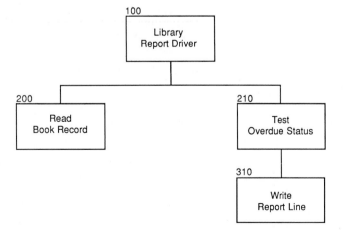

Figure 4.7 Sample Problem Hierarchy Chart

You will note from the sample problem solution that the hierarchy chart in Figure 4.7 gives the reader an idea of the structure of the processing control functions that must be performed in solving the problem. However, the detailed logic statements involved in the actual solution occur as pseudocode instructions for each of the modules shown. The approach in solving the remaining problems in this chapter is to show both the hierarchy charts and the detailed pseudocode statements for each module shown on the charts.

Now that you have seen an actual problem solution, let's discuss how hierarchy charts handle structured programming methodology.

Program Logic Structures

Hierarchy charts incorporate structured programming control structures (sequence, selection and iteration) into the individual modules that are shown on the charts themselves. The structures are represented in the pseudocode statements that describe the activities being performed by each module. Therefore, each of the three basic control structures is permitted in hierarchy chart methodology where necessary via the pseudocode that occurs in each module.

If you need to review how these control structures are implemented using pseudocode methodology, please refer to this same section in Chapter 3.

Advantages and Disadvantages of Hierarchy Charts

Some of the advantages of hierarchy charts are:

- They provide a good conceptual overview of all the major processes being performed in the problem solution

- Only two special symbols are used, the process block and the flow line

- A great deal of flexibility is available in constructing the charts, so it is relatively easy to add, change, or delete modules without disturbing any others

- They provide a good documentation tool for maintaining programs because a programmer can easily visualize the effects of adding, modifying, or deleting functions within the program

- Since each module contained on a hierarchy chart shows the pseudocode statements for performing the module's activities, the statements can generally be translated on a one-for-one basis to a high-level language program statement

- They provide an excellent tool for depicting top-down program design concepts

Some of the disadvantages are:

- Detailed instructions cannot be depicted on the charts but must be presented additionally as pseudocode statements for each module shown

- They provide only a structural view of the problem solution, not a detailed view of the individual logic steps required

- The diagrams can become quite lengthy for complex problems

Summary of Hierarchy Chart Procedures

The following list is a summary of the steps to be followed in using hierarchy charts to solve a logic problem.

1. Determine what is the required output of the problem: a report, the result of a calculation, a message, a file, for example.

2. Determine what input data has been provided by the problem.

3. List, either mentally or on a piece of paper, each of the major processes that must be performed in order to transform the input data to the desired output.

4. Determine which processes should be placed in the driver module and determine the proper sequence in which they should be performed.

5. Draw the first block or box on the hierarchy chart and label it as the driver module for the problem with a label number of 100 (see Figure 4.2).

6. Group all of the major processes being performed directly under the control of the driver module on the second level of the hierarchy chart. The first block being performed by the driver module should be the leftmost block on Level 2. Each of the other processes in the driver module should occur as blocks on Level 2 and follow in sequence moving in a left-to-right direction along Level 2. Label each module on this level with a number beginning with a 2 (prefix number) and a descriptive narrative label of the process itself inside the block.

7. Repeat the methodology of step 6 for as many levels and as many modules as are required to depict all processes necessary to solve the problem. Be sure to label all modules with the appropriate prefix level number and narrative process description.

8. After completing the hierarchy chart, develop on a separate page or pages the module pseudocode for each module shown on the chart.

Now move on and apply what you've learned by solving the standard problem set. Good luck!

PROBLEM SOLUTIONS

➤ Problem 1—Lease Versus Buy ◄

Ajax Manufacturing Company has the option to purchase outright or lease (with an option to buy at lease-end) a computer system to aid in its business operations. If Ajax purchases the system for $10,000, it will finance the full amount for four years at a 10% interest rate.

> **NOTE:** Simple Interest (I) = Principal (P) × Rate (R) × Time Period (T).

> If Ajax leases the equipment for four years and decides to purchase at lease-end, the monthly cost will be $250 with a final payment of $3000. Which option should Ajax choose in order to minimize the total cost of the computer system? The problem solution should satisfy varying lease versus buy input information.

In reviewing this problem, notice that the only output requirement is to identify the recommended option for procuring a computer system for Ajax. You need to calculate the costs of the two available options and then compare those costs in order to make a recommendation. Since you have all of the data available to make the necessary calculations, identify what processing modules you need to show on the hierarchy chart in order to solve the problem.

Of course, the first module will be the driver module, which will contain the following processes to be performed:

1. Input all purchase option and lease-purchase option data

2. Calculate the purchase cost of the system

3. Calculate the lease-purchase cost of the system

4. Compare two options and print out recommendation

5. Stop processing

The completion of these processes will produce the desired solution to the problem. The hierarchy chart showing these processes is shown in Figure 4.8.

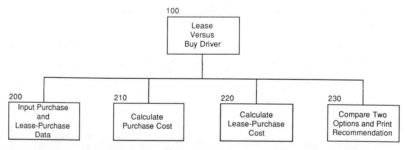

Figure 4.8 Lease Versus Buy Problem Hierarchy Chart

You now need to develop the pseudocode for the five processing modules required for this problem. This pseudocode follows in Figure 4.9.

This completes the hierarchy chart solution for this problem. Now that you've finished the hierarchy chart for this problem, which option should Ajax choose? When you plug in all the numbers and do the calculations, you will see that the recommendation is the purchase option because its cost ($14,000) is less than the lease-purchase option ($15,000).

LEASE VERSUS BUY DRIVER
1. Input all purchase and lease-purchase option data.
2. Calculate purchase cost.
3. Calculate lease-purchase cost.
4. Compare two options and print out recommendation.
5. Stop processing.

INPUT PURCHASE AND LEASE-PURCHASE DATA
1. Input purchase price.
2. Input interest rate.
3. Input time period.
4. Input monthly lease cost.
5. Input number of payments.
6. Input lump sum cost.

CALCULATE PURCHASE COST
1. Calculate finance cost:
   Finance cost = purchase price times interest rate times time period
2. Calculate purchase cost:
   Purchase cost = purchase price plus finance cost

CALCULATE LEASE-PURCHASE COST
1. Calculate total lease cost:
   Total lease cost = monthly lease cost times number of payments
2. Calculate lease-purchase cost = total lease cost plus lump sum cost

COMPARE TWO OPTIONS AND PRINT RECOMMENDATION
1. If the total cost of the purchase option is greater than the total cost of the lease-purchase option
        then
                print "THE RECOMMENDED OPTION IS THE LEASE-PURCHASE OPTION"
                stop processing
        else
                print "THE RECOMMENDED OPTION IS THE PURCHASE OPTION"
                stop processing.

Figure 4.9 Pseudocode for Standard Problem 1 Modules

▶ Problem 2—Payroll ◀

Easymoney Inc. desires to generate their current manual payroll via computer. The information collected every payroll period includes the employee social security number, pay rate, hours worked, and total other deductions. The payroll department would like a report listing these items: employee social security number, hours worked, pay rate, gross pay, FICA withheld (6.13% of gross pay), federal tax withheld (20% of gross pay), total other deductions and net pay.

Once again, the output requirement for this problem is a report showing various pieces of payroll information for the company's employees. All of the required input data is provided for making the necessary computations, so identify the major processes that should be invoked in the driver module and shown on the hierarchy chart. These processes are:

1. Input employee pay record

2. Calculate gross pay

3. Calculate taxes to be withheld

4. Calculate net pay

5. Write report line

6. Stop processing

The hierarchy chart for these modules is shown in Figure 4.10.

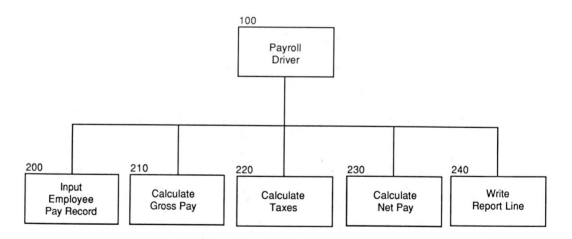

Figure 4.10 Payroll Problem Hierarchy Chart

Now develop the pseudocode for each of the modules shown on the previous hierarchy chart. Please refer to Figure 4.11.

PAYROLL DRIVER
1. Set END-OF-FILE INDICATOR = 'NO'.
2. Input employee pay record.
3. Calculate gross pay for the employee.
4. Calculate taxes to be withheld for the employee.
5. Calculate net pay for the employee.
6. Write a report line for the employee.
7. Perform step 2 through step 6 until all employees have been processed, i.e., END-OF-FILE = 'YES'.
8. Stop processing.

INPUT EMPLOYEE PAY RECORD
1. Read EMPLOYEE PAY RECORD:
   - social security number
   - hours worked
   - hourly pay rate
   - total other deductions
2. If last record has been read
      then
            set END-OF-FILE indicator = 'YES'.

CALCULATE GROSS PAY
1. If hours worked is greater than 40
      then
            overtime pay = (hours worked minus 40) times 1.5 times hourly pay rate
      else
            overtime pay = 0.
2. Calculate gross pay for the employee:
   Gross pay = hourly pay rate times 40 plus overtime pay

Figure 4.11 Pseudocode for Standard Problem 2 Modules

```
CALCULATE TAXES
1. Calculate FICA tax for the employee:
   FICA tax = gross pay times 0.0613
2. Calculate federal tax for the employee:
   Federal tax = gross pay times 0.20

CALCULATE NET PAY
1. Calculate net pay for the employee:
   Net pay = gross pay minus FICA tax minus federal tax minus total other deductions

WRITE REPORT LINE
1. If the line-count for this page has been exceeded,
      then write new page heading information.
2. Write a report line for the employee including the following items:
   - social security number
   - hours worked
   - hourly pay rate
   - gross pay
   - FICA tax
   - federal tax
   - total other deductions
   - net pay
```

Figure 4.11 Pseudocode for Standard Problem 2 Modules (continued)

▶ Problem 3—Health and Diet ◀

Bedford Waistwatcher's Association requests that a program be written to motivate members to stay on their diet. One of the staple diet items recommended is yogurt. If a member follows the Association diet strictly, a large amount of yogurt can be consumed over a short period of time. The cost effectiveness of buying yogurt or making yogurt at home should be evaluated. The data needed to provide an analysis is store cost of yogurt per cup, cost of yogurt maker if made at home, cost of home ingredients per cup, and number of cups. An analysis should show the number of cups, home cost, store cost, and savings or loss per cup.

In reviewing the problem statement, you can see that you are being asked to compare the cost of two ways of obtaining yogurt. This means that you must perform the following processes (which should be shown in the driver module):

1. Input data for yogurt cost comparison

2. Calculate yogurt costs for both alternatives

3. Compare the two costs of obtaining yogurt for the range of cups specified

4. Stop processing

Please review the hierarchy chart depicting these modules in Figure 4.12.

The pseudocode for the modules shown on the previous hierarchy chart is contained in Figure 4.13.

This completes the hierarchy chart solution for Standard Problem 3.

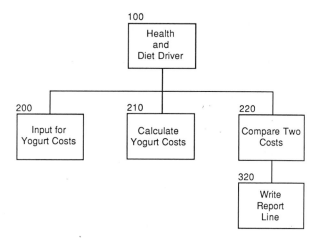

Figure 4.12 Health and Diet Problem Hierarchy Chart

HEALTH AND DIET DRIVER
1. Input data for yogurt cost comparison.
2. Calculate yogurt costs.
3. Compare the two costs of obtaining yogurt and print out a recommendation.
4. Perform step 2 and step 3 for the range 1 to the number of cups specified.
5. Stop processing.

INPUT DATA FOR YOGURT COST
1. Input store cost of yogurt per cup.
2. Input home cost of ingredients per cup.
3. Input cost of yogurt maker if made at home.
4. Input number of cups.

CALCULATE YOGURT COSTS
1. Calculate the home cost of yogurt:
    Home cost = current number of cups times the home cost of ingredients per cup plus the cost of
                the yogurt maker
2. Calculate the store cost of yogurt:
    Store cost = current number of cups times the store cost of yogurt per cup

Figure 4.13 Pseudocode for Standard Problem 3 Modules

```
COMPARE TWO COSTS
1. If the home cost of yogurt is equal to the store cost
      then
            write a report line showing zero savings/loss
      else
            continue to step 2.
2. If the home cost of yogurt is less than the store cost
      then
            write a report line showing savings
      else
            write a report line showing loss.

WRITE REPORT LINE
1. If the line-count for this page has been exceeded,
      then write new page heading information.
2.   Write a report line showing the following items:
     - current number of cups
     - home cost
     - store cost
     - zero savings/loss or savings or loss
```

Figure 4.13 Pseudocode for Standard Problem 3 Modules (continued)

▶ Problem 4—Daily Sales ◀

Vidal Blass is the owner of Obnoxious Telephone Sales. Vidal has had up to 20 employees solicit sales via telephone on a specific day. Vidal would like to produce a sales summary report at the end of each business day to determine which salespeople generate the most revenue. Employees make a phone sale, write the sales information down on a receipt with their name and the total sale, and place the receipt in a bin shared by all of the employees. At the end of the day, all of the receipts are gathered and the summary report produced by entering the name and sales amount from each receipt. The first activity the computer will perform is to sort all input records in name order. (Assume that no two salespeople have the same name.) The sales summary will list the total sales by each name and the grand total sales for the day's business activities.

Develop the logic to provide this summary report. This problem solution requires an output report showing daily sales for each salesperson and a grand total for all daily sales. List the major processes that need to be called by the driver module and shown on the hierarchy chart. These processes are:

1. Input salesperson sales receipt record

2. Check for salesperson name change and accumulate individual and daily total sales

3. Write a grand total line for daily sales

4. Stop processing

The hierarchy chart for these modules is shown in Figure 4.14.

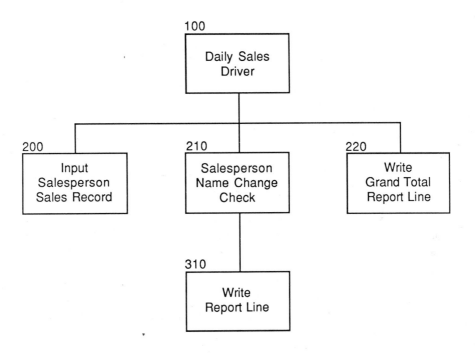

Figure 4.14 Daily Sales Problem Hierarchy Chart

Now develop the pseudocode for each of the modules shown on the previous hierarchy chart. This pseudocode is shown in Figure 4.15.

DAILY SALES DRIVER
1. Set END-OF-FILE indicator = 'NO'.
2. Input salesperson sales receipt record.
3. Check for salesperson name change and accumulate individual and grand total sales.
4. Perform step 2 through step 3 until all salespeople have been processed, i.e., END-OF-FILE = 'YES'.
5. Write a grand total line for daily sales.
6. Stop processing.

INPUT SALESPERSON SALES RECORD
1. Read SALESPERSON SALES RECORD:
   - salesperson name
   - sales amount from each individual sales receipt
2. If last record has been read
      then
            set END-OF-FILE indicator = 'YES'.

SALESPERSON NAME CHANGE CHECK
1. If the salesperson name has changed
      then
            write a report line for the current salesperson,
            add the current salesperson's daily sales total to grand total sales for all sales-
               people,
            set the individual salesperson daily sales total equal to the sales amount from the first daily
               sales receipt for the new salesperson just processed,
      else
            add the current salesperson's sales amount from the current sales receipt to the individual
               salesperson daily sales total.

WRITE REPORT LINE
1. If the line-count for this page has been exceeded,
      then write new page heading information.
2. Write a report line for the employee including the following items:
   - salesperson name
   - daily sales total

WRITE GRAND TOTAL REPORT LINE
1. Write a report line for the company showing grand total sales for all salespeople.

Figure 4.15 Pseudocode for Standard Problem 4 Modules

▶ Problem 5—House Construction ◀

Well-Bilt Homes Inc. would like you to design a program which enables builders to calculate home building costs based on prospective room sizes. This program is interactive; it allows the user to input the number of rooms desired and the individual room dimensions (length and width only). The building cost per square foot is based on the following:

1000 square feet or less	$60 per square foot
1001–2000 square feet	$50 per square foot
More than 2000 square feet	$40 per square foot

Develop the logic to compute the building cost of the house.

First analyze the problem to determine the output requirements. The user wishes to see the following information about the desired house:

- The number of rooms in the house

- The dimension (length and width) in feet of each room

- The square footage for each room

- The total square footage of the house

- The total building cost for the house

Next identify the major processes that need to be performed in the problem solution. These processes, as always, will appear in the driver module and on the hierarchy chart, and are as follows:

1. Input and print the number of rooms desired for the house

2. Input room dimensions for each room

3. Calculate and accumulate square footage for each room

4. Write a report line showing individual room statistics

5. Determine the building cost per square foot based on total square footage for the house

6. Calculate the total cost of the house

7. Write a report line showing summary information about the house

8. Stop processing

Please refer to the hierarchy chart for these processes in Figure 4.16.

Now that you've reviewed the hierarchy chart, develop the pseudocode for each of the required modules. This pseudocode is shown in Figure 4.17.

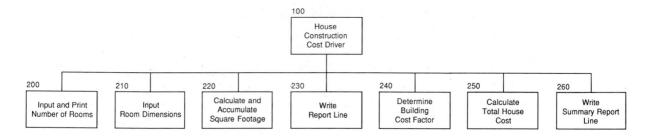

Figure 4.16 House Construction Problem Hierarchy Chart

HOUSE CONSTRUCTION COST DRIVER
1. Input and print the number of rooms desired for the house.
2. Input room dimensions for each room.
3. Calculate and accumulate the square footage for each room.
4. Write a report line for each room.
5. Perform step 2 through step 4 for the number of rooms specified in step 1.
6. Determine building cost per square foot.
7. Calculate the total cost of the house.
8. Write a summary report line.
9. Stop processing.

INPUT AND PRINT NUMBER OF ROOMS
1. Input the number of rooms desired for the house.
2. Output (or print) the number of rooms.

INPUT ROOM DIMENSIONS
1. Input the length and width dimensions for the current room being processed.

CALCULATE AND ACCUMULATE SQUARE FOOTAGE
1. Calculate the square footage for the room just processed:
   Room square footage = length times width
2. Add room square footage to total square footage for the house:
   Total square footage = total square footage plus room square footage

WRITE REPORT LINE
1. Write a report line for the room just processed showing:
   - room length
   - room width
   - room square footage

Figure 4.17 Pseudocode for Standard Problem 5 Modules

DETERMINE BUILDING COST FACTOR
1. If the total square footage of the house is greater than 2000 square feet, then use a building cost factor of $40 per square foot.
2. If the total square footage of the house is greater than 1000 square feet, but less than 2001 square feet, then use a building cost factor of $50 per square foot.
3. If the total square footage of the house is less than 1001 square feet, then use a building factor of $60 per square foot.

CALCULATE TOTAL HOUSE COST
1. Calculate total cost of the house:
   Cost = total square footage times building cost factor per square foot

WRITE SUMMARY REPORT LINE
1. Write a summary report line showing the following items:
   - total square footage of the house
   - building cost per square foot
   - total building cost of the house.

Figure 4.17 Pseudocode for Standard Problem 5 Modules (continued)

▶ Problem 6—Personnel Statistics ◀

The chairman of the board of Eldorado Enterprises Inc. has requested a report from the Personnel Department that will show various types of information about the company's work force. This report should provide the following:

1. The total number of males and females (SEX CODE = M for males, F for females)

2. The total number of employees by the following age categories (BIRTHDAY YEAR)
   a. less than 21
   b. 21–30
   c. 31–40
   d. 41–50
   e. 51–60
   f. 61–70
   g. over 70

3. The total number of people who have been with the company for 10 years or more (SENIORITY CODE = 3, 4, or 5)

4. The total number of engineers (OCCUPATION CODE = 7) in the company

In analyzing this problem, notice that the output requirement of this problem is a report showing all of the requested employee information. To produce this report, you will have to make several different tests and add to several accumulators for all employees who meet the specified criteria. The major processes or modules required for solving this problem are:

1. Input today's year

2. Input employee personnel record

3. Determine employee sex and accumulate

4. Determine employee age and accumulate by age category

5. Determine employee seniority and accumulate

6. Determine engineer category and accumulate

7. Generate a report showing the employee statistics

8. Stop processing

The hierarchy chart depicting these processing modules is shown in Figure 4.18. Please review the chart now.

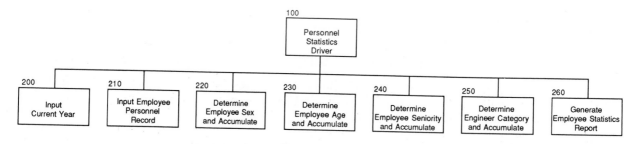

Figure 4.18 Personnel Statistics Hierarchy Chart

Now that you've looked at the hierarchy chart, go through the pseudocode for each of the required modules. Refer to Figure 4.19.

PERSONNEL STATISTICS DRIVER
1. Set END-OF-FILE indicator = 'NO'.
2. Input current year.
3. Input employee personnel record.
4. Determine employee sex and accumulate.
5. Determine employee age and accumulate by age category.
6. Determine employee seniority and accumulate.
7. Determine engineer category and accumulate.
8. Perform step 3 through step 7 until all employees have been processed, i.e., END-OF-FILE indicator = 'YES'.
9. Generate a report showing all employee statistics.
10. Stop processing.

INPUT CURRENT YEAR
1. Input today's year.

INPUT EMPLOYEE PERSONNEL RECORD
1. Read EMPLOYEE PERSONNEL RECORD.
2. If last record has been read
    then
        set END-OF-FILE indicator = 'YES'.

DETERMINE EMPLOYEE SEX AND ACCUMULATE
1. If sex code is equal to 'M'
    then
        add 1 to male accumulator
    else
        add 1 to female accumulator.

DETERMINE EMPLOYEE AGE AND ACCUMULATE BY AGE CATEGORY
1. Calculate employee's age in years:
   Age = today's year minus birthday year
2. If age is greater than 70 add 1 to over-70 accumulator.
3. If age is greater than 60, but less than 71 add 1 to 61-70 accumulator.
4. If age is greater than 50, but less than 61 add 1 to 51-60 accumulator.
5. If age is greater than 40, but less than 51 add 1 to 41-50 accumulator.
6. If age is greater than 30, but less than 41 add 1 to 31-40 accumulator.
7. If age is greater than 20, but less than 31 add 1 to 21-30 accumulator.
8. If age is less than 21 add 1 to under-21 accumulator.

DETERMINE EMPLOYEE SENIORITY AND ACCUMULATE
1. If seniority code is equal to 3 or 4 or 5 add 1 to 10-year seniority accumulator.

DETERMINE ENGINEER CATEGORY AND ACCUMULATE
1. If occupation code is equal to 07 add 1 to engineer-count accumulator.

Figure 4.19 Pseudocode for Standard Problem 6 Modules

GENERATE EMPLOYEE STATISTICS REPORT
1. Write a report showing the following employee information:
   - total number of males
   - total number of females
   - total number of employees over 70
   - total number of employees between 61 and 70
   - total number of employees between 51 and 60
   - total number of employees between 41 and 50
   - total number of employees between 31 and 40
   - total number of employees between 21 and 30
   - total number of employees under 21
   - total number of employees who have 10 or more years seniority in the company; and
   - total number of engineers in the company.

Figure 4.19   Pseudocode for Standard Problem 6 Modules (continued)

This completes the hierarchy chart solution for this problem as well as the standard problem set for this chapter. You should now be comfortable with the hierarchy chart as a logic development tool. Now let's move on to a set of walk-throughs which use sample data in solving some of the standard problems that have been discussed.

Hierarchy Chart Walk-Through

This section of the chapter shows solutions to two problems from the standard problem set using sample data values for the variables.

► Problem 3—Health and Diet ◄

The following data is provided for determining whether or not to purchase yogurt from a store or to make it at home.

Store cost per cup of yogurt = $1.50

Home cost of ingredients per cup = $1.00

Cost of yogurt maker = $10.00

Number of cups of yogurt required = 30

Please refer to Figure 4.13 for the logic used to compare the cost of the two methods for obtaining yogurt.

Module 200—Input Data for Yogurt Cost

1. Input the previous data.

Case 1: Number of Cups = 1
Module 210—Calculate Yogurt Costs

1. Home Cost of Yogurt = Current Number of Cups times Home Cost of Ingredients per
Cup plus Yogurt Maker Cost
= 1 × $1.00 + $10.00
= $11.00

2. Store Cost of Yogurt = Current Number of Cups times Store Cost per Cup
= 1 × $1.50
= $1.50

Module 220—Compare Two Costs

Since the Home Cost ($11.00) is greater than the Store Cost ($1.50), the report line generated by
Module 320 would appear as follows:

CUP	HOME COST	STORE COST	SAVINGS/LOSS
1	$11.00	$1.50	−$9.50

Case 2: Number of Cups = 20
Module 210—Calculate Yogurt Costs

1. Home Cost of Yogurt = 20 × $1.00 + $10.00
= $30.00

2. Store Cost of Yogurt = 20 × $1.50
= $30.00

Module 220—Compare Two Costs

Since the Home Cost ($30.00) equals the Store Cost ($30.00), the report line generated by
Module 320 would appear as follows:

CUP	HOME COST	STORE COST	SAVINGS/LOSS
20	$30.00	$30.00	$.00

Case 3: Number of Cups = 30
Module 210—Calculate Yogurt Costs
1. Home Cost of Yogurt = 30 × $1.00 + $10.00
                                        = $40.00

2. Store Cost of Yogurt = 30 × $1.50
                                        = $45.00

Module 220—Compare Two Costs
Since the Store Cost ($45.00) is greater than the Home Cost ($40.00), the report line generated by Module 320 would appear as follows:

CUP	HOME COST	STORE COST	SAVING/LOSS
30	$40.00	$45.00	$5.00

Thus, our analysis for this set of problem data has shown that one should purchase yogurt from the store for quantities up to 20 cups; for quantities greater than 20 cups, it is more cost beneficial to make the yogurt at home.

► Problem 5—House Construction ◄

The following data is provided for the desired house:

Number of rooms in house = 5
Living Room: 20′ × 18′
Dining Room: 14′ × 14′
Kitchen: 15′ × 10′
Bedroom #1:   18′ × 15′
Bedroom #2:   15′ × 15′

Please refer to Figure 4.17 for the logic used to determine the house construction costs for this house.

Module 200—Input and Print Number of Rooms
1. Input 5

2. Print NUMBER OF ROOMS FOR THIS HOUSE IS 5

Module 210—Input Room Dimensions
1. Input 20′, 18′

Module 220—Calculate and Accumulate Square Footages

1. Room Square Footage = Length times Width
                         = 20 × 18
                         = 360 sq. ft.

2. Total Square Footage = Total Square Footage plus Room Square Footage
                         = 0 + 360
                         = 360 sq. ft.

Module 230—Write Report Line

ROOM LENGTH	ROOM WIDTH	ROOM SQ. FOOTAGE
20′	18′	360 sq. ft.

Modules 210, 220 and 230 would be processed four more times for the remaining room dimensions. After the other four rooms are processed, the total square footage computed for the house is 1201 square feet. Module 240 would then be processed as follows:

Module 240—Determine Building Cost Factor

1. Since the total square footage is less than 2000, but greater than 1000 square feet (1201), the building cost factor is $50.00 per square foot.

Module 250—Calculate Total House Cost

1. Cost = Total Square Footage times Building Cost Factor per Square Foot
         = 1201 sq. ft. × $50
         = $60,050

Module 260—Write Summary Report Line

TOTAL SQUARE FOOTAGE	BUILDING COST (per sq. ft.)	TOTAL HOUSE BUILDING COST
1201	$50.00	$60,050

SUMMARY

In this chapter, you learned that a hierarchy chart is a logic development tool that uses blocks and connecting lines as components to depict program structure.

The rules for hierarchy charts are as follows:

- Rectangles (blocks) must be used to represent the major processes to be performed in the hierarchy chart.

- Modules should be labeled with an appropriate description of the function of the module and a module label number.

- A module must be connected to another module or modules using a flow line.

- A hierarchy chart must begin with a main control (driver) module as the only module on the first logical level.

- Each processing level within a hierarchy chart must be subordinate to the processing level above it.

- Logical processing flow proceeds in a top-down, left-to-right fashion starting with the driver module.

- Use pseudocode statements as appropriate to define the specific processes that are being performed by each module in the chart.

The advantages of hierarchy charts as a logic development tool are:

- They provide a good conceptual overview of all the major processes being performed in the problem solution.

- They provide a great deal of flexibility in constructing the charts, so it is relatively easy to add, change, or delete modules without disturbing any others.

- They provide a good documentation tool for maintaining programs because a programmer can easily visualize the effects of adding, modifying, or deleting functions within the program.

- They provide an excellent means for depicting top-down program design concepts.

The disadvantages are:

- They do not provide detailed instructions on the chart. These must be presented additionally as pseudocode statements for each module shown.

- They provide only a structural view of the problem solution, not a detailed view of the individual logic steps required.

A hierarchy chart is an excellent tool for documenting program structure and major processing functions. It is used extensively in the commercial business environment.

REVIEW QUESTIONS

MULTIPLE CHOICE
1. One component of hierarchy charts is the flow line. The other is:
    a. a decision symbol
    b. a circle
    c. a process block or rectangle
    d. a parallelogram

2. Which term does not logically relate to hierarchy charts?
   a. flow lines
   b. modules
   c. processing blocks
   d. decision symbols

3. Hierarchy charts are divided into units called logical:
   a. levels
   b. columns
   c. plateaus
   d. continuums

4. A module in a hierarchy chart is connected to other modules by the use of:
   a. dotted lines
   b. connecting loops
   c. flow lines
   d. dashed lines

5. Hierarchy charts typically use one of the following as a part of the logic development process:
   a. programming statements
   b. notes
   c. pseudocode
   d. special indicators

FILL IN THE BLANK

1. A hierarchy chart has one and only one __driver__ *or main control* module.

2. Each processing level within a hierarchy chart must be __subordinate__ *to* the processing level above it.

3. In a hierarchy chart, logical processing flow proceeds in a top-down, __left to right__ direction.

4. Hierarchy charts provide an excellent means for depicting __conceptual__ *design overview* program design concepts.

5. A module on a hierarchy chart is labeled with a descriptive name and a __level__ *module label* number.

SHORT ANSWER

1. Explain the term *hierarchy chart*.

2. Explain the relationship between hierarchy charts and pseudocode.

3. List and explain the use of the components of hierarchy charts.

4. Explain the advantages of hierarchy charts as a logic development tool.

5. Explain the disadvantages of hierarchy charts as a logic development tool.

EXERCISES

1. Fast Eddie's Credit Company needs a report that will show all customers who have exceeded their account credit limits. Eddie's office records show the following data on each account:

   1. Account number

   2. Customer name

   3. Customer address

   4. Current account balance

   5. Account credit limit

   Develop the logic required to produce a report that shows the above information on all over-limit customers.

2. A salesperson receives a commission on 15% of all sales if he or she has sold at least $200,000 worth of merchandise during a month but only 7.5% if the sales are less than $200,000. Show the logic required to process a record containing a sales amount, calculate the commission, and print out the commission amount to be paid.

3. Shady Lady Mortgage Company requires an insurance down payment on all its mortgages based on the following schedule:

   5% on the first $25,000

   3% on the remaining balance

   Develop the logic required for a program to compute the down payment required by the mortgagee and list the mortgagee's account number and name. The input data record will contain the name, account number, and mortgage amount fields.

4. The Keller Land and Cattle Company needs a computer program that will calculate the cost per square foot of various tracts of land. The input data for this calculation will be the tract dimensions (length and width) in feet and the total cost of the tract. Show the logic to make the required calculation and print out the resulting cost.

5. The Personnel Director at your company would like you to produce a report that shows the total number of males in the company who earn more than $35,000 per year and the total number of females who earn less than $20,000 per year. Develop the logic to provide this report showing all employees by social security number in these categories. Your input data fields will be employee social security number, sex code (male = 1, female = 2), and gross annual salary.

The IPO Chart

OBJECTIVES

Upon completion of this chapter, you should be able to:

- Define the term IPO chart
- List and discuss the advantages and disadvantages of the IPO chart as a logic development tool
- Identify and use the rules and constraints associated with the IPO chart
- Solve word problems using the IPO chart as a logic development tool

Introduction

An IPO chart is an *input-process-output* chart, hence the acronym IPO. An IPO chart is both a logic development tool and a documentation tool. Physically, an IPO chart is a diagram or schematic consisting of three columns depicting the three activities of any programming process: input, process, and output. In each of these columns are statements or clauses which identify each of the specific requirements or tasks that are necessary to complete each of the three activities. An overview of the IPO technique is presented first and each of the six standard problems are solved to illustrate the power of the IPO chart as a logic development tool in problem solving.

It should be noted that the IPO methodology was first developed by IBM Corporation and was introduced in literature as HIPO (Hierarchical-Input-Process-Output) charts. The explanation of the IPO technique as presented in this text has been simplified and condensed. The major points of the methodology are presented here in the same manner as they have been presented by these authors in an actual classroom environment.

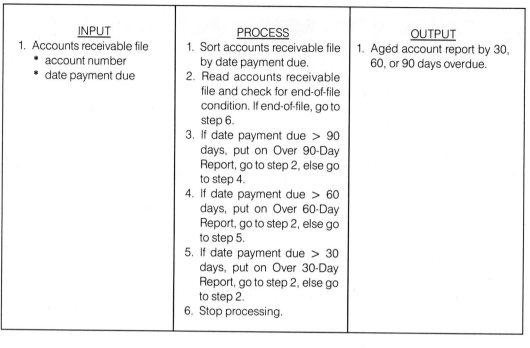

INPUT	PROCESS	OUTPUT

1. Accounts receivable file
    * account number
    * date payment due
	1. Sort accounts receivable file by date payment due.
	2. Read accounts receivable file and check for end-of-file condition. If end-of-file, go to step 6.
	3. If date payment due > 90 days, put on Over 90-Day Report, go to step 2, else go to step 4.
	4. If date payment due > 60 days, put on Over 60-Day Report, go to step 2, else go to step 5.
	5. If date payment due > 30 days, put on Over 30-Day Report, go to step 2, else go to step 2.
	6. Stop processing.
		1. Aged account report by 30, 60, or 90 days overdue.

Figure 5.1 Sample IPO Chart—Aged Accounts Receivable Report

Components

The best way to introduce an IPO chart is to provide an example of one. As you can see from Figure 5.1, an IPO chart uses no special symbols but is divided into three columns.

Rules and Constraints

The rules for using IPO charts are relatively simple. The first action that is required is to draw three columns and label them from left to right as INPUT, PROCESS, and OUTPUT. The next step is to start with the OUTPUT column and fill in what is to be produced by the given problem. After completing the OUTPUT column, the INPUT column should be filled in. Under the INPUT column, you should list all of the input sources of data or information that have been provided to you as part of the problem. Finally, the last step required in completing the IPO chart is to list, under the PROCESS column, the required processes that must be performed in order to transform the given input into the desired output. This column is the most difficult and time-consuming portion of the IPO chart to complete. However, without it you would not be able to solve the problem successfully.

Now let's go back and review the sample problem shown in Figure 5.1.

Sample Problem

Before you can analyze the sample IPO chart, you need to look at the problem that this IPO chart is attempting to solve. A simple problem whose solution is being presented by this IPO chart might be as follows:

The Accounting Manager of XYZ Company wants you to provide a report which will show all accounts that are 30, 60, or more than 90 days overdue. The report should show the account number and date payment due for all overdue accounts.

The first step in using an IPO chart to solve a problem begins with the rightmost or OUTPUT column. In analyzing any problem, you should make sure that you understand clearly what the expected results or output should be. Look back at the problem statement again. What is it specifically that the accounting manager wants? In this particular problem it is easy to see that it is nothing more than a report. Pretty easy, but look further at the request.

You know that it is a report that is requested, but your job is to determine what is on the report. Once again, it's easy to see that the report should show all accounts that are 30, 60, or 90 days overdue. In order to provide the desired information, you must be able to determine what data is available to work with, where that data is, and what processes you must go through in order to produce the desired report. This leads to the remaining two columns on the IPO chart, the INPUT and PROCESS columns.

As you can see under the INPUT column on the IPO chart, there is only one entry, the accounts receivable file. This means that the data that you are looking for in order to produce the report is contained in the accounts receivable file. You know this because there are two data fields (preceded by asterisks) shown underneath the accounts receivable file: account number and date payment due. In looking again at the OUTPUT column, notice that the desired report requests only the account number and those accounts overdue by 30, 60, or 90 days. This information can be produced by using only these two fields. Therefore, the INPUT column of the IPO chart needs only to show one entry to enable you to complete the accounting manager's request. Now that you have finished the OUTPUT and INPUT columns on the IPO chart, it's time to complete the middle or PROCESS column.

As you already know, the PROCESS column is the portion of the IPO chart that is used to depict the logic necessary to take the available input, process it, and produce the required output. This column normally requires more time to complete than either of the other two columns because of the amount of thought required to actually list the individual tasks that must be performed to solve the problem.

In order to generate the report for accounts overdue by specific time periods (30, 60, or 90 days), you must be able to group all accounts together based on the dates when their respective payments are due (here it is assumed that you are using a computer to solve this problem). To accomplish the required grouping, you must sort (or order) all accounts on the accounts receivable file by their date payment due field. This task is listed as step 1 under the PROCESS column on the IPO chart.

After the sorting process (or step 1) is completed, you must process or read each account on the accounts receivable file to determine what is in the date payment due field for each account. However, as part of this reading process, you must check to see if you have reached the end of the accounts receivable file so you will know that the reading process is over and the required report is complete. If you have not finished reading all of the accounts, then proceed to step 3 under the PROCESS column.

Step 3 tells you to check the date payment due field to see if the account is more than 90 days overdue. If this condition is TRUE, then list this account on the portion of the report labeled "Accounts Over 90 Days" and return to step 2. However, if this condition is FALSE, then the logic shown under the PROCESS column tells you to proceed to step 4.

Step 4 directs you to check the date payment due field to see if the account is more than 60 days overdue. If this condition is TRUE, then list this account on the portion of our report labeled "Accounts Over 60 Days" and return to step 2. However, if this condition is FALSE, then the logic tells you to proceed to step 5.

Step 5 instructs you to check the date payment due field to see if the account is more than 30 days overdue. If this condition is TRUE, then list this account on the portion of your report labeled "Accounts Over 30 Days" and return to step 2. If this condition is FALSE, then the account is not overdue, this account is not listed, and you proceed as directed to step 2.

Step 6 tells you to stop processing when you have read all of the accounts from the accounts receivable file. At this point, you have produced the accounting report, in three sections, and have successfully completed the report requested by the accounting manager.

Now that you've been through this relatively easy example, let's discuss how IPO charts handle structured programming methodology.

Program Logic Structures

IPO charts incorporate structured programming control structures (sequence, selection and iteration) into the processing steps shown under the PROCESS column of the IPO charts. The structures are represented in the pseudocode statements that describe the activities being performed by each of the numbered steps in the PROCESS column for a given IPO chart. You learned in Chapter 3 that pseudocode supports each of the three structured programming control tools. Since IPO charts use pseudocode to depict the logical processes required to solve problems, you now know that the three basic control structures can be implemented using IPO chart methodology.

If you need to review how these control structures are implemented using pseudocode methodology, please refer to this same section in Chapter 3.

Advantages and Disadvantages of IPO Charts

Some of the advantages of IPO charts are:

- They are easy to read because of the use of English-like statements

- No special symbols are used to represent specific functions

- No specific syntax is required other than the columnar format

- The three columnar headings—INPUT, PROCESS, OUTPUT—aid in the problem analysis process by forcing the placement of pertinent data from a problem statement into its logical group

- Pseudocode statements under the PROCESS column can generally be translated on a one-for-one basis to high-level language program statements

Some of the disadvantages are:

- Charts can become quite lengthy for complex problems

- To present top-down design concepts, IPO charts must usually be used in conjunction with another logic development tool

- Some experience is required before becoming proficient with this methodology

Summary of IPO Chart Procedures

The following list is a summary of the steps to be followed in using IPO charts to solve a logic problem.

1. Determine what is the required output of the problem: a report, the result of a calculation, a message, a file, for example. List, under the OUTPUT column of the chart, all the required output items that have been identified.

2. Determine what input data has been provided by the problem and list each of these data items under the INPUT column of the chart.

3. List, either mentally or on a piece of paper, each of the processes that must be performed in order to take the input data, process it, and provide the desired output.

4. Determine the proper order in which the processes identified in step 3 must be performed.

5. Start with the first process identified in step 4 and label it as step 1 using the appropriate words, clauses, and/or sentences to communicate the activity or action that must be accomplished at this point in the logic. List the labeled step under the PROCESS column on the chart.

6. Repeat step 5 for as many processes as are required to solve the problem. Number each successive process with the next step number in sequence.

Now it's time to move on and solve the standard set of problems. Have fun!

PROBLEM SOLUTIONS

▶ Problem 1—Lease Versus Buy ◀

Ajax Manufacturing Company has the option to purchase outright or lease (with an option to buy at lease-end) a computer system to aid in its business operations. If Ajax purchases the system for $10,000, it will finance the full amount for four years at a 10% interest rate.

NOTE: Simple Interest (I) = Principal (P) × Rate (R) × Time Period (T).

If Ajax leases the equipment for four years and decides to purchase at lease-end, the monthly cost will be $250 with a final payment of $3000. Which option should Ajax choose in order to minimize the total cost of the computer system? The problem solution should satisfy varying lease versus buy input information.

To attack the solution to this problem using the IPO chart technique, start off with the OUTPUT column first as you did in the sample problem.

As you know, the first step in developing the OUTPUT column is to ascertain what the required output is to be. In this problem, you are being asked to perform some calculations so that a comparative decision can be made. The result of these calculations will be two numeric values, one for each alternative. Therefore, the output must identify each alternative and its associated cost. Refer to Figure 5.2.

OUTPUT
1. TOTAL COST FOR THE PURCHASE OPTION = $
2. TOTAL COST FOR THE LEASE-BUY OPTION = $
3. THE RECOMMENDED OPTION IS XXXXXXXXX OPTION

Figure 5.2 OUTPUT Column—Standard Problem 1

See how easy the OUTPUT column is for this problem. At this time, go back and review the problem and determine all of the given information contained in the problem statement. The next step in the analysis is to show all of this given information in the INPUT column of our IPO chart. This column is shown in Figure 5.3.

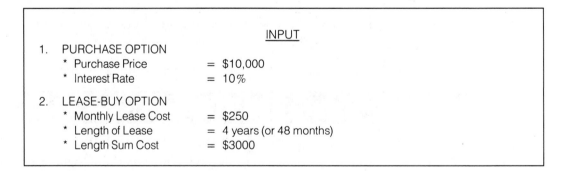

INPUT
1. PURCHASE OPTION
    * Purchase Price   = $10,000
    * Interest Rate   = 10%

2. LEASE-BUY OPTION
    * Monthly Lease Cost   = $250
    * Length of Lease   = 4 years (or 48 months)
    * Length Sum Cost   = $3000

Figure 5.3 INPUT Column—Standard Problem 1

There is not much information available from the statement of the problem. Don't worry about that right now, but continue on with the best part of the IPO chart, the PROCESS column, and see what you can come up with. Refer to Figure 5.4.

PROCESS
1. Input all data for the PURCHASE option.
2. Compute Finance Cost = Purchase Price X Interest Rate X Time Period
3. Compute Total Cost of the PURCHASE option = Purchase Price + Finance Cost
4. Input all data for the LEASE-PURCHASE option.
5. Compute Lease Cost = Monthly Lease Cost X Number of Payments
6. Compute Total Cost of the LEASE-PURCHASE option = Lease Cost + Lump Sum Cost
7. Print the total cost of each option.
8. Compare the total cost of each option.
9. Print a message stating which is the recommended option for Ajax Manufacturing Company.

Figure 5.4 PROCESS Column—Standard Problem 1

This completes our IPO chart for this problem. Did you recognize that all of the above information was given to you in the statement of the problem? Can you see how developing an IPO chart can aid in analyzing and solving a word problem by making you identify what the output requirements are, what the known data is, and what processes must be performed on that data before the correct solution can be obtained?

Oh, let's not forget to actually solve the problem! Figure 5.5 shows how to do the processing specified under our PROCESS column.

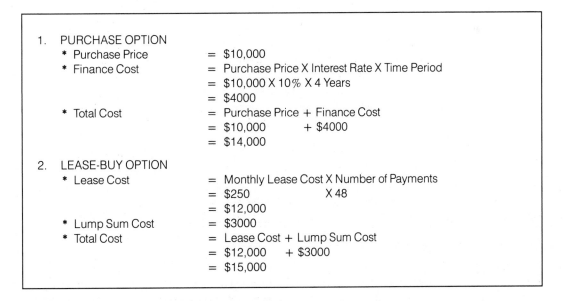

Figure 5.5 Costs for Each Option—Standard Problem 1

Now that you've computed the cost of both options, go back and look at how you would output the program results using the format specified in the OUTPUT column of the IPO chart. This output would appear as shown in Figure 5.6.

LEASE VERSUS BUY ANALYSIS
AJAX MANUFACTURING COMPANY
COMPUTER SYSTEM

TOTAL COST FOR THE PURCHASE OPTION = $14,000
TOTAL COST FOR THE LEASE-BUY OPTION = $15,000
THE RECOMMENDED OPTION IS PURCHASE OPTION

Figure 5.6 Output for Standard Problem 1

▶ Problem 2—Payroll ◀

Easymoney Inc. desires to generate their current manual payroll via computer. The information collected every payroll period includes the employee social security number, pay rate, hours worked, and total other deductions. The payroll department would like a report listing these items: employee social security number, hours worked, pay rate, gross pay, FICA withheld (6.13% of gross pay), federal tax withheld (20% of gross pay), total other deductions, and net pay.

As always, start with the OUTPUT column. In this problem you are asked to provide one report for the company payroll department. Therefore, the OUTPUT column would appear as shown in Figure 5.7. This is all that is required to complete the OUTPUT column. However, if an analyst had prepared this IPO chart, he or she would also attach a report format, labeled REPORT 1, to the chart so that a programmer would be able to use this in developing the print program for this problem.

OUTPUT
1. COMPANY PAYROLL REGISTER FOR PAY PERIOD (See REPORT 1)

Figure 5.7 OUTPUT Column—Standard Problem 2

Now proceed to the INPUT column which would appear as shown in Figure 5.8.

These are all of the data items provided to us to produce the requested report. You must now develop the PROCESS column using the input data items. Refer to Figure 5.9.

INPUT

1. Employee Social Security Number
2. Hourly Pay Rate
3. Hours Worked
4. Total Other Deductions

Figure 5.8 INPUT Column—Standard Problem 2

PROCESS

1. Input employee payroll data items.
2. Check Hours Worked to see if greater than 40.
   - If greater than 40
        Compute Overtime Pay = (Hours Worked - 40) X 1.5 X Hourly Pay Rate
     else
        Overtime Pay = 0
3. Compute Gross Pay = Hourly Pay Rate X 40 + Overtime Pay
4. Compute FICA Withheld = Gross Pay X .0613
5. Compute Federal Tax Withheld = Gross Pay X .20
6. Compute Net Pay = Gross Pay
                      - FICA Withheld
                      - Federal Tax Withheld
                      - Total Other Deductions
7. Write print line on COMPANY PAYROLL REGISTER REPORT showing:
   - Employee Social Security Number
   - Hours Worked
   - Hourly Pay Rate
   - Gross Pay
   - FICA Withheld
   - Federal Tax Withheld
   - Total Other Deductions
   - Net Pay
8. Test for another employee.
   - If there is another employee, go to step 1
     else
        stop processing.

Figure 5.9 PROCESS Column—Standard Problem 2

This completes the IPO chart for this problem.

▶ Problem 3—Health and Diet ◀

Bedford Waistwatchers Association requests that a program be written to motivate members to stay on their diet and show the cost savings that can result from a change in diet. One of the staple diet items recommended is yogurt. If a member follows the Association diet strictly, a large amount of yogurt can be consumed over a short period of time. The cost effectiveness of buying yogurt or making yogurt at home should be evaluated. If a monetary savings can be realized by making yogurt at home versus buying it at the store, how many cups of yogurt must be produced to achieve this savings? The data needed to provide an analysis is store cost of yogurt per cup, cost of yogurt maker if made at home, cost of home ingredients per cup, and number of cups. An analysis should show the home cost, store cost, and savings or loss per cup.

Once again, begin with the OUTPUT column. In this problem you are asked to produce output to show a comparative analysis of the cost of yogurt based on whether it's made at home or bought from a store. To make this analysis possible, our OUTPUT column should appear as shown in Figure 5.10.

OUTPUT

1. BREAK-EVEN ANALYSIS REPORT FOR YOGURT COSTS (See REPORT 1)

Figure 5.10 OUTPUT Column—Standard Problem 3

Proceeding to the INPUT column, it would appear as shown in Figure 5.11.

INPUT

1. Cost of yogurt per cup if purchased from store.
2. Cost of ingredients per cup if homemade.
3. Cost of yogurt-making machine.
4. Number of cups to be consumed.

Figure 5.11 INPUT Column—Standard Problem 3

Since this is all of the data that you would have to work with, proceed to the PROCESS column. Refer to Figure 5.12.

PROCESS

1. Input all data for the yogurt cost comparison.
   - store cost of yogurt per cup
   - home cost of ingredients per cup
   - cost of yogurt maker if made at home
   - number of cups
2. Calculate the home cost of yogurt:
   Home cost = current number of cups times the home cost of ingredients per cup plus the cost of
                     the yogurt maker
3. Calculate the store cost of yogurt:
   Store cost = current number of cups times the store cost of yogurt per cup
4. If the home cost of yogurt is equal to the store cost
       then
           print a report line line showing current number of cups, home cost, store cost, and zero
               savings/loss
   else
       continue to step 5.
5. If the home cost of yogurt is less than the store cost
       then
           compute the savings,
           print a report line showing current number of cups, home cost, store cost, and savings
       else
           compute the loss,
           print a report line showing current number of cups, home cost, store cost, and loss.
6. Perform steps 2 through 5 for the range 1 to the number of cups specified.
7. Stop processing.

Figure 5.12 PROCESS Column—Standard Problem 3

This completes the IPO chart for this problem.

▶ Problem 4—Daily Sales ◀

Vidal Blass is the owner of Obnoxious Telephone Sales. Vidal has had up to 20 employees solicit sales via telephone on a specific day. Vidal would like to produce a sales summary report at the end of each business day to determine which salespeople generate the most revenue. Employees make a phone sale, write the sales information down on a receipt with their name and the total sale, and place the receipt in a bin shared by all of the employees. At the end of the day, all of the receipts are gathered and the summary report produced by entering the name and sales amount from each receipt. The first activity the computer will perform is to sort all input records in name order. (Assume that no two salespeople have the same name.) The sales summary will list the total sales by each name and the grand total sales for the day's business activities.

Develop the logic to provide this summary report. Start with the OUTPUT column. The output required for this problem is a sales report for Mr. Blass. The OUTPUT column on our IPO chart would appear as shown in Figure 5.13. This is all that is required to complete the OUTPUT column. Just as you have seen before, the format for this report would be labeled as REPORT 1 and attached to the IPO chart.

<u>OUTPUT</u>

1. OBNOXIOUS TELEPHONE SALES
      DAILY SALES REPORT
      BY SALESPERSON
      (See REPORT 1)

Figure 5.13 OUTPUT Column—Standard Problem 4

Now proceed to the INPUT column which would appear as shown in Figure 5.14.

<u>INPUT</u>

1. Salesperson Name
2. Sales Amount from Each Individual Sales Receipt

Figure 5.14 INPUT Column—Standard Problem 4

These are the only data items provided in this problem. You must now develop the logic to take this data and generate the requested report. Complete the PROCESS column as shown in Figure 5.15.

PROCESS
1. Input sales data for each salesperson from sales receipt.
2. Check for salesperson name change.
   - If the salesperson name has changed
         then
             print a report line showing daily sales total for the current salesperson,
             add the current salesperson's daily sales total to the total sales accumulator for all
                salespeople,
             set the individual salesperson daily sales total equal to the sales amount from the first
                daily sales receipt for the new salesperson just processed
         else
             add the current salesperson's sales amount from the current sales receipt to the individual
                salesperson daily sales total.
3. Check for more daily sales receipts.
   - If there is another sales receipt, go to step 1
      else
         go to step 4.
4. Process last salesperson's sales
   - Add last salesperson's daily sales total to the total sales accumulator for all salespeople.
   - Print a report line showing the daily sales total for the last salesperson processed.
5. Print a grand total line for total sales for company.
6. Stop processing.

Figure 5.15 PROCESS Column—Standard Problem 4

This completes the IPO chart for Standard Problem 4.

➤ **Problem 5—House Construction** ◄

Well-Bilt Homes Inc. would like you to design a program which enables builders to calculate home building costs based on prospective room sizes. This program is interactive; it allows the user to input the number of rooms desired and the individual room dimensions (length and width only). The building cost per square foot is based on the following:

1000 square feet or less	$60 per square foot
1001–2000 square feet	$50 per square foot
More than 2000 square feet	$40 per square foot

Develop the logic to compute the building cost of the house.

As always, begin by analyzing the output requirements. You are being asked to produce a listing of all the items shown in the OUTPUT column of Figure 5.16. These are the specific output items that are needed to solve the requirements of this problem. If a specific format is required for these items, the format for the report would be labeled as REPORT 1 and attached to the IPO chart.

OUTPUT

1. Number of Rooms in the House.
2. Room Dimensions (Length and Width) in Feet of Each Room
3. Square Footage for Each Room
4. Total Square Footage for the House
5. Total Building Cost for the House

Figure 5.16 OUTPUT Column—Standard Problem 5

The INPUT column for this problem would show all of the input items as provided by the problem. This column would appear as shown in Figure 5.17. As you can see from Figure 5.17, there are only two input data items provided in the problem. You must now figure out how to derive the requested output information as stated in the problem. Complete the PROCESS column as shown in Figure 5.18.

INPUT

1. Number of Rooms Desired
2. Room Dimensions (Length and Width) in Feet

Figure 5.17 INPUT Column—Standard Problem 5

This completes the IPO chart for Problem 5.

<u>PROCESS</u>

1. Input the number of desired rooms.
2. Print an ouput line showing the desired number of rooms.
3. Input room dimensions (length and width) in feet.
4. Compute room square footage.
    - Room Square Footage = Length X Width
5. Accumulate overall square footage for the house.
    - Total Square Footage = Total Square Footage plus Room Square Footage
6. Print an output line showing the current room being processed:
    - Room Length
    - Room Width
    - Room Square Footage
7. Perform steps 3 through 6 for the number of rooms specified in step 1.
8. Check Total Square Footage to determine a building cost factor.
    - If the total square footage is greater than 2000 square feet
    then
        building cost factor = $40 per square foot.
    - If the total square footage is greater than 1000 square feet, but less than 2001 square feet
    then
        building cost factor = $50 per square foot.
    - If the total square footage is less than 1001 square feet
    then
        building cost factor = $60 per square foot.
9. Calculate total house building cost.
    Total Building Cost = total square footage times building cost factor per square foot
10. Print an output line showing the total square footage for the house.
11. Print an output line showing the building cost per square foot.
12. Print an output line showing the total building cost of the house.
13. Stop processing.

Figure 5.18 PROCESS Column—Standard Problem 5

Problem 6—Personnel Statistics

The chairman of the board of Eldorado Enterprises Inc. has requested a report from the Personnel Department that will show various types of information about the company's work force. This report should provide the following:

1. The total number of males and females (SEX CODE = M for males, F for females)

2. The total number of employees by the following age categories (BIRTHDAY YEAR)
   a. less than 21
   b. 21–30
   c. 31–40
   d. 41–50
   e. 51–60
   f. 61–70
   g. over 70

3. The total number of people who have been with the company for 10 years or more (SENIORITY CODE = 3, 4, or 5)

4. The total number of engineers (OCCUPATION CODE = 7) in the company

As usual, start with the OUTPUT column. In this problem, you are asked to provide a report for the chairman of the board. The OUTPUT column would contain one entry. Refer to Figure 5.19. This is all that is required to complete the OUTPUT column. Just as in the previous problem, the format for this report would be labeled as REPORT 1 and attached to the IPO chart. (Refer to report layout for Problem 6 in Chapter 1.)

OUTPUT
1. STATISTICAL WORK FORCE ANALYSIS PROFILE (See REPORT 1)

Figure 5.19 OUTPUT Column—Standard Problem 6

The INPUT column for this problem would appear as shown in Figure 5.20.

These are all of the personnel data items provided to produce the requested report. You must now figure out how to process these data items in order to produce the required output. Let's complete the PROCESS column as shown in Figure 5.21.

```
                                 INPUT
   1.  Sex Code
   2.  Birthday Year
   3.  Seniority Code
   4.  Occupation Code
```

Figure 5.20 INPUT Column—Standard Problem 6

```
                                 PROCESS
   1.  Input today's year and employee personnel data items.
   2.  Check Sex Code.
       - If 'M', Add 1 to Male Counter
         else Add 1 to Female Counter.
   3.  Compute age in years by subtracting the Birthday Year from today's year.
       If age greater than 70, Add 1 to Over-70 Counter
       else
       If age greater than 60, Add 1 to 61-70 Counter
       else
       If age greater than 50, Add 1 to 51-60 Counter
       else
       If age greater than 40, Add 1 to 41-50 Counter
       else
       If age greater than 30, Add 1 to 31-40 Counter
       else
       If age greater than 20, Add 1 to 21-30 Counter
       else
           Add 1 to Under-21 Counter.
   4.  Check Seniority Code.
       - If code = 3, 4 or 5, Add 1 to 10-Year Counter.
   5.  Check Occupation Code.
       - If code = 07, Add 1 to Engineer Counter.
   6.  Test for another employee.
       - If there is another employee, go to step 1
         else
             go to step 7.
   7.  Print the report using the data contained in the above counters.
   8.  Stop processing.
```

Figure 5.21 PROCESS Column—Standard Problem 6

This completes the standard problem set for this chapter. At this time, you should be very familiar with the IPO chart as a logic development tool for problem solving. Now let's work through some of the standard problems using some typical data values.

IPO Chart Walk-Through

This section of the chapter shows solutions to two problems from the standard problem set using sample data values for the variables.

▶ Problem 2—Payroll ◀

The following data is provided for two typical employees of Easymoney Inc:

Employee Number	Social Security Number	Hours Worked	Hourly Pay Rate	Total Other Deductions
1	456-78-9999	60	$7.00	$50.00
2	345-10-8787	40	10.00	50.00

Please refer to Figure 5.9 for the logic used to compute the employee's individual pay.

Employee #1:

1. Input 456-78-9999, 60, $7.00, $50.00

2. Since Hours Worked is greater than 40,
$$\text{Overtime Pay} = (\text{Hours Worked} - 40) \times 1.5 \times 7.00$$
$$= (60 - 40) \times 1.5 \times 7.00$$
$$= \$210.00$$

3. Gross Pay = Hourly Pay Rate times 40 plus Overtime Pay
$$= \$7.00 \times 40 + \$210.00$$
$$= \$490.00$$

4. FICA Withheld = Gross Pay times 0.0613
$$= \$490.00 \times 0.0613$$
$$= \$30.04$$

5. Federal Tax Withheld = Gross Pay times 0.20
$$= \$490.00 \times 0.20$$
$$= \$98.00$$

6. Net Pay = Gross Pay − FICA Withheld − Federal Tax Withheld − Total Other Deductions
$$= \$490.00 - \$30.04 - \$98.00 - \$50.00$$
$$= \$311.96$$

7. Write a Report Line:

Social Security Number	Hours Worked	Hourly Pay Rate	Gross Pay	FICA Tax	FED Tax	Total Other Deductions	Net Pay
456-78-9999	60	7.00	490.00	30.04	98.00	50.00	311.96

Employee #2:

1. Input 345-10-8787, 40, $10.00, $50.00

2. Since Hours Worked is not greater than 40, Overtime Pay = 0.

3. Gross Pay = Hourly Pay Rate times 40 plus Overtime Pay
   = $10.00 × 40 + 0
   = $400.00

4. FICA Withheld = Gross Pay times 0.0613
   = $400.00 × 0.0613
   = $24.52

5. Federal Tax Withheld = Gross Pay times 0.20
   = $400.00 × 0.20
   = $80.00

6. Net Pay = Gross Pay − FICA Withheld − Federal Tax Withheld
   − Total Other Deductions
   = $400.00 − $24.52 − $80.00 − $50.00
   = $245.48

7. Write a Report Line:

Social Security Number	Hours Worked	Hourly Pay Rate	Gross Pay	FICA Tax	FED Tax	Total Other Deductions	Net Pay
345-10-8787	40	10.00	400.00	24.52	80.00	50.00	245.48

This completes the walk-through for this problem.

► Problem 6—Personnel Statistics ◄

The following data for the employees of Eldorado Enterprises Inc. is provided for this problem:

Sex Code	Birthday Year	Seniority Code	Occupation Code
M	1950	3	07
F	1967	2	09
M	1935	4	07
F	1942	5	10
F	1960	1	05
M	1958	1	02

Please refer to Figure 5.21 for the logic used in solving this problem.

Input Today's Year, 1986.

Employee #1:

1. Input M, 1950, 3, 07

2. Since the Sex Code = M, add 1 to the Male Counter.

3. Compute age in years = Today's Year − Birthday Year
$$= 1986 - 1950$$
$$= 36$$
Since the age is greater than 30, add 1 to the 31–40 Counter.

4. Since the Seniority Code = 3, add 1 to 10-Year Counter.

5. Since the Occupation Code = 07, add 1 to Engineer Counter.

Employee #2:

1. Input F, 1967, 2, 09

2. Since the Sex Code = F, add 1 to the Female Counter.

3. Compute age in years = Today's Year − Birthday Year
$$= 1986 - 1967$$
$$= 19$$
Since the age is less than 21, add 1 to the Under-21 Counter.

4. Since the Seniority Code = 2, do not add 1 to 10-Year Counter.

5. Since the Occupation Code = 09, do not add 1 to Engineer Counter.

Employee #3:

1. Input M, 1935, 4, 07

2. Since the Sex Code = M, add 1 to the Male Counter.

3. Compute age in years = Today's Year − Birthday Year
$$= 1986 - 1935$$
$$= 51$$
Since the age is greater than 50, add 1 to 51–60 Counter.

4. Since the Seniority Code = 4, add 1 to 10-Year Counter.

5. Since the Occupation Code = 07, add 1 to Engineer Counter.

Employee #4:

1. Input F, 1942, 5, 10

2. Since the Sex Code = F, add 1 to the Female Counter.

3. Compute age in years = Today's Year − Birthday Year
                         = 1986 − 1942
                         = 44

Since the age is greater than 40, add 1 to 41–50 Counter.

4. Since the Seniority Code = 5, add 1 to 10-Year Counter.

5. Since the Occupation Code = 10, do not add 1 to Engineer Counter.

Employee #5

1. Input F, 1960, 1, 05

2. Since the Sex Code = F, add 1 to Female Counter.

3. Compute age in years = Today's Year − Birthday Year
                         = 1986 − 1960
                         = 26

Since the age is greater than 20, add 1 to 21-30 Counter.

4. Since the Seniority Code = 1, do not add 1 to 10-Year Counter.

5. Since the Occupation Code = 05, do not add 1 to Engineer Counter.

Employee #6:

1. Input M, 1958, 1, 02

2. Since the Sex Code = M, add 1 to Male Counter.

3. Compute age in years = Today's Year − Birthday Year
                         = 1986 − 1958
                         = 28

Since the age is greater than 20, add 1 to 21-30 Counter.

4. Since the Seniority Code = 1, do not add 1 to 10-Year Counter.

5. Since the Occupation Code = 02, do not add 1 to Engineer Counter.

Since there are no more employees to be processed, proceed as directed in step 7 of Figure 5.21 and print a report showing the data that has just been processed.

ELDORADO ENTERPRISES INC.
PERSONNEL STATISTICAL REPORT

```
TOTAL NUMBER OF MALES = 3
TOTAL NUMBER OF FEMALES = 3
TOTAL EMPLOYEES OVER 70 = 0
TOTAL EMPLOYEES BETWEEN 61 AND 70 = 0
TOTAL EMPLOYEES BETWEEN 51 AND 60 = 1
TOTAL EMPLOYEES BETWEEN 41 AND 50 = 1
TOTAL EMPLOYEES BETWEEN 31 AND 40 = 1
TOTAL EMPLOYEES BETWEEN 21 AND 30 = 2
TOTAL EMPLOYEES UNDER 21 = 1
```

TOTAL NUMBER OF EMPLOYEES WITH 10 YEARS OR MORE SENIORITY = 3
TOTAL NUMBER OF EMPLOYEES WHO ARE ENGINEERS = 2

This completes the logic walk-through for this problem using IPO charts.

SUMMARY

In this chapter, you learned that an IPO chart is a logic development tool and documentation tool combined. An IPO chart is a diagram or schematic consisting of three columns depicting the three activities of the programming process: input, process, and output. In each of the columns on the chart are statements, clauses, or items which identify each of the specific requirements or tasks which are necessary to complete each of the three activities.

The components of the IPO chart are three columns labeled as INPUT, PROCESS, and OUTPUT with the statements, clauses, or items contained in each column. These components are used in conjunction with the following rules:

- After drawing the three columns labeled as INPUT, PROCESS, and OUTPUT, start with the OUTPUT column and fill in what is to be produced by the given problem.

- Next, under the INPUT column, list all of the input sources of data or information that has been provided to you as part of the problem.

- Finally, list under the PROCESS column, the required processes that must be performed in order to transform the given input into the desired output. The processes should be listed in the sequence in which they should be performed.

The advantages of the IPO chart as a logic development tool are:

- It is easy to read because of the use of English-like statements.

- It does not use any special symbols to represent specific functions.

- It does not require a specific syntax other than the columnar format.

- The three column headings, INPUT, PROCESS, and OUTPUT, aid in the problem-analysis process by forcing the placement of pertinent data from a problem statement into its logical group.

- The pseudocode statements under the PROCESS column can generally be translated on a one-for-one basis to high-level language program statements.

The disadvantages are:

- IPO charts can become quite lengthy for complex problems.

- To present top-down design concepts, IPO charts must usually be used in conjunction with another logic development tool.

- IPO charts require some experience before one becomes proficient with the methodology.

The IPO chart is a handy tool for documenting program functions and is used widely in the commercial business environment.

REVIEW QUESTIONS

MULTIPLE CHOICE

1. Which of the following special symbols is used in an IPO chart?
    a. blocks
    b. flow lines
    c. dotted lines
    d. none of the above

2. Which of the following control structures cannot be shown with IPO charts?
    a. iteration
    b. transformance
    c. sequence
    d. selection

3. Which of the following is a component of IPO charts?
    a. flow lines
    b. blocks
    c. columns
    d. parallelograms

4. Which term does not logically relate to IPO charts?
    a. INPUT
    b. PROCESS
    c. OUTPUT
    d. BLOCK

5. IPO charts use which one of the following as a part of the logic development process?
    a. programming statements
    b. pseudocode
    c. special symbols
    d. blocks

FILL IN THE BLANK

1. An IPO chart has _____ columns.

2. An IPO chart uses _____ in the PROCESS column to show the steps necessary to solve a problem.

3. The _____ column of an IPO chart shows all the input data that has been provided as part of the problem statement.

4. The IPO chart is generally easy to read because of the use of _____-like statements in the PROCESS column.

5. IPO charts must usually use another logic development tool, pseudocode, to present _____ program design concepts.

SHORT ANSWER

1. Explain the term *IPO chart*.

2. Explain the relationship between IPO charts and pseudocode.

3. List and explain the use of the components of IPO charts.

4. What are the advantages of the IPO chart as a logic development tool?

5. What are the disadvantages of the IPO chart as a logic development tool?

EXERCISES

1. The Galaxy School District is interested in comparing the pay of its instructors with those of other school districts around the country. You have been asked to develop a computer program that will compute the average annual salary of teachers for all elementary, junior high, and high schools within the district. Your input data will consist of a code (1 = elementary, 2 = junior high, and 3 = senior high) for type of school and an annual salary for each teacher. Develop the logic to show the average pay for teachers for each category of school within the school district.

2. The James Bond Travel Agency desires a computer program that will keep track of all customers who have paid to go on specific cruises. Your input data will consist of a customer name, address, cruise number, and amount paid. Prepare the logic required to generate a report that will show each of the input data items for a given customer.

3. The State Board of Education is interested in seeing a report that will show the number of students within a school district who are failing (grade below 60) at least one course. The input data used to generate such a report is the following:

    1. student number

    2. course grade

   Develop the logic required to produce such a report.

4. Jim Bob's Car Rental Agency would like a computer program that computes the average gas mileage of its fleet of cars based on the type of car. The input data that is provided to you for solving this problem is the car type, miles driven, and gallons of gasoline used for each car owned by Jim Bob. Develop the logic required to print a report showing the average miles per gallon by type of car.

5. Develop the logic to compute and print the sales commission for each salesperson of the Windy City TV Sales Company. The commission is calculated based on the following schedule:

less than $100	7% of sales price
$100 to $500	6% of sales price
more than $500	5% of salesprice

   Your input data consists of a salesperson's name and sales amount. Generate a report to show total commission amounts by individual salespeople.

The Nassi-Shneiderman Chart

OBJECTIVES

After studying this chapter, you should be familiar with the following concepts:

- The symbols or components used by a Nassi-Shneiderman chart

- The various rules and limits the tool must follow to solve a problem

- How to represent the three program logic structures (sequence, selection, and repetition) with a Nassi-Shneiderman chart

- The advantages and disadvantages of employing Nassi-Shneiderman charts as a logic development tool

- The general logical steps to follow when solving any problem with this technique

- How to solve word problems using the Nassi-Sneiderman chart as a logic development tool

Introduction

The Nassi-Shneiderman chart is a logic development tool introduced by I. Nassi and Ben Shneiderman in 1973. The technique uses two basic symbols to represent the logic structure, the rectangle and triangle. These symbols readily display the three program logic structures discussed in earlier chapters. This tool combines characteristics employed in two other logic tools, the flowchart and pseudocode. Due to these characteristics, a Nassi-Shneiderman chart is commonly referred to as a *structured flowchart* or *structured pseudocode*.

Components

The Nassi-Shneiderman chart consists of a large rectangle separated into smaller rectangles and triangles to depict the detailed processes needed to solve the problem. Each rectangle or triangle contains pseudocode statements describing the function occurring in that symbol. The chart is read in top-down order. Figure 6.1 is a simplified Nassi-Shneiderman chart showing the activities that occur when withdrawing money from an automatic teller machine.

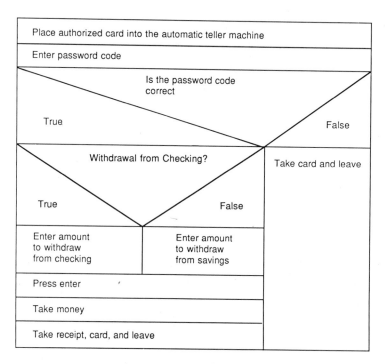

Figure 6.1 Example of Simplified Nassi-Shneiderman Chart

Notice that all sections are incorporated into one large rectangle that serves as the border for the entire solution. A decision or selection instruction is represented by dividing a rectangle into three triangles. The middle triangle specifies the condition that is being tested (for example, is the password code correct). The outer triangles display the two possible results, TRUE or FALSE (yes or no), of a decision instruction. A line separates the path of instructions to follow when the result is TRUE or FALSE. As you can see, this tool provides the detail of a flowchart, but initially it may be harder to distinguish how the symbols interrelate. The detail needed for you to fully comprehend how a Nassi-Shneiderman chart functions is discussed shortly.

As with some of the other logic tools discussed in this text (Warnier-Orr diagram and Structure Chart), the Nassi-Shneiderman chart must be used in correlation with a data dictionary. The data dictionary specifies the particulars associated with each data element (data name, data type, and data element length) and its relevancy to data records or other data items. Figure 6.2 contains a sample data dictionary entry for an accounts receivable record.

For data-type designation, C represents character data and N represents numeric data. The data dictionary eliminates confusion about data items and how they are defined when listed in a Nassi-Shneiderman chart.

```
ACCOUNTS.RECEIVABLE.RECORD      <=====   Data label or record name

    ACCOUNT.NUMBER        --   NNNNN or N(5)
    TRANSACTION.TYPE      --   NN
    TRANSACTION.DATE      --   CCCCCCCC or C(8)    ⇒ 8 charecters
    AMOUNT.OF.SALE        --   NNNN.NN
```

Figure 6.2 Sample Data Dictionary Entry

Rules and Constraints

The rules for drawing a Nassi-Shneiderman chart are not complex because only two basic symbols are used. A Nassi-Shneiderman chart is read in top-down order, but the reader has an option in the order of reading symbols in the case of a decision or iteration structure. Figure 6.3 shows the most basic Nassi-Shneiderman structure.

1	Instruction
2	Instruction
3	Instruction
4	Instruction
5	Instruction

Figure 6.3 Sequential Execution of Nassi-Shneiderman Instructions

The number in the left side of each rectangle signifies the execution order of each symbol.

> **NOTE:**   This symbol-numbering convention is used to explain Nassi-Shneiderman concepts throughout this chapter. Its use is optional in a final solution.

You start at the top and proceed downward. As you are aware, the logic can get much more complex. The selection or decision structure provides an option for the reader in determining what symbol should be executed next. Figure 6.4 illustrates the instruction execution order with a selection symbol.

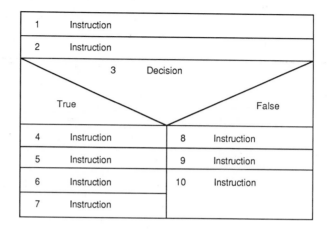

Figure 6.4 Example of Selection Structure

The middle triangle specifies the condition that is being tested; the result can only be TRUE or FALSE. The two outer triangles allude to the TRUE or FALSE path to follow based on the test results. If decision 3 is TRUE, instructions 4–7 are executed; if it is FALSE, instructions 8–10 are executed. The direction you wish to proceed on the basis of the decision (TRUE or FALSE path) and, therefore, the selection of the next instruction to execute is based on your discretion. Here is the same decision (Figure 6.5) with a different numbering sequence.

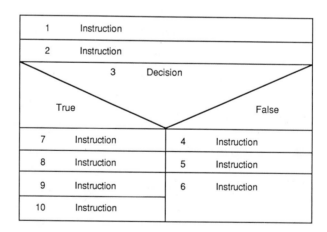

Figure 6.5 Alternate Selection Structure Representation

If decision 3 is TRUE, instructions 7–10 are performed. If FALSE, instructions 4–6 are executed. The other rule to be aware of involves the varying sizes of the symbols and how that affects their execution order. To emphasize this concept, study Figure 6.6, which appends additional instructions to Figure 6.5.

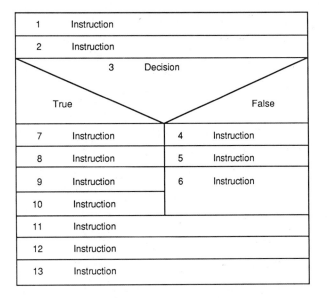

Figure 6.6   Illustration of the Varying Symbol Sizes and How They Affect Execution

The last three instructions (11–13) are executed regardless of the result of the previous decision (instruction 3). If the decision was TRUE, instructions 7–10 are executed. Conversely, if the decision was FALSE, instuctions 4–6 are executed. Be aware of the symbol size and how that could impact the execution order of instructions.

Program Logic Structures

We have already discussed the first of the three program logic structures, sequential execution of instructions. If you need to review, turn back to Figure 6.3. Now we will examine the last two program logic structures: selection and repetition.

A general discussion of the representation of the selection or decision logic structure is presented in Figures 6.4 and 6.5. To clear up any remaining confusion, a concrete example should help. Assume a tennis wholesaler distributes tennis rackets to various retailers. Suppose he wants to entice volume sales for a particular racket by offering a 5% discount on all orders above 300 tennis rackets. The Nassi-Shneiderman solution to this problem is shown in Figure 6.7.

There will be circumstances when the result of a decision calls for no action. Figure 6.8 modifies the previous example to represent this action. The variable DISCOUNT is initially set to zero. When the test is made to determine if QTY exceeds 300, no action is necessary when the result is FALSE. Another option in addition to placing NULL or NO ACTION in the rectangle is to leave the symbol blank.

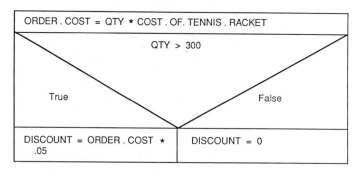

Figure 6.7 Sample Problem Illustrating Selection

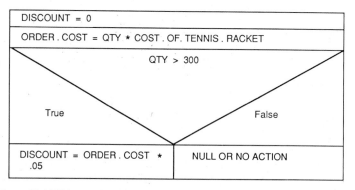

Figure 6.8 Selection with NULL or NO ACTION Option

One can also nest decision symbols inside of other decision symbols. Let's alter the discount procedure of Figure 6.7 to compare against more specific QTY values. If QTY is:

300 or less, the discount percentage is 0%

301 to 500, the discount percentage is 5%

greater than 500, the discount percentage is 10%

The selection structure would change to incorporate a nested decision (decision within a decision) structure (Figure 6.9).

The original test has not changed from Figure 6.7: if QTY is less than or equal to 300, the discount amount is zero. The TRUE side of the decision has changed: if QTY is greater than 300, it can fall into two possible ranges, 301–500 or greater than 500. Based on the result of the comparison, the appropriate discount percentage is applied.

Refer to Figure 6.10 to view the last program logic structure, repetition. To represent repetitive instructions, an outer rectangle contains the word DOWHILE or REPEAT and the condition that is tested against (for example, DOWHILE there are more records in the file or DOWHILE COUNTER < 25). As long as the condition is TRUE, the symbols embedded inside this outer rectangle can contain simple instructions, decision symbols, or nested repetitive structures.

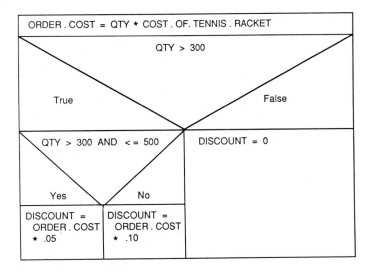

Figure 6.9 Example of Nested Decision Structure

```
DOWHILE  condition is true
        Instruction
        Instruction
        Instruction
        Instruction
        END DOWHILE
```

Figure 6.10 Example of Repetitive Logic Structure

Advantages and Disadvantages of Nassi-Shneiderman Charts

Some of the advantages of Nassi–Shneiderman charts are:

- The diagramming rules within the technique require the use of structured or modular programming concepts. (If necessary review Program Design section in Chapter 1.) All instructions are enclosed in special symbols which graphically depict each function as one of the three logic structures: sequence, selection, and repetition.

- The technique is easy to learn because only two basic symbols are used, the rectangle and triangle.

- Complex, nested selection structures can be represented in a simple concise manner.

- These charts provide a superb method of program documentation.

- The transformation from Nassi-Shneiderman problem solution to program code is a relatively straightforward process.

Some of the disadvantages of Nassi-Shneiderman charts are:

- Nassi-Shneiderman charts do not promote modularity. They are so detail-oriented it is difficult to break a solution into specific modules by function. The entire solution is enclosed by one big rectangle which can be viewed as a module.

- Nassi-Shneiderman charts are difficult to maintain. If logic needs to be modified for an existing Nassi-Shneiderman chart, the entire diagram must be redrawn.

- Complex problems may require more than one-page solutions.

- Drawing and enclosing symbols into one neat and visually correct solution can be a tedious process.

Summary of Nassi-Shneiderman Chart Procedures

When solving problems with Nassi-Shneiderman charts, the following general steps should be observed.

1. Identify the required input and output variables in two separate sequence (rectangle) symbols.

2. List the processes necessary to convert the input to the desired output.

3. Determine which parts of the solution may need to be included in a repetitive structure to handle a variable number of input records.

4. Incorporate all of the structures identified in earlier steps into one cohesive solution (one large rectangle divided into the integrated symbols).

5. Assign test values to the input variables and walk through the solution to discern if the desired output is achieved.

PROBLEM SOLUTIONS

This section contains the solutions to the six problems using the Nassi-Shneiderman methodology. Remember, the purpose of these solutions is to provide you with examples to assist you in solving problems at the end of this chapter or from other sources. Each problem solution consists of four parts:

1. Restatement of the problem

2. Solution narrative

3. Nassi-Shneiderman chart

4. Data dictionary

To promote readability, the variables defined in the data dictionary are underlined in each Nassi-Shneiderman chart. A new convention will be used just for these solutions: within each symbol (rectangle or triangle) a number appears in the left-hand corner. This numbering scheme identifies each symbol within the Nassi-Shneiderman chart to allow reference to individual symbols within the solution narrative. This numbering convention is one of many used by Nassi-Shneiderman charts, and will assist you in understanding the solutions.

▶ Problem 1—Lease Versus Buy ◀

Ajax Manufacturing Company has the option to purchase outright or lease (with an option to buy at lease-end) a computer system to aid in its business operations. If Ajax purchases the system for $10,000, it will finance the full amount for four years at a 10% interest rate.

> **NOTE:** Simple Interest (I) = Principal (P) × Rate (R) × Time Period (T).

If Ajax leases the equipment for four years and decides to purchase at lease-end, the monthly cost will be $250 with a final payment of $3000. Which option should Ajax choose in order to minimize the total cost of the computer system? The problem solution should satisfy varying lease versus buy input information.

Symbols 1 and 2 read the respective PURCHASE and LEASE.BUY records. Symbols 3 and 4 calculate PURCHASE.OPTION.COST and LEASE.BUY.OPTION.COST based on the values read from the previous records. Symbols 5 through 7 write the report headings, prepare the PURCHASE.OPTION.COST and LEASE.BUY.OPTION.COST report lines, and actually write these report lines. Symbol 8 determines which option cost is cheaper and, based on that determination, writes the recommended option in Symbol 9 or 10.

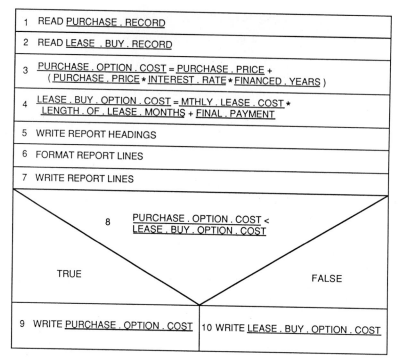

1 READ <u>PURCHASE . RECORD</u>

2 READ <u>LEASE . BUY . RECORD</u>

3 <u>PURCHASE . OPTION . COST</u> = <u>PURCHASE . PRICE</u> +
    (<u>PURCHASE . PRICE</u> * <u>INTEREST . RATE</u> * <u>FINANCED . YEARS</u>)

4 <u>LEASE . BUY . OPTION . COST</u> = <u>MTHLY . LEASE . COST</u> *
    <u>LENGTH . OF . LEASE . MONTHS</u> + <u>FINAL . PAYMENT</u>

5 WRITE REPORT HEADINGS

6 FORMAT REPORT LINES

7 WRITE REPORT LINES

8 <u>PURCHASE . OPTION . COST</u> <
   <u>LEASE . BUY . OPTION . COST</u>

TRUE   FALSE

9 WRITE <u>PURCHASE . OPTION . COST</u>   10 WRITE <u>LEASE . BUY . OPTION . COST</u>

Figure S6.1 Problem 1 Solution

```
<<DATA DICTIONARY>>

PURCHASE.RECORD                          REPORT.ITEMS
   PURCHASE.PRICE        NNNNN.NN            PURCHASE.OPTION.COST    NNNNN.NN
   INTEREST.RATE         N.NN                LEASE.BUY.OPTION.COST   NNNNN.NN
   FINANCED.YEARS        NN


LEASE.BUY.RECORD
   MTHLY.LEASE.COST           NNN.NN
   LENGTH.OF.LEASE.MONTHS     NN
   FINAL.PAYMENT              NNNN.NN
```

► Problem 2—Payroll ◄

Easymoney Inc. desires to generate their current manual payroll via computer. The information collected every payroll period includes the employee social security number, pay rate, hours worked, and total other deductions. The payroll department would like a report listing these items: employee social security number, hours worked, pay rate, gross pay, FICA withheld (6.13% of gross pay), federal tax withheld (20% of gross pay), total other deductions, and net pay.

Symbols 1 through 3 assign beginning values to certain variables and read the first EMPLOYEE.RECORD. Symbols 4 through 20 comprise a DOWHILE loop that continues until all records have been read. There are three main activities in this loop:

1. The payroll-related variables are calculated (symbols 5–8).

2. The LINE.CTR is checked for end-of-page condition (symbols 9–12), the REPORT.LINE is written (symbols 13 and 14), and LINE.CTR incremented (symbol 15).

3. The next EMPLOYEE.RECORD is read and the end-of-file condition is checked (symbols 16–19).

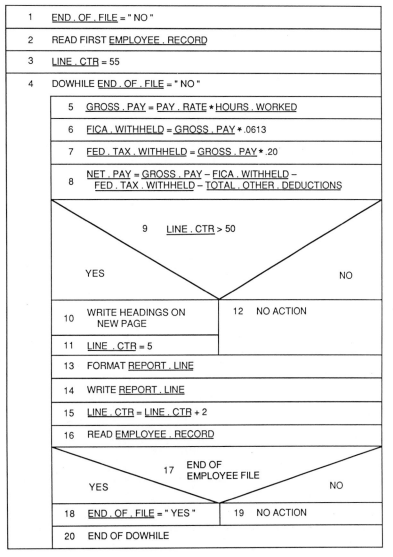

Figure S6.2 Problem 2 Solution

```
<<DATA DICTIONARY>>
```

```
EMPLOYEE.RECORD                                REPORT.LINE
    SOCIAL.SEC.NUMBER         N(9)                  SOCIAL.SEC.NUMBER         N(9)
    PAY.RATE                  NN.NN                 HOURS.WORKED              NN.N
    HOURS.WORKED              NN.N                  PAY.RATE                  NN.NN
    TOTAL.OTHER.DEDUCTIONS    NNNN.NN               GROSS.PAY                 NNNN.NN
                                                    FICA.WITHHELD             NNN.NN
                                                    FED.TAX.WITHHELD          NNNN.NN
                                                    TOTAL.OTHER.DEDUCTIONS    NNNN.NN
                                                    NET.PAY                   NNNN.NN

MISCELLANEOUS VARIABLES
    END.OF.FILE               CCC
    LINE.CTR                  NN
```

► Problem 3—Health and Diet ◄

Bedford Waistwatchers Association requests that a program be written to motivate members to stay on their diet and show the cost savings that can result from a change in diet. One of the staple diet items recommended is yogurt. If a member follows the Association diet strictly, a large amount of yogurt can be consumed over a short period of time. The cost effectiveness of buying yogurt or making yogurt at home should be evaluated. If a monetary savings can be realized by making yogurt at home versus buying it at the store, how many cups of yogurt must be produced to achieve this savings? The data needed to provide an analysis is store cost of yogurt per cup, cost of yogurt maker if made at home, cost of home ingredients per cup, and number of cups. An analysis should show the home cost, store cost, and savings or loss per cup.

Symbols 1–3 perform the housekeeping activities: YOGURT.RECORD is read, CUP.NUMBER is set equal to 1, and LINE.CTR is assigned the value 55 to ensure that when the LINE.CTR is checked in symbol 8, the first report heading is printed. Symbols 4–16 are enclosed within a DOWHILE loop and repeated as long as the incremented CUP.NUMBER is less than or equal to the entered (from YOGURT.RECORD) NUMBER.OF.CUPS. Symbols 5–7 calculate the variable values that will be printed later. Symbol 8 determines if LINE.CTR is greater than 50 (end-of-page condition). If TRUE, report headings are printed on a new page and LINE.CTR is initialized to 5 (symbols 9 and 10). Symbols 12–14 prepare REPORT.LINE for printing, print REPORT.LINE, and increment LINE.CTR by 2 to keep track of the last line printed on by the current REPORT.LINE. Symbol 15 adds 1 to CUP.NUMBER. The value in this variable controls how many times the DOWHILE loop is repeated.

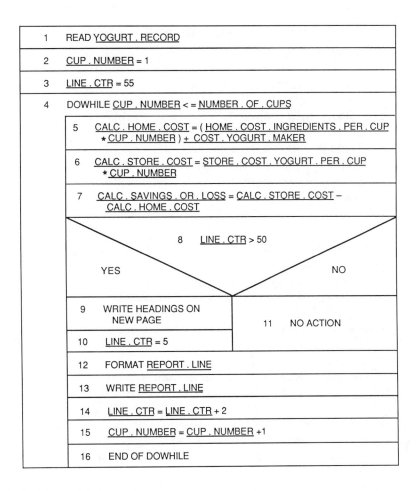

Figure S6.3 Problem 3 Solution

<<DATA DICTIONARY>>

YOGURT.RECORD		REPORT.LINE	
STORE.COST.YOGURT.PER.CUP	NN.NN	CUP.NUMBER	NN
COST.YOGURT.MAKER	NN.NN	CALC.HOME.COST	NNN.NN
HOME.COST.INGREDIENTS.PER.CUP	NN.NN	CALC.STORE.COST	NNN.NN
NUMBER.OF.CUPS	NN	CALC.SAVINGS.OR.LOSS	NNN.NN

WORK.VARIABLES
   LINE.CTR   NN

► Problem 4—Daily Sales ◄

Vidal Blass is the owner of Obnoxious Telephone Sales. Vidal has had up to 20 employees solicit sales via telephone on a specific day. Vidal would like to produce a sales summary report at the end of each business day to determine which salespeople generate the most revenue. Employees make a phone sale, write the sales information down on a receipt with their name and the total sale, and place the receipt in a bin shared by all of the employees. At the end of the day, all of the receipts are gathered and the summary report produced by entering the name and sales amount from each receipt. The first activity the computer will perform is to sort all input records in name order. (Assume that no two salespeople have the same name.) The sales summary will list the total sales by each name and the grand total sales for the day's business activities.

The daily sales problem involves control-break logic (see Chapter 1 if you need to review). The initialization activities occur in symbols 1–6. END.OF.FILE is set to NO to prepare for the loop which occurs starting at symbol 7. TOTAL.SALES and GRAND.TOTAL.SALES are two accumulator variables that are assigned the value zero. To prepare for printing the first report heading, LINE.CTR is set to 55. The first SALES.RECEIPT.RECORD is read (symbol 5) and preparation for control-break processing occurs in symbol 6, where PREV.SALESPER-SON.NAME (the previous control-field variable) is assigned the first SALESPERSON.NAME (current control-field variable) value.

The DOWHILE loop stretches from symbol 7 to 26. This loop will repeat while END.OF.FILE contains the value "NO." The END.OF.FILE value can only change when the end of sales receipts file test (symbol 21) is TRUE. SALESPERSON.NAME is compared to PREV.SALESPERSON.NAME (symbol 8) to determine if a control break has occurred (a new salesperson name has been read). If TRUE, the total sales amount for the current salesperson is incremented by the amount stored in the AMT.OF.SALE variable (symbol 9). If the test is FALSE, the LINE.CTR is checked to see if the bottom of page has been reached, which requires a new report heading (symbols 10–13). The REPORT.LINE for the previous salesperson is prepared (symbol 14). Then the REPORT.LINE is written and the LINE.CTR incremented to keep track of where this REPORT.LINE was printed on the page (symbols 15 and 16). Symbols 17 and 18 prepare for the new salesperson read in and initiate control-break processing logic for this salesperson. TOTAL.SALES is set equal to AMT.OF.SALE and the current SALESPERSON.NAME value is assigned to PREV.SALESPERSON.NAME. PREV.SALESPERSON.NAME is used as the comparison value for the next sales record read. Symbol 19 keeps a running total in GRAND.TOTAL.SALES with the accumulation of the AMT.OF.SALE value. The next SALES.RECEIPT.RECORD is read in symbol 20 and the end-of-file condition is tested in symbol 21.

Symbols 27 and 28 prepare the GRAND.TOTAL.LINE for printing. (What this entails depends on the programming language used with this logic tool.) The GRAND.TOTAL.LINE is then printed.

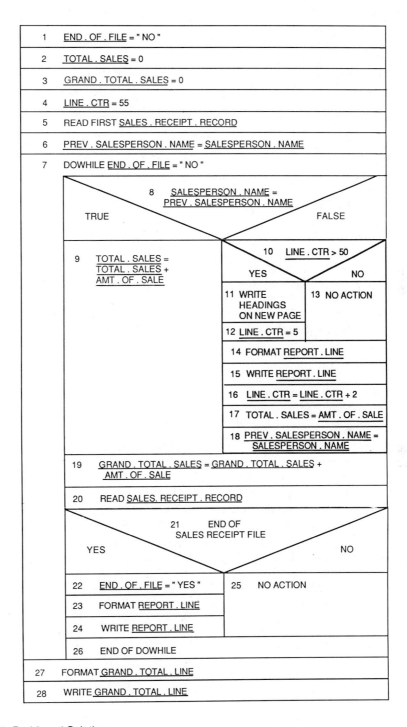

Figure S6.4 Problem 4 Solution

```
<<DATA DICTIONARY>>

SALES.RECEIPT.RECORD                           REPORT.LINE
     SALESPERSON.NAME      C(20)                   SALESPERSON.NAME      C(20)
     AMT.OF.SALE           NNN.NN                  TOTAL.SALES           NNNN.NN

GRAND.TOTAL.LINE
     GRAND.TOTAL.SALES     N(5).NN

WORK.VARIABLES
     END.OF.FILE           CCC
     LINE.CTR              NN
     PREV.SALESPERSON.NAME C(20)
```

▶ Problem 5—House Construction ◀

Well-Bilt Homes Inc. would like you to design a program which enables builders to calculate home building costs based on prospective room sizes. This program is interactive; it allows the user to input the number of rooms desired and the individual room dimensions (length and width only). The building cost per square foot is based on the following:

1000 square feet or less	$60 per square foot
1001–2000 square feet	$50 per square foot
More than 2000 square feet	$40 per square foot

Develop the logic to compute the building cost of the house.

Symbols 1–5 perform the start-up activities: the NUMBER.OF.ROOMS is entered, the accumulation variable TOTAL.HOUSE.SQ.FT is set to zero, and the report headings are printed. Symbols 6–12 form a REPEAT loop which performs operations on each room. The room length and width are entered (symbol 7), the room square footage is calculated (symbol 8) and the REPORT.LINE is printed (symbols 9 and 10). A running total of square footage is accumulated in symbol 11.

The TOTAL.HOUSE.SQ.FT value is tested to determine the COST.PER.SQ.FT (symbols 13–17). The total cost of the house is calculated and the output lines are printed (symbols 18–21).

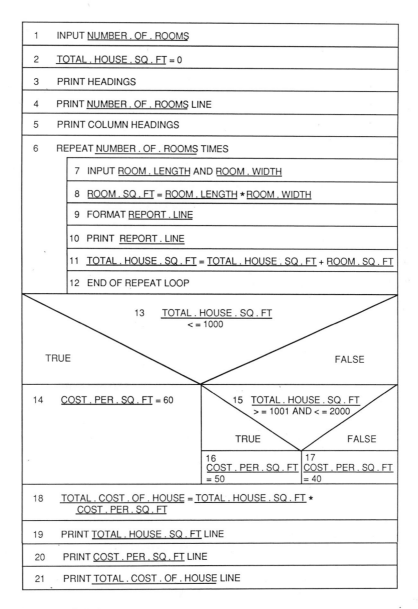

1	INPUT NUMBER . OF . ROOMS
2	TOTAL . HOUSE . SQ . FT = 0
3	PRINT HEADINGS
4	PRINT NUMBER . OF . ROOMS LINE
5	PRINT COLUMN HEADINGS
6	REPEAT NUMBER . OF . ROOMS TIMES

7	INPUT ROOM . LENGTH AND ROOM . WIDTH
8	ROOM . SQ . FT = ROOM . LENGTH * ROOM . WIDTH
9	FORMAT REPORT . LINE
10	PRINT REPORT . LINE
11	TOTAL . HOUSE . SQ . FT = TOTAL . HOUSE . SQ . FT + ROOM . SQ . FT
12	END OF REPEAT LOOP

13   TOTAL . HOUSE . SQ . FT
< = 1000

TRUE   FALSE

14 COST . PER . SQ . FT = 60	15 TOTAL . HOUSE . SQ . FT > = 1001 AND < = 2000
	TRUE FALSE
	16 COST . PER . SQ . FT = 50	17 COST . PER . SQ . FT = 40

18   TOTAL . COST . OF . HOUSE = TOTAL . HOUSE . SQ . FT * COST . PER . SQ . FT

19   PRINT TOTAL . HOUSE . SQ . FT LINE

20   PRINT COST . PER . SQ . FT LINE

21   PRINT TOTAL . COST . OF . HOUSE LINE

Figure S6.5 Problem 5 Solution

```
<<DATA DICTIONARY >>
```

NUMBER.OF.ROOMS	NN	REPORT.LINE	
ROOM.LENGTH	NN	ROOM.LENGTH	NN
ROOM.WIDTH	NN	ROOM.WIDTH	NN
TOTAL.HOUSE.SQ.FT	N(5)	ROOM.SQ.FT	NNNN
COST.PER.SQ.FOOT	NNN.NN		
TOTAL.COST.OF.HOUSE	N(6).NN		

▶ Problem 6—Personnel Statistics ◀

The chairman of the board of Eldorado Enterprises Inc. has requested a report from the Personnel Department that will show various types of information about the company's work force. This report should provide the following:

1. The total number of males and females (SEX CODE = M for males, F for females)

2. The total number of employees by the following age categories (BIRTHDAY YEAR)
   a. less than 21
   b. 21–30
   c. 31–40
   d. 41–50
   e. 51–60
   f. 61–70
   g. over 70

3. The total number of people who have been with the company for 10 years or more (SENIORITY CODE = 3, 4, or 5)

4. The total number of engineers (OCCUPATION CODE = 7) in the company

This problem deals with multiple decisions, multiple counter variables, and repetition. The housekeeping activities occur in symbols 1–4: the looping control variable END.OF.FILE is assigned the value NO, all counter variables are initialized to zero, the input values are read for TODAYS.YEAR and for the first PERSONNEL.RECORD.

The DOWHILE loop begins at symbol 5 and concludes with symbol 44. AGE is calculated in symbol 6. This result is compared with the breakdown AGE ranges (AGE less than 21, 21 to 30, etc.), and the proper counter variable is incremented based on these tests (symbols 7–27). In symbols 28–33 the SEX.CODE is checked for male or female and the appropriate counter variable is updated. The SENIORITY.CODE is tested to determine if an employee has been with the company more than 10 years. If TRUE, the proper counter variable is incremented (these activities occur in symbols 34–36). If OCCUPATION.CODE is 7, that employee is an engineer and the TOTAL.ENGINEERS counter variable is updated (symbols 37–39). The next PERSONNEL.RECORD is read and the end-of-file situation checked in symbols 40–43.

After the DOWHILE loop is complete, the report is printed in symbols 45–50.

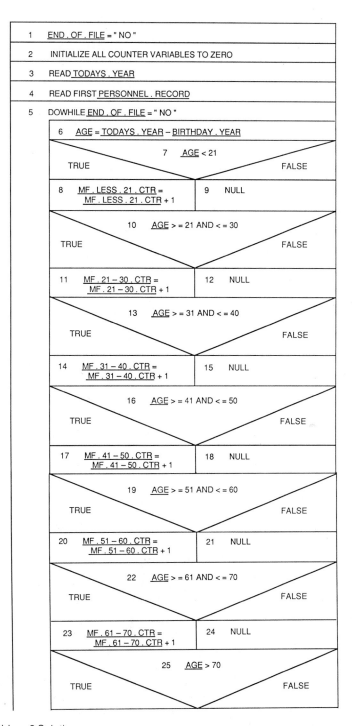

Figure S6.6 Problem 6 Solution

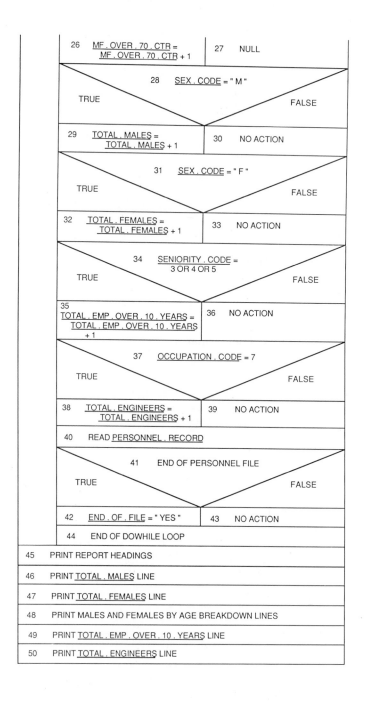

Figure S6.6 Problem 6 Solution (continued)

<<DATA DICTIONARY>>

PERSONNEL.RECORD		COUNTER.VARIABLES	
SEX.CODE	C	TOTAL.MALES	N(5)
BIRTHDAY.YEAR	NN	TOTAL.FEMALES	N(5)
SENIORITY.CODE	N	MF.LESS.21.CTR	N(4)
OCCUPATION.CODE	N	MF.21-30.CTR	N(4)
		MF.31-40.CTR	N(4)
		MF.41-50.CTR	N(4)
OTHER.VARIABLES		MF.51-60.CTR	N(4)
TODAYS.YEAR	NN	MF.61-70.CTR	N(4)
END.OF.FILE	CCC	MF.OVER.70.CTR	N(4)
AGE	NN	TOTAL.EMP.OVER.10.YEARS	N(4)
		TOTAL.ENGINEERS	N(4)

Nassi-Shneiderman Walk-Through

This section is designed to show the techniques used to verify that the problem solution functions correctly. This process involves plugging some values into the variables and actually "walking through" the Nassi-Shneiderman solutions. You should use this technique to verify your Nassi-Shneiderman solution for correctness.

The first two problems will be verified. Refer back to these completed problem solutions because the symbol reference numbers will be used in this walk-through. The remaining four problems can be verified by you to provide additional practice.

► Problem 1—Lease Versus Buy ◄

SYMBOL 1:   PURCHASE.PRICE = 6000.00
INTEREST.RATE = 0.08
FINANCED.YEARS = 5

SYMBOL 2:   MTHLY.LEASE.COST = 150.00
LENGTH.OF.LEASE.MONTHS = 60
FINAL.PAYMENT = 1800.00

SYMBOL 3:   PURCHASE.OPTION.COST = 8400
(6000 + (6000 * 0.08 * 5))

SYMBOL 4:   LEASE.BUY.OPTION.COST = 10,800
((150 * 60) + 1800)

SYMBOLS 5-7: Will write the report headings and a separate report line for PURCHASE.OPTION.COST and LEASE.BUY.OPTION.COST

SYMBOL 8:   PURCHASE.OPTION.COST < LEASE.BUY.OPTION.COST
8400 < 10,000

SYMBOL 9:   The test in symbol 8 is TRUE, so the PURCHASE.OPTION.COST (8400) is written.

▶ Problem 2—Payroll ◀

SYMBOL 1: END.OF.FILE = "NO"

SYMBOL 2: SOCIAL.SEC.NUMBER = 222345555
PAY.RATE = 12.50
HOURS.WORKED = 40.0
TOTAL.OTHER.DEDUCTIONS = 83.00

SYMBOL 3: LINE.CTR = 55

SYMBOL 4: END.OF.FILE is equal to "NO" which allows the symbols within the loop to be executed.

SYMBOL 5: GROSS.PAY = 500.00
(12.50 * 40)

SYMBOL 6: FICA.WITHHELD = 30.65
(500 * 0.0613)

SYMBOL 7: FED.TAX.WITHHELD = 100.00
(500 * 0.20)

SYMBOL 8: NET.PAY = 286.35
(500 − 30.65 − 100 − 83)

SYMBOL 9: The LINE.CTR is greater than 50 so symbols 10 and 11 are executed.

SYMBOL 10: Report headings are printed on a new page

SYMBOL 11: LINE.CTR = 5

SYMBOLS 13–14: The REPORT.LINE is readied for printing and is printed (what this entails depends on the programming language used)

SYMBOL 15: LINE.CTR = 7
(5 + 2)

SYMBOL 16: SOCIAL.SEC.NUMBER = 214576532
PAY.RATE = 16.00
HOURS.WORKED = 25.5
TOTAL.OTHER.DEDUCTIONS = 42.65

SYMBOL 17: If this was the end of the employee file, symbol 18, which changes the END.OF.FILE variable to "YES," would be executed and the DOWHILE loop would end. Otherwise, no action is taken.

SYMBOL 19:   No action.

SYMBOL 4:   END.OF.FILE is equal to "NO" which allows the symbols within
                  the loop to be executed.

SYMBOL 5:   GROSS.PAY = 408.00
                  (16.00 * 25.5)

SYMBOL 6:   FICA.WITHHELD = 25.01
                  (408.00 * 0.0613)

SYMBOL 7:   FED.TAX.WITHHELD = 81.60
                  (408.00 * 0.20)

SYMBOL 8:   NET.PAY = 258.74
                  (408 − 25.01 − 81.60 − 42.65)

SYMBOL 9:   The LINE.CTR is not greater than 50 so symbol 12 (no action) is
                  executed.

SYMBOL 12:   No action.

SYMBOLS   The REPORT.LINE is readied for printing and is printed (what
13–14:   this entails depends on the programming language used)

SYMBOL 15:   LINE.CTR = 9
                  (7 + 2)

SYMBOL 16:   SOCIAL.SEC.NUMBER = 420566812
                  PAY.RATE = 7.25
                  HOURS.WORKED = 37.5
                  TOTAL.OTHER.DEDUCTIONS = 22.48

SYMBOL 17:   If this was the end of the employee file, symbol 18, which changes
                  the END.OF.FILE variable to "YES," would be executed and the
                  DOWHILE loop would end. Otherwise, no action is taken.

SYMBOL 19:   No action.

All of the above activities would repeat until the end-of-file condition goes into effect in symbols 17 and 18.

SUMMARY

This chapter introduced you to the components, rules for use, and functions of the Nassi-Shneiderman logic development technique. What feature does this technique offer over some of the other logic tools discussed in this textbook? The Nassi-Shneiderman chart is a combination of two logic tools, the flowchart and pseudocode. You are not forced to memorize a multitude of symbols as with flowcharting. And the technique allows the freedom of incorporating pseudocode into the context of two simple symbols, the rectangle and triangle.

The advantages of the Nassi-Shneiderman chart as a logic development tool are:

- All instructions are enclosed in a special symbol which graphically depicts the functions of the symbol.

- The technique is easy to learn because only two basic symbols are used, the rectangle and triangle.

- Complex, nested selection structures can be represented in a straightforward manner.

- These charts provide a superb method of program documentation.

- The transformation from Nassi-Shneiderman problem solution to program code is a relatively simple process.

The disadvantages are:

- Modularity is not emphasized due to the detail orientation of the Nassi-Shneiderman chart. The final solution is enclosed in one big rectangle (module).

- The completed Nassi-Shneiderman chart is difficult to maintain: modifications require the entire diagram to be redrawn.

- Moderately complex problems may require more than one-page solutions.

- Drawing and enclosing symbols into one neat and visually correct solution can be a tedious process.

This tool could be used by someone who does not like the detail and restrictions imposed by flowcharting, and conversely feels that pseudocode is nonstandardized and allows the user too much liberty. In the computer industry, the Nassi-Shneiderman chart is slowly gaining more popularity in the northern and eastern geographical areas of the United States.

REVIEW QUESTIONS

MULTIPLE CHOICE

1. The two basic symbols used to represent logic structure within the Nassi-Shneiderman chart are:
    - a. rectangle
    - b. circle
    - c. square
    - d. triangle
    - e. both a and d

2. The Nassi-Shneiderman chart incorporates features from which two other logic tools?
    a. flowchart and pseudocode
    b. Warnier-Orr and flowchart
    c. structure chart and pseudocode
    d. IPO chart and flowchart

3. The Nassi-Shneiderman chart is also referred to as:
    a. structured pseudocode
    b. structured IPO chart
    c. structured flowchart
    d. "lazy" structure chart
    e. both a and c

4. Which one of the following items is not used with Nassi-Shneiderman charts?
    a. data dictionary
    b. pseudocode
    c. special symbols
    d. all of the above

5. Which one of the following statements is true?
    a. Nassi-Shneiderman charts are easy to maintain.
    b. Nassi-Shneiderman charts use a large number of special symbols.
    c. Moderately complex Nassi-Shneiderman solutions may require more than one page.
    d. All of the above statements are false.

FILL IN THE BLANK

1. A Nassi-Shneiderman chart is read in ___top down___ order.

2. For selection representation, an alternative requiring no action should contain the word _____ or NO ACTION.

3. The ___repetition___ logic structure is represented with the word DOWHILE followed by smaller rectangle symbols.

4. To submerge one selection logic structure within another selection logic structure is referred to as _____.

5. To represent a decision, logic structure requires ___3___ triangles to be drawn.

SHORT ANSWER

1. Why would you use the Nassi-Shneiderman technique to solve problems instead of other logic tools discussed in this text?

2. Are there any circumstances under which the Nassi-Shneiderman method would not be the proper logic tool for problem solution?

3. Do you think this logic tool will eventually be accepted as the computer industry standard for problem solution and documentation? Why or why not?

4. In your opinion what changes should be made to the Nassi-Shneiderman procedure to improve the methodology?

5. Discuss how the Nassi-Shneiderman technique implements the three program logic structures.

EXERCISES

1. A prime number is a number divisible by only one and itself. Obviously, even numbers (except two) cannot be prime numbers since they are always divisible by two. Therefore, any number with a final digit of 0, 2, 4, 6, or 8 is not a prime number. Write the logic to find and count the prime numbers between 1 and 100 in the report format shown below.

SAMPLE REPORT FORMAT

```
            PRIME NUMBERS BETWEEN 1 AND 100

            NN      NN     NN      NN      NN

            .       .      .       .       .

            NN      NN     NN      NN      NN


            THERE ARE NN PRIME NUMBERS BETWEEN 1 AND 100.
```

2. Some countries in addition to the United States record temperature in Celsius degrees instead of Fahrenheit degrees. If you were going to vacation in one of those countries for the summer, you may want a report listing the temperature in Celsius and Fahrenheit degrees. The formula to convert Celsius to Fahrenheit is:

$$F = (9/5 * C) + 32$$

F is Fahrenheit degrees and C is Celsius degrees. Write the logic to produce the Fahrenheit equivalent for the Celsius degrees 0 through 100.

SAMPLE REPORT FORMAT:

<pre>
            CONVERT CELSIUS TO FAHRENHEIT

            CELSIUS   FAHRENHEIT

               0   NNN

               .   "

               .   .

               .   .

             100   NNN
</pre>

3. Write the logic to read 100 records consisting of one variable. The format of that variable is NNNN. Produce a report containing this information:

SAMPLE REPORT FORMAT:

<pre>
              ANALYSIS OF 100 NUMBERS

      THE LOWEST NUMBER IS: NNNN
      THE HIGHEST NUMBER IS: NNNN
      THE AVERAGE VALUE FOR ALL NUMBERS IS: NNNN
</pre>

4. Wallstreet Investors Company wishes to write a program to analyze the stock portfolio of individual clients. One client can own many different stocks and this program will make a recommendation of which stocks to keep or sell and give the total value of the current stocks the client possesses. The input for each stock portfolio is stock number, number of shares, purchase price of stock, and current market value of stock. The output will display for each stock number the number of shares, purchase price of stock, market value of stock, gain or loss in dollars for the total shares, and a recommendation to keep or sell the stock. If the gain or loss variable is negative, the status field should print SELL; otherwise, the stock status prints KEEP. Grand totals should show total shares of stock, total dollar purchase price, total dollar market value, and total dollar gain or loss. Develop the logic necessary to solve this problem.

SAMPLE REPORT FORMAT:

WALLSTREET INVESTORS COMPANY
STOCK PORTFOLIO ANALYSIS

STOCK NUMBER	NUMBER OF SHARES	PURCHASE PRICE PER STOCK	MARKET VALUE PER STOCK	GAIN OR LOSS	STATUS
NNNN	NNNN	$NNN.NN	$NNN.NN	$NNNN.NN	CCCC
.	.	:	.	.	"
.	.	.	.	.	.
.	.	.	.	.	.
NNNN	NNNN	$NNN.NN	$NNN.NN	$NNNN.NN	CCCC

```
TOTAL SHARES OF STOCK:          NNNNN
TOTAL DOLLAR PURCHASE PRICE:    $NNNNN.NN
TOTAL DOLLAR MARKET VALUE:      $NNNNN.NN
TOTAL DOLLAR GAIN OR LOSS:      $NNNNN.NN
```

5. Harry and Larry's Boat Rentals rents sailboats, canoes, and pedal boats to customers visiting Lake Tippywangle. A competitor, Karen's Carefree Boats, has recently opened a similar operation on the other side of the lake. In hopes of gaining an edge over their competitor, Harry and Larry are recording information on each boat rental. At the end of the day this data is keyed into the following record format:

```
RENTAL NUMBER     NNNN
RENTAL STATUS     C       —   "B" for begin of rental
                              "E" for end of rental

BOAT TYPE         C       —   "S" for sailboat
                              "C" for canoe
                              "P" for pedal boat

TIME              NNNN    —   Military time; for example,
                              1 PM is 1300 hours
```

For each rental there are two records: one when the boat is checked out (rental status = B) and one when the boat is returned (rental status = E). The file is sorted by rental number and rental status to ensure that the rental number has the beginning record followed by the appropriate ending record. From this file Harry and Larry want this report at the end of each day:

SAMPLE REPORT FORMAT:

```
            HARRY AND LARRY'S BOAT RENTAL
                 DAILY STATISTICS

         NUMBER OF TOTAL RENTALS:   NNNN
         NUMBER OF SAILBOATS RENTED:   NNNN
         NUMBER OF CANOES RENTED:   NNNN
         NUMBER OF PEDAL BOATS RENTED:   NNNN


         LONGEST BOAT RENTAL TIME:   NN.NN HOURS
         SHORTEST BOAT RENTAL TIME:   NN.NN HOURS
         AVERAGE BOAT RENTAL TIME:   NN.NN HOURS
```

6. Melvin's Market Research Company maintains a demographic file containing information for over two million inhabitants in a three-city area. Each record contains the following information:

First Name	C(15)	
Last Name	C(15)	
Street	C(20)	
City	C(20)	
State	CC	
Zip Code	N(5)	
Phone Number	N(8)	
Sex	C	(M = Male; F = Female)
Age	NN	
Dwelling Code	C	(A = Apartment, H = Home, D = Duplex)

Melvin wants to conduct phone research for persons meeting this criteria:

1. Last name begins with the letters M–Z

2. Lives in the Norfolk city limits

3. Is between the ages 22–35

4. Lives in a home

Produce the logic that will assist Melvin in generating the following report.

SAMPLE REPORT FORMAT:

```
                    MELVINS'S MARKET RESEARCH COMPANY
           MARKET STUDY FOR NORFOLK RESIDENTS WHO LIVE IN A HOME

FIRST                LAST                 STREET            AGE  PHONE
NAME                 NAME

XXXXXXXXXXXXXXX      XXXXXXXXXXXXXXX      XXXXXXXXXXXXXX    NN   NNN-NNNN
      .                    .                   .             .      .
      .                    .                   .             .      .
      .                    .                   .             .      .
XXXXXXXXXXXXXXX      XXXXXXXXXXXXXXX      XXXXXXXXXXXXXX    NN   NNN-NNNN

TOTAL NUMBER OF PEOPLE: NNN,NNN
```

REFERENCES

I. Nassi and B. Shneiderman, "Flowchart techniques for structured programming," ACM SIGPLAN Notices vol. 8 no. 8, p. 12 (August 1973).

The Warnier-Orr Diagram

OBJECTIVES

After reading this chapter, you should be able to:

- Define and use the components of a Warnier-Orr diagram
- Understand the rules and constraints specific to a Warnier-Orr diagram
- Implement the three program logic structures with the techniques available in the Warnier-Orr diagram program development logic tool
- List the advantages and disadvantages of Warnier-Orr diagrams
- Solve complex problems with the Warnier-Orr diagram methodology

Introduction

The Warnier Diagram is a program design methodology developed by Jean-Dominique Warnier in Paris during the mid 1970s. Kenneth Orr refined and enhanced some of the concepts introduced by Warnier. From this sharing of ideas between both individuals, the final product, the Warnier-Orr diagram, was born. The Warnier-Orr diagram is a technique that can be used at the program level (the emphasis of this book) or at the system level (the collection of programs or processes that make up the entire system). This logic tool is often referred to as a "lazy" hierarchy chart, or a hierarchy chart turned on its side. The diagram consists of a few symbols that can be used in a manner that allows the user a great deal of creativity and flexibility.

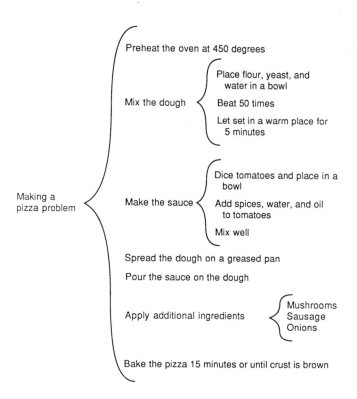

Figure 7.1 Use of Warnier-Orr Brackets to Make a Pizza

Components

Warnier-Orr diagrams consist of a series of brackets drawn from left-to-right that continue until all requirements of the particular problem are completed. Each bracket consists of pseudocode-type statements that are executed in order from top to bottom. In the terminology of some of the other logic tools covered in this book (hierarchy charts or structure charts), you can view the bracket as performing the same role as a module. Figure 7.1 is a simplified Warnier-Orr diagram to demonstrate the steps necessary to make a pizza. (The recipe may not seem tasty, but it should help you to understand the concept.)

The steps are followed in a left-to-right, top-down order. If you are thinking that this logic tool looks easy, hang on, it will get more challenging. These brackets are combined with other special symbols to depict the order in which the activities (pseudocode) will be executed.

The data dictionary must be included with a Warnier-Orr diagram to convey to the reader the type of data item (numeric or character) and data name that is used to identify that item within the brackets. Figure 7.2 presents a typical data dictionary entry.

Without the data dictionary, the data or variable names identified in the diagram will not be clear and concise.

```
INVENTORY.RECORD              <=======   Data label or record name

    PART.NUMBER          --    CCCCC or C(5)
    PART.DESCRIPTION     --    CCCCCCCCCCCCCCCCCCCCCCCCC or C(25)
    QUANTITY.ON.HAND     --    NNNNN or N(5)
    SAFETY.STOCK.LEVEL   --    N(4)
    UNIT.PRICE           --    NNNN.NN
```

Figure 7.2 Example of a Data Dictionary Entry

Rules and Constraints

1. A Warnier-Orr diagram is read in left-to-right, top-down order. A bracket can consist of any number of pseudocode instructions. Figure 7.3 illustrates the execution order. Proceed from bracket to bracket in a left-to-right order, evaluating the instructions within each bracket in sequence from top to bottom.

2. On the left side of each bracket in the Warnier-Orr diagram there must be a label describing the function of that bracket. This label also specifies how often the instructions to the right of the bracket will be repeated by placing in parentheses under each label a variable or integer value.

A bracket repeated once:

Label   {   OR   Label   {
                                  (1)

A bracket repeated a constant number of times:

Label   {   OR   Label   {
(10)   (6)

A bracket repeated a variable number of times:

Label   {   OR   Label   {
(Var)   (N)

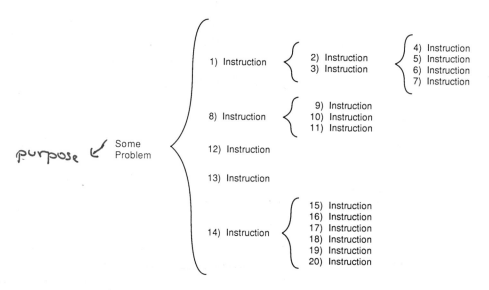

Figure 7.3 Warnier-Orr Diagram Showing the Left-to-Right, Top-Down Order of Execution

3. The first (or leftmost) label of a Warnier-Orr diagram always states the purpose of the diagram or name of the problem and thus is repeated only one time.

4. You know what appears to the left of a bracket; the next item to consider is what appears on the right side of a bracket. There are two objects that are on the right side of a bracket: a label which is followed by another bracket (known as *nesting brackets* as each bracket is read in order from left to right), or a pseudocode instruction. Labels and their function have already been analyzed so let's take a closer look at the pseudocode instructions. Instructions can be straightforward: add three variables named A, B and C and store the result in a variable named D; or read a record from a file. Instructions can also be used to make decisions or set up a loop (repetitive process). Refer to the next section to look at the procedures used by Warnier-Orr diagrams to show decisions and repetitive activities.

5. In a Warnier-Orr diagram there are no limits to the number of brackets shown in the diagram or the number of instructions (or labels) within a bracket. A Warnier-Orr diagram can be used without difficulty to solve a simple or very complex problem.

6. To address a common question asked by individuals when first using a Warnier-Orr diagram, "When do I create another bracket, and should it be drawn to the right of the current bracket or should this bracket move down and start a new level in the diagram?" Before answering this question, view the skeleton Warnier-Orr diagram in Figure 7.4.

When drawing a Warnier-Orr diagram, think of breaking the logic tool down into levels. In Figure 7.4 an example of one level is bracket 2 through bracket 2B, another level is bracket 4. As you can see, a level can be divided into one or more brackets. You can view each bracket as a task within a level. A level performs one type of activity, such as editing all of the numeric fields within a record to ensure that they are positive, or opening files for input or output and assigning variables an initial value.

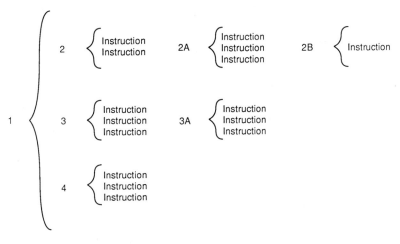

Figure 7.4 Warnier-Orr Diagram Illustrating Levels of Brackets

When solving a problem, identify the activities that must occur to achieve the requirements of the problem. If you have determined that an activity is divided into more than one task, then the next bracket and its instructions will be placed to the right of the current bracket at the same level. An example of this is brackets 3 through 3A in Figure 7.4. If a new activity has emerged, that activity is shown down at the next level. If you are confused, just remember one rule of thumb: the more practice you have with Warnier-Orr diagrams, the easier it will be to determine exactly where a bracket should be placed.

Program Logic Structures

How do Warnier-Orr diagrams implement the three program logic structures: sequence, selection, and repetition? You have already seen how a Warnier-Orr diagram sequentially executes instructions in a left-to-right, top-down order. If you need to refresh your memory, examine Figure 7.3.

To illustrate the second logic structure, selection, we need to define some new symbols. In most high-level programming languages, an IF statement is used to make a decision. This IF statement is evaluated to see if it is TRUE or FALSE. For instance, if the local theatre was showing a movie rated R and wanted to validate the age of people entering the theatre, the program statements may look something like this:

```
IF AGE IS 18 OR OVER THEN
    ACCEPT MONEY FOR ADMISSION TO MOVIE
    GIVE THE PERSON A TICKET
    ADMIT PERSON TO MOVIE
ELSE
    TELL THE PERSON THEY ARE TOO YOUNG TO ENTER THE MOVIE
    ADVISE PERSON TO CALL PARENT OR AN OLDER FRIEND
```

Obviously, the above "program code" is not written in any particular programming language, but the general concept is available in most programming languages. A condition is tested (a person's age is 18 or over) and evaluated to be either TRUE or FALSE. If TRUE, the next statement or statements after the reserved word THEN are executed until the reserved word ELSE is encountered. If the condition is FALSE, the statement or statements after the reserved word ELSE are executed.

A Warnier-Orr diagram would represent the above "program code" as shown in Figure 7.5(a). The (0,1) underneath the AGE 18 OR OVER statement signifies that the instructions within the bracket to the right of this statement will be executed 0 or 1 time. The ⊕ symbol means that the statements are mutually exclusive: when one of the statements is TRUE, the other statement is FALSE. The bar or line over the bottom statement means NOT AGE 18 OR OVER, and the bracket to the right of this statement is executed 0 or 1 time based on whether the statement is TRUE or FALSE. An alternative method to represent a conditional logic structure is shown in Figure 7.5(b). You can drop the (0,1) and use the ⊕ symbol by itself and replace the bar or line with the word NOT. Figure 7.5(c) contains a third technique to depict a conditional logic structure.

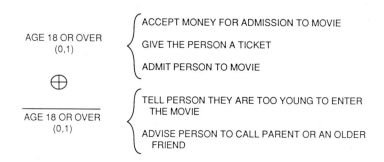

Figure 7.5a Example to Illustrate How the Selection Logic Structure Appears

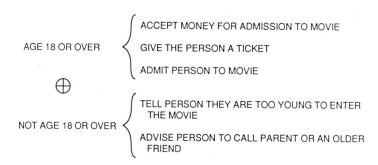

Figure 7.5b Example to Illustrate an Alternate Method of the Selection Logic Structure

How could a Warnier-Orr diagram represent testing a situation where, if the condition was TRUE, you wanted to do certain processes; otherwise, if the condition was FALSE, you wanted to do nothing? Look at Figure 7.6(a) to see an example in which a person's sex is tested. All this particular test is interested in is if the person is a male. If TRUE, add 1 to a variable called MALE.COUNTER; otherwise, if the condition was FALSE, do nothing. To show in a Warnier-Orr diagram when you want no action to occur as the result of a test, use the word SKIP. Another method to accomplish the same objective is shown in Figure 7.6(b).

If you want to test for just one condition, test for only that condition with one bracket.

You previously saw examples of how to use the logic structure repetition or iteration. Refer back to item 2 in the "Rules and Constraints" section if you need a review.

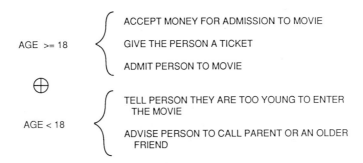

Figure 7.5c Example of a Third Method of the Selection Logic Structure

MALE
(0, 1)   {   ADD 1 TO MALE.COUNTER

⊕

‾‾‾‾‾
MALE
(0, 1)   {   SKIP

Figure 7.6a Example of a Condition Using SKIP

MALE
(0, 1)   {   ADD 1 TO MALE.COUNTER

Figure 7.6b Same Objective Without Using SKIP

One repetitive structure not discussed in item 2 appears like this:

Label
(conditional expression)

Some type of conditional expression is tested such as COUNTER < 85 or END.OF.FILE = "NO." As long as this condition is TRUE, the activities within the bracket are repeated. When the condition is FALSE, the bracket is no longer repeated. Some action occurs inside of the bracket to change this condition to ensure that you do not have an endless loop.

Advantages and Disadvantages of Warnier-Orr Diagrams

- These diagrams break down the problem solution into components that follow a hierarchical or structured order (left-to-right, then top-down). This allows the reader to grasp the activities that are involved in solving the problem.

- Warnier-Orr diagrams employ only a few basic symbols. The user of this technique spends more time trying to solve the problem than being concerned with remembering confusing symbols, rules, and guidelines.

- The information within each bracket can be as detailed or general as the user wishes. There are no hard and fast rules that must be obeyed. This allows a great deal of flexibility for the person using a Warnier-Orr diagram.

- They provide excellent program documentation for other programmers as well as the person who wrote the original diagram and may need to refer back to it six months later (in which time the person may have forgotten the specific details included in the diagram).

- One can easily see how the different data variables are used within the diagram. With the use of a data dictionary, the manipulation of the data is normally not difficult to track.

- Warnier-Orr diagrams can be used to design systems as well as individual programs within a system.

One disadvantage of Warnier-Orr diagrams is: Initially, a person who is used to other logic techniques (hierarchy chart or structure chart) may have a period of adjustment. These techniques are read top-down, left-to-right in direct contrast to the Warnier-Orr diagram which is read in left-to-right, top-down order.

Summary of Warnier-Orr Diagram Procedures

When learning how to solve a problem with a new logic tool, the most common question asked is, "What is my first step?". The following is a list of general steps to follow when using Warnier-Orr diagrams to develop problem solutions.

1. Define all input and output data dictionary variables. Before attempting to solve a problem you must clearly identify the desired input and output data items. As you proceed through the next steps, you will need to define other intermediate data dictionary variables.

2. Identify all activities or levels that must occur to satisfy problem requirements. These activities can be listed in any order. Go through a "brainstorming" period when coming up with activities.

3. Once all levels have been identified, reorder this list into its logical execution order and determine how many times each level is repeated. For levels that are repetitive (looping) it is valid to list general tasks that may occur within that bracket even though they will not be shown in the diagram until step 5.

4. Name each activity with a descriptive label. Write this label down and draw a bracket to the right of this label.

5. To the right of each bracket drawn in step 4, list all of the tasks that should occur within that bracket.

6. At this time you should have a "skeleton" Warnier-Orr diagram outlining all activities required to solve the problem. At this point, if the problem is relatively simple, you could be finished with the diagram. If the problem is more complex, you would not be able to write a program from this diagram yet. How you read a road map would be a good analogy. When you have reached step 5, you have found the city. The next steps will allow you to locate the specific street and decide on the best way to get to that street.

    The rest of the process is fairly straightforward. Look at each activity that you have defined and ask yourself this question. Do I need to break this activity down into more detail? If the answer is yes, draw a bracket and list to the right of this bracket all entries that should occur there. Repeat this process until you can answer no to the above question.

    When you answer no to this question, proceed down the remaining list of activities, following the above procedure until you have exhausted the list.

All of the steps involved in solving a problem using a Warnier-Orr diagram have been discussed. To enable you to experience the pleasure of going through these steps, some challenging problems have been provided at the end of this chapter.

PROBLEM SOLUTIONS

The remainder of the chapter is devoted to the detailed narrative and solution for each of the problems described in Chapter 1. All of the problems are solved in the sequence of steps listed in the previous summary section. Within the Warnier-Orr diagram solutions, all data items defined in the data dictionary are underlined to be more easily identified by the reader. Have fun!

▶ Problem 1—Lease Versus Buy ◀

Ajax Manufacturing Company has the option to purchase outright or lease (with an option to buy at lease-end) a computer system to aid in its business operations. If Ajax purchases the system for $10,000, it will finance the full amount for four years at a 10% interest rate.

> **NOTE:** Simple Interest (I) = Principal (P) × Rate (R) × Time Period (T).

If Ajax leases the equipment for four years and decides to purchase at lease-end, the monthly cost will be $250 with a final payment of $3000. Which option should Ajax choose in order to minimize the total cost of the computer system? The problem solution should satisfy varying lease versus buy input information.

Step 1:

Define all input, output, and intermediate data dictionary variables needed to solve the lease versus buy problem.

```
<<DATA DICTIONARY>>
```

```
PURCHASE.RECORD                             REPORT.ITEMS
    PURCHASE.PRICE      NNNNN.NN                PURCHASE.OPTION.COST    NNNNN.NN
    INTEREST.RATE       N.NN                    LEASE.BUY.OPTION.COST   NNNNN.NN
    FINANCED.YEARS      NN


LEASE.BUY.RECORD
    MTHLY.LEASE.COST            NNN.NN
    LENGTH.OF.LEASE.MONTHS      NN
    FINAL.PAYMENT               NNNN.NN
```

Steps 2 and 3:

Identify all activities that must occur to satisfy the lease versus buy problem requirements. Group these activities into their logical execution order and determine how many times the activity should be repeated. The problem requirements ask for a recommendation based on just one input record, so the following activities will occur only once:

1. READ PURCHASE AND LEASE RECORDS (1)

2. CALCULATE PURCHASE COST (1)

3. CALCULATE LEASE COST (1)

4. WRITE REPORT HEADINGS, FINAL COST FIGURES, AND MAKE RECOMMENDATION (1)

Step 4:

Take each activity listed in Steps 2 and 3 above and name it with a descriptive label. Write this label name down and draw a bracket to the right of the label (Figure S7.1.4).

Step 5:

To the right of each bracket drawn in Step 4, list all of the tasks that should occur within that bracket. There are four main activities: read purchase and lease records, calculate purchase cost, calculate lease cost, and write the recommended option. Figure S7.1.5 displays these activities in appropriate Warnier-Orr format.

Step 6:

This step refines the items derived in earlier steps and provides the final solution for the lease versus purchase problem. Identify the activities that need to be broken down into more detail. For this problem, the only activity that should be divided into more detail is how to recommend an option in the WRITE REPORT bracket. Figure S7.1.6 illustrates the changes to the WRITE REPORT bracket. The rest of the solution is unchanged from what appears in Figure S7.1.5.

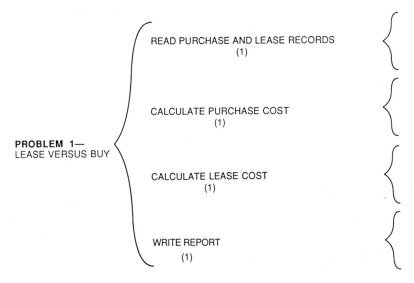

Figure S7.1.4 Problem 1 Solution—Step 4

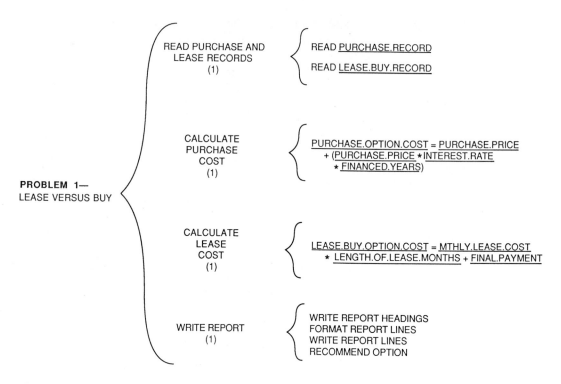

Figure S7.1.5   Problem 1 Solution—Step 5

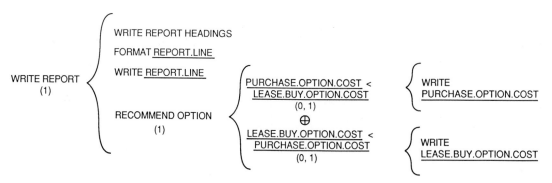

Figure S7.1.6   Problem 1 Solution—Step 6

Problem 2—Payroll

Easymoney Inc. desires to generate their current manual payroll via computer. The information collected every payroll period includes the employee social security number, pay rate, hours worked, and total other deductions. The payroll department would like a

> report listing these items: employee social security number, hours worked, pay rate, gross pay, FICA withheld (6.13% of gross pay), federal tax withheld (20% of gross pay), total other deductions, and net pay.

Step 1:
   Define all input, output, and intermediate data dictionary variables necessary to solve this payroll problem.

`<<DATA DICTIONARY>>`

EMPLOYEE.RECORD			REPORT.LINE	
SOCIAL.SEC.NUMBER	N(9)		SOCIAL.SEC.NUMBER	N(9)
PAY.RATE	NN.NN		HOURS.WORKED	NN.N
HOURS.WORKED	NN.N		PAY.RATE	NN.NN
TOTAL.OTHER.DEDUCTIONS	NNNN.NN		GROSS.PAY	NNNN.NN
			FICA.WITHHELD	NNN.NN
			FED.TAX.WITHHELD	NNNN.NN
			TOTAL.OTHER.DEDUCTIONS	NNNN.NN
			NET.PAY	NNNN.NN

MISCELLANEOUS VARIABLES	
END.OF.FILE	CCC
LINE.CTR	NN

Steps 2 and 3:
   Identify all levels that must occur to satisfy payroll problem requirements. Once that has been achieved, change the order of this list into their logical sequence necessary to solve the problem. It may take a few attempts to place the items in the proper order. For example, initialization activities (setting variables to proper beginning values and reading the first record on the file) must occur before you can calculate gross pay, net pay, and so on for each record in the file.

1.   INITIALIZATION ACTIVITIES (1)

2.   PROCESS EMPLOYEE FILE—FOR EACH RECORD IN THE EMPLOYEE FILE DO:
   a.   CALCULATE GROSS.PAY
   b.   CALCULATE NET.PAY
   c.   WRITE REPORT.LINE
   d.   GET NEXT EMPLOYEE.RECORD

Step 4:
   Take each activity listed in Steps 2 and 3 above and use it as a label for each bracket drawn (Figure S7.2.4). This problem reads and manipulates all records in the file. To detect an end-of-file condition, the solution uses a variable called END.OF.FILE. The variable is assigned an initial value of NO, meaning that the end-of-file condition has not been reached. Each time a record is read (GET), the diagram checks that record to see if it is the last one on the file. If so, the value YES is assigned to the variable END.OF.FILE, and the PROCESS EMPLOYEE FILE bracket will no longer be repeated.

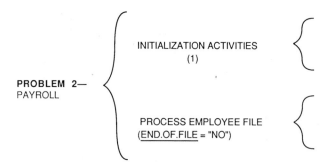

Figure S7.2.4 Problem 2 Solution—Step 4

Step 5:

To the right of each bracket drawn in step 4 all of the tasks that should occur within that bracket are listed (Figure S7.2.5).

For this example, the PROCESS EMPLOYEE FILE bracket is further divided into the detailed tasks needed to calculate the employee's salary information and to produce a report.

Step 6:

Identify the activities which need to be broken down into more detail. In this problem most of the work is done in the PROCESS EMPLOYEE FILE bracket. It is the only bracket that needs to be broken down into more detail. Figure S7.2.6 shows the expanded PROCESS EMPLOYEE FILE bracket.

The activities that occur are:

1. Calculate gross pay

2. Calculate net pay

3. Write report line

4. Read next EMPLOYEE.RECORD

The only bracket needing further elaboration is the WRITE REPORT.LINE bracket. In this bracket, the variable LINE.CTR is checked against a constant value of 50. If the test is TRUE (number of lines printed on the page is > 50), a new page with appropriate headings is printed. Notice also that the LINE.CTR is incremented by 2 each time REPORT.LINE is printed. The payroll problem specifications require each report line to be double-spaced (report line separated by a blank line), so the LINE.CTR variable is increased by 2 to reflect the blank line printed along with the report line. This problem solution is now complete.

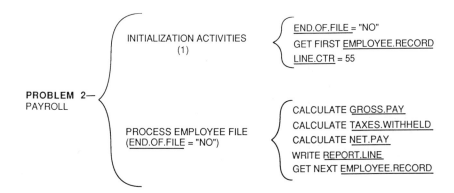

Figure S7.2.5 Problem 2 Solution—Step 5

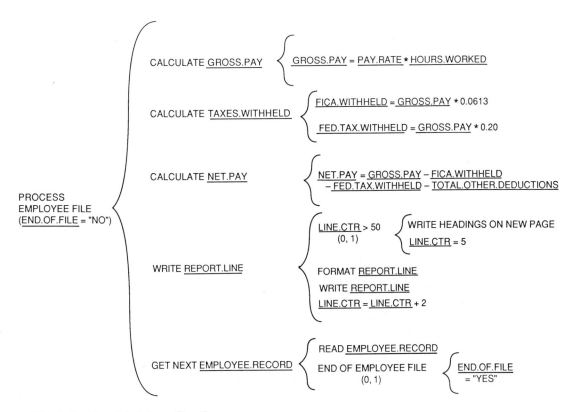

Figure S7.2.6 Problem 2 Solution—Step 6

▶ Problem 3—Health and Diet ◀

Bedford Waistwatchers Association requests that a program be written to motivate members to stay on their diet and show the cost savings that can result from a change in diet. One of the staple diet items recommended is yogurt. If a member follows the Association diet strictly, a large amount of yogurt can be consumed over a short period of time. The cost effectiveness of buying yogurt or making yogurt at home should be evaluated. If a monetary savings can be realized by making yogurt at home versus buying it at the store, how many cups of yogurt must be produced to achieve this savings? The data needed to provide an analysis is store cost of yogurt per cup, cost of yogurt maker if made at home, cost of home ingredients per cup, and number of cups. An analysis should show the home cost, store cost, and savings or loss per cup.

Step 1:

Define all input, output, and work data dictionary variables to solve the problem. Obviously, all of these variables cannot be defined in Step 1; some variables will not become apparent until Steps 5 and 6. In Step 1, list as many variables as you think are necessary and add to this list as needed later.

```
<<DATA DICTIONARY>>
```

```
YOGURT.RECORD                                 REPORT.LINE
    STORE.COST.YOGURT.PER.CUP      NN.NN          CUP.NUMBER              NN
    COST.YOGURT.MAKER              NN.NN          CALC.HOME.COST          NNN.NN
    HOME.COST.INGREDIENTS.PER.CUP  NN.NN          CALC.STORE.COST         NNN.NN
    NUMBER.OF.CUPS                 NN             CALC.SAVINGS.OR.LOSS    NNN.NN

WORK.VARIABLES
    LINE.CTR                       NN
```

Steps 2 and 3:

Identify all activities that must occur to satisfy problem requirements. Once that has been achieved, change the order of this list into the logical sequence necessary to solve the problem. There are two main activities: start-up (initialization) and the actual calculation and printing of the variable values.

1. START-UP ACTIVITIES (1)

2. CALCULATE AND PRINT COST FIELDS (NUMBER.OF.CUPS)

Step 4:

Use the activity names in Steps 2 and 3 as labels for the brackets (Figure S7.3.4). Notice that the CALCULATE AND PRINT COST FIELDS bracket is repeated by the variable NUMBER.OF.CUPS read in the START-UP ACTIVITIES bracket.

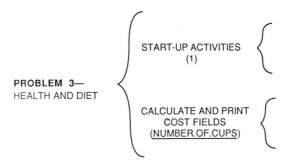

Figure S7.3.4 Problem 3 Solution—Step 4

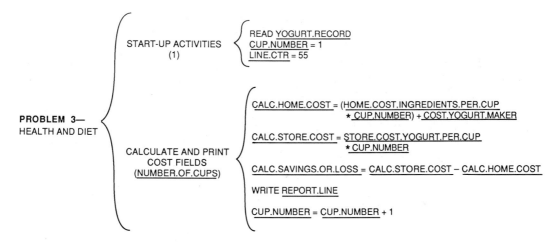

Figure S7.3.5 Problem 3 Solution—Step 5

Step 5:

To the right of each bracket drawn in Step 4, list all of the tasks that should occur within that bracket (Figure S7.3.5). In the START-UP ACTIVITIES, YOGURT.RECORD is read, CUP.NUMBER is set to 1, and LINE.CTR is initialized to 55 to force the first heading group to print at the top of a new page. (See Figure S7.3.6 to observe how LINE.CTR is used.) The CALCULATE and PRINT COST FIELDS bracket is repeated based on the value read from YOGURT.RECORD (stored in the variable NUMBER.OF.CUPS).

Step 6:

Identify the activities that need to be broken down into more detail. The only activity that needs to be divided into further detail is the WRITE REPORT LINE bracket to check if the variable LINE.CTR exceeds a value larger than the last line that can be printed on a page (check for page break). Every time the REPORT.LINE is written, LINE.CTR is increased by 2 to account for the double spacing of the output. The solution for this bracket is provided on Figure S7.3.6. The rest of the diagram remains as presented in Figure S7.3.5.

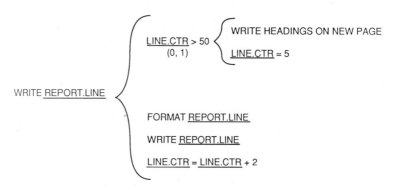

Figure S7.3.6 Problem 3 Solution—Step 6

▶ Problem 4—Daily Sales ◀

Vidal Blass is the owner of Obnoxious Telephone Sales. Vidal has had up to 20 employees solicit sales via telephone on a specific day. Vidal would like to produce a sales summary report at the end of each business day to determine which salespeople generate the most revenue. Employees make a phone sale, write the sales information down on a receipt with their name and the total sale, and place the receipt in a bin shared by all of the employees. At the end of the day, all of the receipts are gathered and the summary report produced by entering the name and sales amount from each receipt. The first activity the computer will perform is to sort all input records in name order. (Assume that no two salespeople have the same name.) The sales summary will list the total sales by each name and the grand total sales for the day's business activities.

Step 1:

Define all input, output, and work data dictionary variables. As you proceed with the problem solution to Steps 5 and 6, other variables are identified and included in the data dictionary. This step allows you to take a "first cut" at creating variables.

```
<<DATA DICTIONARY>>

SALES.RECEIPT.RECORD                          REPORT.LINE
    SALESPERSON.NAME        C(20)                 SALESPERSON.NAME        C(20)
    AMT.OF.SALE            NNN.NN                  TOTAL.SALES            NNNN.NN

GRAND.TOTAL.LINE
    GRAND.TOTAL.SALES      N(5).NN

WORK.VARIABLES
    END.OF.FILE                   CCC
    LINE.CTR                      NN
    PREVIOUS.SALESPERSON.NAME     C(20)
```

Steps 2 and 3:

Identify all levels that must occur to satisfy problem requirements. This is a brainstorming step: list all the activities as they come to mind and do not be concerned about the order. Once that has been achieved, change the order of this list into its logical sequence necessary to solve the problem.

1. START-UP ACTIVITIES (1)

2. PROCESS SALES RECEIPT FILE—FOR EACH SALES RECEIPT RECORD DO:

    a. COMPARE CURRENT SALESPERSON.NAME TO PREVIOUS.SALESPERSON.NAME
    b. UPDATE GRAND.TOTAL.SALES
    c. READ NEXT SALES.RECEIPT.RECORD

3. WRITE GRAND.TOTAL.LINE (1)

Step 4:

Take each activity listed in Steps 2 and 3 above and use it as a label for each bracket drawn (Figure S7.4.4). All records in the file are read and processed in the same manner as in problem 2. This problem will put into practice a concept introduced in Chapter 1, control breaks. Refer back to Chapter 1 if you need to refresh your memory. The control field from the input record is SALESPERSON.NAME, the data item that will store the previous control field value is PREVIOUS.SALESPERSON.NAME. These two variables are compared to detect a name change which means that a control break has occurred. The result of this action will be revealed in later steps within the COMPARE SALESPERSON.NAME TO PRE-VIOUS.SALESPERSON.NAME bracket.

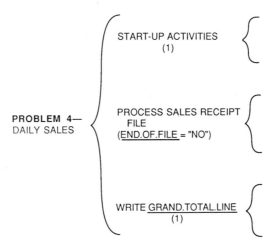

Figure S7.4.4 Problem 4 Solution—Step 4

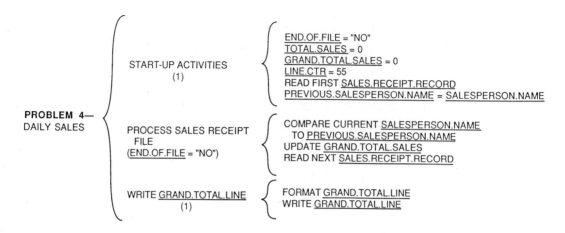

Figure S7.4.5 Problem 4 Solution—Step 5

Step 5:

To the right of each bracket drawn in Step 4, list all of the tasks that should occur within that bracket (Figure S7.4.5). START-UP ACTIVITIES initializes variables to proper values (for example, assigning LINE.CTR the numeric value 55 to ensure the first heading will be printed later in this Warnier-Orr diagram), reads the first record, and sets up the control break comparison variable (or key) PREVIOUS.SALESPERSON.NAME. PROCESS SALES RECEIPT FILE reads all records on the file (processes records while the conditional expression END.OF.FILE = "NO" is true), compares the current record's name to the control break key name (what occurs here is explained in Step 6), and updates grand total sales field.

Step 6:

If necessary, divide the remaining activities into more detail. The only bracket that needs to be further subdivided is the PROCESS SALES RECEIPT FILE. Figure S7.4.6 illustrates how that bracket is expanded; the rest of Figure S7.4.5 is unchanged.

In the COMPARE CURRENT SALESPERSON.NAME TO PREVIOUS.SALES-PERSON.NAME bracket, if the comparison is TRUE, the TOTAL.SALES field for the control break is accumulated. If FALSE, the LINE.CTR is checked for a page break, the detail line for the current salesperson is printed and processing for the new control break salesperson begins (TOTAL.SALES is set equal to current salesperson's AMT.OF.SALE and the control break key PREVIOUS.SALESPERSON.NAME, is assigned the current SALESPER-SON.NAME). The only bracket that may need further explanation is READ NEXT SALES.RECEIPT.RECORD. Why is the report line written? With control break logic, at end of file you need to process the last control field value; otherwise, the sales totals for the last salesperson would not appear on the report. The only time that REPORT.LINE is written is when a control break (SALESPERSON.NAME NOT = PREVIOUS.SALESPERSON.NAME) occurs. Control breaks are a tricky procedure!

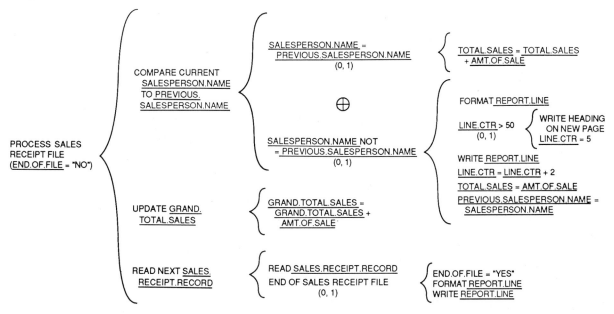

Figure S7.4.6 Problem 4 Solution—Step 6

► Problem 5—House Construction ◄

Well-Bilt Homes Inc. would like you to design a program which enables builders to calculate home building costs based on prospective room sizes. This program is interactive; it allows the user to input the number of rooms desired and the individual room dimensions (length and width only). The building cost per square foot is based on the following:

1000 square feet or less	$60 per square foot
1001–2000 square feet	$50 per square foot
More than 2000 square feet	$40 per square foot

Develop the logic to compute the building cost of the house.

Step 1:

Define all input, output, and work data dictionary variables required to calculate square footage for any house based on number of rooms and their respective length and width.

```
<<DATA DICTIONARY>>

NUMBER.OF.ROOMS          NN          REPORT.LINE
ROOM.LENGTH              NN             ROOM.LENGTH        NN
ROOM.WIDTH               NN             ROOM.WIDTH         NN
TOTAL.HOUSE.SQ.FT        N(5)           ROOM.SQ.FT         NNNN
COST.PER.SQ.FOOT         NNN.NN
TOTAL.COST.OF.HOUSE      N(6).NN
```

Steps 2 and 3:

Identify all activities that must occur to satisfy program requirements and place them in logical order. This problem is different from the previous problems since you read the number of rooms in the START-UP ACTIVITIES bracket and manipulate each room based on the entered room length and width in the PROCESS ROOMS bracket.

1. START-UP ACTIVITIES (1)

2. PROCESS ROOMS: FOR EACH ROOM:

    a. INPUT ROOM LENGTH AND WIDTH
    b. CALCULATE ROOM SQUARE FOOTAGE
    c. PRINT REPORT LINE
    d. UPDATE TOTAL

3. DETERMINE COST PER SQUARE FOOT (1)

4. DETERMINE FINAL COST (1)

5. PRINT FINAL LINES (1)

Step 4:

Use the activities in Steps 2 and 3 as labels for appropriate brackets (Figure S7.5.4). There are five main activities (brackets) that are considered in more detail in Step 5.

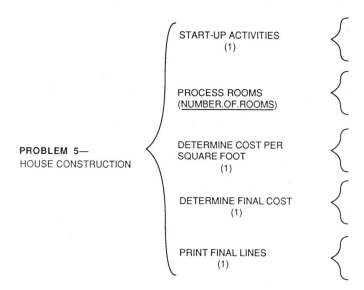

Figure S7.5.4 Problem 5 Solution—Step 4

Step 5:

To the right of each bracket drawn in Step 4, list all of the tasks that should occur within that bracket (Figure S7.5.5). START-UP ACTIVITIES receives the NUMBER.OF.ROOMS and prints the headings. PROCESS.ROOMS reads in ROOM.LENGTH and ROOM.WIDTH, NUMBER.OF.ROOMS times. For each room the square footage is calculated, the detailed room information is printed, and the square footage total is accumulated. The remaining activities are more fully disclosed in Step 6.

Step 6:

If necessary, break down the remaining activities into more detailed brackets. The final solution is displayed in Figure S7.5.6.

DETERMINE COST PER SQUARE FOOT bracket looks at the TOTAL.HOUSE.SQ.FT variable for one of three ranges: less than or equal to 1000 square feet, 1001 to 2000 square feet, or greater than 2000 square feet. The final cost is calculated in the next bracket (DETERMINE FINAL COST) and the total cost is printed (PRINT FINAL LINES).

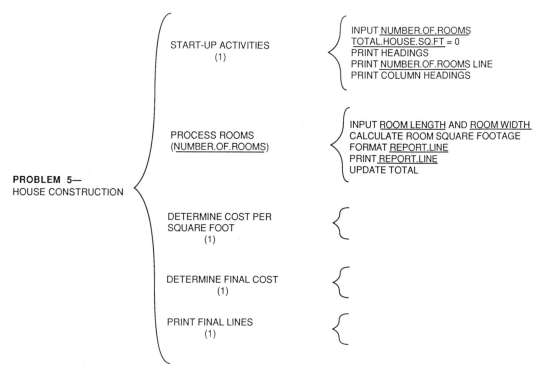

Figure S7.5.5 Problem 5 Solution—Step 5

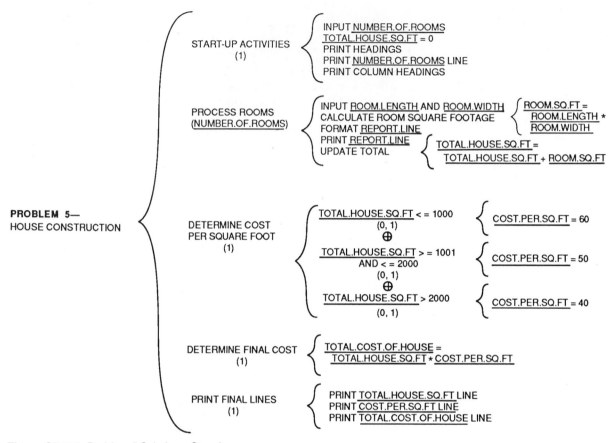

Figure S7.5.6 Problem 5 Solution—Step 6

► Problem 6—Personnel Statistics ◄

The chairman of the board of Eldorado Enterprises Inc. has requested a report from the Personnel Department that will show various types of information about the company's work force. This report should provide the following:

1. The total number of males and females (SEX CODE = M for males, F for females)

2. The total number of employees by the following age categories (BIRTHDAY YEAR)
    a. less than 21
    b. 21–30
    c. 31–40
    d. 41–50
    e. 51–60
    f. 61–70
    g. over 70

> 3. The total number of people who have been with the company for 10 years or more (SENIORITY CODE = 3, 4, or 5)
>
> 4. The total number of engineers (OCCUPATION CODE = 7) in the company

Step 1:

This problem illustrates the usage of multiple counters. The first step defines input, output, and work data dictionary variables.

```
<<DATA DICTIONARY>>
```

PERSONNEL.RECORD		COUNTER.VARIABLES	
SEX.CODE	C	TOTAL.MALES	N(5)
BIRTHDAY.YEAR	NN	TOTAL.FEMALES	N(5)
SENIORITY.CODE	N	MF.LESS.21.CTR	N(4)
OCCUPATION.CODE	N	MF.21-30.CTR	N(4)
		MF.31-40.CTR	N(4)
		MF.41-50.CTR	N(4)
OTHER.VARIABLES		MF.51-60.CTR	N(4)
TODAYS.YEAR	NN	MF.61-70.CTR	N(4)
END.OF.FILE	CCC	MF.OVER.70.CTR	N(4)
AGE	NN	TOTAL.EMP.OVER.10.YEARS	N(4)
		TOTAL.ENGINEERS	N(4)

Steps 2 and 3:

Identify all activities that must occur to satisfy problem requirements and place them in logical order. There are three primary activities: BEGINNING ACTIVITIES reads the first record and initializes variables; PROCESS PERSONNEL FILE inspects each record, calculates the employee's age and updates counter variables; and PRINT REPORT.

1. BEGINNING ACTIVITIES (1)

2. PROCESS PERSONNEL FILE: FOR EACH RECORD ON PERSONNEL FILE:

   a. CALCULATE AGE
   b. CHECK FOR SEX AND AGE
   c. CHECK FOR EMPLOYEES OVER 10 YEARS
   d. CHECK FOR ENGINEERS
   e. GET NEXT PERSONNEL.RECORD

3. PRINT REPORT

Step 4:

Take each activity listed in Steps 2 and 3 above and use that as a label for each bracket drawn (Figure S7.6.4). This problem will read and process all records in the file in the same manner as some of the earlier problems. The main concept conveyed in this example is how to manipulate many counter variables. (To review how counters work, look back in Chapter 1.)

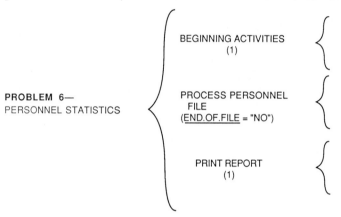

Figure S7.6.4 Problem 6 Solution—Step 4

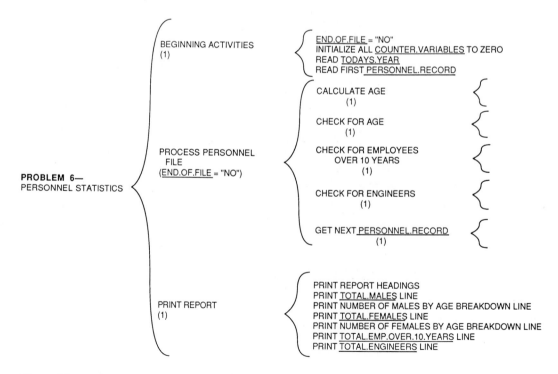

Figure S7.6.5 Problem 6 Solution—Step 5

Step 5:

To the right of each bracket drawn in Step 4, list all of the tasks that should occur within that bracket (Figure S7.6.5) The brackets BEGINNING ACTIVITIES and PRINT REPORT are self-explanatory. The PROCESS PERSONNEL FILE bracket needs to be further explored. For each record read, these tasks occur: the age is calculated and tested for a range (the age counter variable is updated); there is a check of employee length of service; and there is a check for engineer.

Step 6:

If necessary, break down the remaining activities into more detailed brackets. The only brackets that need to be further subdivided are within PROCESS PERSONNEL FILE (see Figure S7.6.6). The rest of the solution in Figure S7.6.5 is unchanged.

Examine the methods used to implement the activities discussed in Step 5. Pay close attention to the decisions and how the counter variables are incremented for age, length of service, and engineer status.

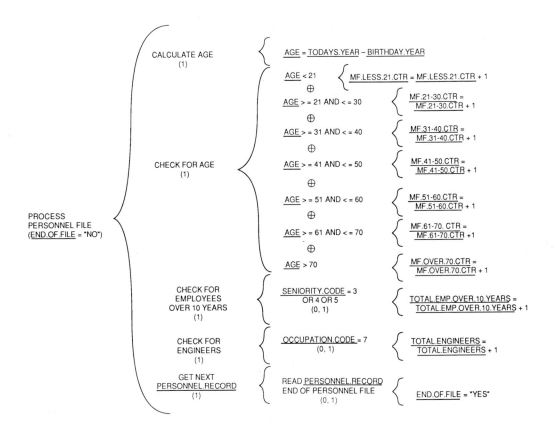

Figure S7.6.6 Problem 6 Solution—Step 6

Warnier-Orr Diagram Walk-Through

This section demonstrates the Warnier-Orr diagram walk-through or verification process for problems 3 and 4. You should follow this process to test your solutions for accuracy. Refer to the completed problems since those bracket names and variable names are used in this walk-through. Bracket names are underlined and nested brackets (bracket within a bracket) are indented within an outer bracket. What this section illustrates is how to plug values in the variables referenced in each bracket.

► Problem 3—Health and Diet ◄

START-UP ACTIVITIES:
STORE.COST.YOGURT.PER.CUP = .40
COST.YOGURT.MAKER = 12.95
HOME.COST.INGREDIENTS.PER.CUP = .04
NUMBER.OF.CUPS = 75
CUP.NUMBER = 1
LINE.CTR = 55

CALCULATE AND PRINT COST FIELDS:
CALC.HOME.COST = 12.99
((.04 * 1) + 12.95)

CALC.STORE.COST = .40
(.40 * 1)

CALC.SAVINGS.OR.LOSS = −12.59
(.40 − 12.99)

WRITE REPORT.LINE:
LINE.CTR is greater than 50 so
   headings are written.

LINE.CTR = 5

The REPORT.LINE is written with
   CUP.NUMBER, CALC.SAVINGS.OR.LOSS, etc.

LINE.CTR = 7
(5 + 2)

CUP.NUMBER = 2
(1 + 1)

The CALCULATE AND PRINT COST FIELDS bracket is repeated NUMBER OF CUPS (75) times. Walk through this bracket one more interation. (We don't have space to walk through the logic 75 times.)

CALCULATE AND PRINT COST FIELDS:
CALC.HOME.COST = 13.03
((.04 * 2) + 12.95)

CALC.STORE.COST = .80
(.40 * 2)

CALC.SAVINGS.OR.LOSS = −12.23
(.80 − 13.03)

WRITE REPORT.LINE:
LINE.CTR is less than 50 so
   no new headings are written.

The REPORT.LINE is written with
   CUP.NUMBER, CALC.SAVINGS.OR.LOSS, etc.

LINE.CTR = 9
(7 + 2)

CUP.NUMBER = 3
(2 + 1)

If needed, walk through a few more iterations of the CALCULATE AND PRINT COST FIELDS brackets; otherwise, proceed to the next walk-through problem.

► Problem 4—Daily Sales ◄

START-UP ACTIVITIES:
END.OF.FILE = "NO"
TOTAL.SALES = 0
GRAND.TOTAL.SALES = 0
LINE.CTR = 55
SALESPERSON.NAME = "JOSEPH"
AMT.OF.SALE = 200.00
PREVIOUS.SALESPERSON.NAME = "JOSEPH"

PROCESS SALES RECEIPT FILE:
The PROCESS.SALES RECEIPT FILE is repeated until the last record on the file is read (END.OF.FILE is assigned the value "YES").

COMPARE CURRENT SALESPERSON.NAME TO PREVIOUS.SALESPERSON.NAME:
SALESPERSON.NAME ("JOSEPH") is equal to PREVIOUS.SALESPERSON.NAME
   ("JOSEPH") so:
      TOTAL.SALES = 200.00
      (0.00 + 200.00)

UPDATE GRAND.TOTAL.SALES
GRAND.TOTAL.SALES = 200.00
(0 + 200.00)

READ NEXT SALES.RECEIPT.RECORD:
SALESPERSON.NAME = "JOSEPH"
AMT.OF.SALE = 400.00
This SALES.RECEIPT.RECORD is not the last record on the
file, thus PROCESS.SALES.RECEIPT FILE bracket is repeated.

PROCESS SALES RECEIPT FILE:

COMPARE CURRENT SALESPERSON.NAME TO
PREVIOUS.SALESPERSON.NAME:

SALESPERSON.NAME = PREVIOUS.SALESPERSON.NAME
SALESPERSON.NAME ("JOSEPH") is equal to PREVIOUS.SALESPERSON.NAME
("JOSEPH") so:
TOTAL.SALES = 600.00
(200.00 + 400.00)

UPDATE GRAND.TOTAL.SALES
GRAND.TOTAL.SALES = 600.00
(400.00 + 200.00)

READ NEXT SALES.RECEIPT.RECORD:
SALESPERSON.NAME = "ANDREW"
AMT.OF.SALE = 750.00
This SALES.RECEIPT.RECORD is not the last record on the file, thus
PROCESS.SALES.RECEIPT FILE bracket is repeated.

PROCESS SALES RECEIPT FILE:

COMPARE CURRENT SALESPERSON.NAME TO
PREVIOUS.SALESPERSON.NAME:

SALESPERSON.NAME NOT = PREVIOUS.SALESPERSON.NAME
SALESPERSON.NAME ("ANDREW") is not equal to PREVIOUS.SALESPERSON.NAME
("JOSEPH") so:
REPORT.LINE is readied for printing
(these activities are dependent
on the programming language)

LINE.CTR > 50:
LINE.CTR with a value of 55 is greater
than 50 so:
HEADINGS are written on new page
LINE.CTR = 5

REPORT.LINE is written

LINE.CTR = 7
(5 + 2)

TOTAL.SALES = 750.00

PREVIOUS.SALESPERSON.NAME = "ANDREW"

UPDATE GRAND.TOTAL.SALES
GRAND.TOTAL.SALES = 1350.00
(600.00 + 750.00)

READ NEXT SALES.RECEIPT.RECORD:
SALESPERSON.NAME = Last record on file
AMT.OF.SALE = Last record on file

This is the last record on the file so:
     END.OF.FILE = "YES"
     REPORT.LINE is formatted and written

WRITE GRAND.TOTAL.LINE
The GRAND.TOTAL.LINE is formatted and is written with the value of 1350.00. Since all records on the file have been read, the solution logic ends processing at this time. This problem exposed you to control-break logic.

SUMMARY

Now that you have reached the end of the chapter, briefly review the material presented concerning Warnier-Orr diagrams. Warnier-Orr diagrams consist of a series of brackets drawn from left to right until all problem requirements are completed. Each bracket consists of pseudocode-type statements that are executed in order from top to bottom. These components are used with an established set of rules:

- On the left side of each bracket there must be a label describing the function of that bracket.

- The first (or leftmost) label is repeated only one time and states the purpose of the diagram or name of the problem.

- Two objects appear on the right side of a bracket: a label followed by another bracket (known as nesting brackets) or a pseudocode instruction.

- There are no limits on the number of brackets or pseudocode instructions in one diagram.

The advantages of the Warnier-Orr diagram as a logic development tool are:

- The reader can quickly grasp the activities involved in a problem.

- It employs only a few basic symbols.

- The information in each bracket can be as detailed or general as the user wishes.

- It provides an excellent means of program documentation.

- The function and use of data variables are distinct.

- The tool can be used to design systems as well as individual programs within a system.

The disadvantages are:

- A person who is used to other logic tools (such as the hierarchy chart or structure chart) may have an adjustment period because the tools differ in execution order.

The solutions to the six problems reinforce the concepts of top-down design or functional decomposition discussed in Chapter 1 and illustrated in other chapters. Problem solutions are developed in stages, beginning with the general stages (functions) that must occur to solve problems and then expanding these functions into more detailed instructions that eventually meet all of the problem requirements. The more comfortable you become with this approach (the Warnier-Orr diagram forces you in that direction), the easier it will be to solve any type of problem that eventually leads to the development of a computer program fulfilling the stated input and output objectives.

REVIEW QUESTIONS

MUTIPLE CHOICE
1. The Warnier-Orr diagram is similar to the
   a. Hierarchy Chart
   b. Structure Chart
   c. IPO Chart
   d. None of the above

2. Warnier-Orr diagrams were
   a. initially designed by Jean-Dominique Warnier and Ken Orr
   b. originally developed to assist only in system design
   c. intended to replace the structure chart logic development tool
   d. all of the above
   e. none of the above

3. On the left side of each bracket in the Warnier-Orr diagram
   a. there is an optional label describing the function of the bracket
   b. there must be a label describing the function of that bracket
   c. there must be a descriptive label preceded by a bracket
   d. all of the above

4. Which of the following statement(s) are false?
    a. A Warnier-Orr diagram has no limits to the number of brackets shown in the diagram or the number of instructions (or labels) within a bracket.
    b. Warnier-Orr diagrams cannot represent the three program logic patterns: sequence, selection, and repetition.
    c. Warnier-Orr diagrams can be used to design systems as well as individual programs within a system.
    d. The data dictionary must be included with a Warnier-Orr diagram.

5. Which of the following statement(s) are true?
    a. Jean-Dominique Warnier originally developed the Warnier diagram in the mid 1970s.
    b. A Warnier-Orr diagram is read in left-to-right, top-down order.
    c. The first bracket states the purpose of the diagram or name of the problem and only appears one time.
    d. All of the above.

FILL IN THE BLANK

1. The Warnier-Orr diagram is a technique that can be used at the program level and _____ level.

2. The Warnier-Orr diagram is often referred to as a _____ chart turned on its side.

3. A Warnier-Orr diagram is read in left-to-right, _____ order.

4. There are two objects that can appear on the right side of a bracket: a label or a _____ instruction.

5. If a (0,1) appears underneath a statement, the instructions within the bracket to the right of this statement will be executed _____ times.

SHORT ANSWER

1. The Warnier-Orr diagram is often referred to as a "lazy" hierarchy chart. How are the two logic tools similar? How do they differ?

2. For some problems Warnier-Orr diagrams are superior to other programming logic tools. Support or dispute the previous statement.

3. Discuss the different alternatives available to represent the selection logic control structure with Warnier-Orr diagrams.

4. What is the function of a bracket in Warnier-Orr diagrams?

5. Discuss the advantages and disadvantages of solving problems using the Warnier-Orr technique.

EXERCISES

1. Vic's Video Rentals has a file which contains the following information on each video cassette movie in stock: movie number, movie title, date rented, date returned, renter's name, renter's address, and renter's telephone number. Vic wants you to write a program to list in the following format all movies that have been rented and not returned. If a movie has a value in the DATE RENTED field, but the DATE RETURNED field is blank, then that movie is not in the store. Vic also wants the report to give him the total number of movies not returned.

SAMPLE REPORT FORMAT:

```
                          VIC'S VIDEO RENTALS
                        MOVIES CURRENTLY RENTED

MOVIE   MOVIE TITLE          DATE      DATE      RENTER'S          RENTER'S
NUM                          RENTED    RETURNED  NAME              TELEPHONE NUM

NNNN    CCCCCCCCCCCCCCCCCCC  CC/CC/CC  CC/CC/CC  CCCCCCCCCCCCCCC   CCC-CCCC

NNNN    CCCCCCCCCCCCCCCCCCC  CC/CC/CC  CC/CC/CC  CCCCCCCCCCCCCCC   CCC-CCCC

NNNN    CCCCCCCCCCCCCCCCCCC  CC/CC/CC  CC/CC/CC  CCCCCCCCCCCCCCC   CCC-CCCC

NNNN    CCCCCCCCCCCCCCCCCCC  CC/CC/CC  CC/CC/CC  CCCCCCCCCCCCCCC   CCC-CCCC

NNNN    CCCCCCCCCCCCCCCCCCC  CC/CC/CC  CC/CC/CC  CCCCCCCCCCCCCCC   CCC-CCCC

NNNN    CCCCCCCCCCCCCCCCCCC  CC/CC/CC  CC/CC/CC  CCCCCCCCCCCCCCC   CCC-CCCC

NNNN    CCCCCCCCCCCCCCCCCCC  CC/CC/CC  CC/CC/CC  CCCCCCCCCCCCCCC   CCC-CCCC

NNNN    CCCCCCCCCCCCCCCCCCC  CC/CC/CC  CC/CC/CC  CCCCCCCCCCCCCCC   CCC-CCCC

TOTAL NUMBER OF MOVIES CURRENTLY RENTED:   NNN
```

2. The owner of Green Acres Lawn Service has purchased a personal computer to help him manage his business. He wants you to write a program to build a file containing information on all current monthly customers. He currently keeps all of this data on 3 × 5-inch index cards. Since he has approximately 4000 customers, there is a high probability of

input error from the information on the cards. The prime objective of your program is to build a file containing "clean" records. Your program must edit the input data in this manner:

Field	Type	Edit
Customer number	NNNN	numeric, range: 1–9999
Customer name	C(25)	only alphabetic characters
Customer address	C(30)	only alphabetic/numeric characters
Type of grass	N	only 1–6
Approximate lawn sq ft	N(5)	numeric, range: 0–10,000
Type of chemical treatment	N	only 1–4
Mthly billing amount	NNN.NN	numeric, range: > 0 and < 250

You must produce two reports: one to list valid records written to the file, and one to list errors that did not pass the edit checks.

```
SAMPLE REPORT FORMAT 1:


                    GREEN ACRES LAWN SERVICE
                    LISTING OF CUSTOMER FILE

CUSTOMER NO:                        NNNN
CUSTOMER NAME:                      CCCCCCCCCCCCCCCCCCCCCCCCC
CUSTOMER ADDRESS:                   CCCCCCCCCCCCCCCCCCCCCCCCCCCCCC
TYPE OF GRASS:                      N
LAWN SQUARE FOOTAGE:                NNNNN
TYPE OF CHEMICAL TREATMENT:         N
MONTHLY BILLING AMOUNT:             NNN.NN

CUSTOMER NO:                        NNNN
CUSTOMER NAME:                      CCCCCCCCCCCCCCCCCCCCCCCCC
CUSTOMER ADDRESS:                   CCCCCCCCCCCCCCCCCCCCCCCCCCCCCC
TYPE OF GRASS:                      N
LAWN SQUARE FOOTAGE:                NNNNN
TYPE OF CHEMICAL TREATMENT:         N
MONTHLY BILLING AMOUNT:             NNN.NN


            .                   .
            .                   .
            .                   .
```

SAMPLE REPORT FORMAT 2:

GREEN ACRES LAWN SERVICE
CUSTOMER FILE EXCEPTIONS

CUSTOMER NUMBER   FIELD IN ERROR

    NNNN   CCCCCCCCCCCCCCCCCCCCCCCCCCCCCCCCCCCCCCCCCCCCC

    NNNN   CCCCCCCCCCCCCCCCCCCCCCCCCCCCCCCCCCCCCCCCCCCCC

    NNNN   CCCCCCCCCCCCCCCCCCCCCCCCCCCCCCCCCCCCCCCCCCCCC

    NNNN   CCCCCCCCCCCCCCCCCCCCCCCCCCCCCCCCCCCCCCCCCCCCC

    NNNN   CCCCCCCCCCCCCCCCCCCCCCCCCCCCCCCCCCCCCCCCCCCCC

     .   .

     .   .

     .   .

3. Stanley's Shady Used Cars wants you to write a program that will calculate monthly car payments for customers. Stanley has a policy that he will finance cars for only one, two, or three years. To show the customer the possible differences in monthly payments, Stanley would like a one-page report to be generated in the format listed below. The input information is customer name, balance owed, and interest rate. (Format is NN.NN. For example, 14.25% is entered as 14.25.) The formula to calculate monthly payments is:

$$\text{Mthly amount} = \text{Interest rate} / 1200$$

$$\text{Number payments} = \text{Years} * 12$$

$$\text{Payment} = \frac{\text{Mthly amount} (1 + \text{Mthly amount})^{\text{Number payments}}}{(1 + \text{Mthly amount})^{\text{Number payments}} - 1} \times \text{Balance Owed}$$

<u>SAMPLE REPORT FORMAT:</u>

```
                    STANLEY'S SHADY USED CARS
                 MONTHLY CAR PAYMENT COMPARISON REPORT

             CUSTOMER NAME: CCCCCCCCCCCCCCCCCCCCCCCCCC

             BALANCE OWED:  NNNNN

             INTEREST RATE: NN.NN

             MONTHLY PAYMENTS FOR ONE YEAR:     NNNN.NN

             MONTHLY PAYMENTS FOR TWO YEARS:    NNNN.NN

             MONTHLY PAYMENTS FOR THREE YEARS:  NNNN.NN
```

4. Sarah's Shiny New Cars is the largest new car dealership in the state with over 4000 cars and trucks in inventory. The sales manager wants you to write a program to produce a profile of current inventory. The record consists of the following fields and their respective format:

   Model number - C(20)

   Serial number - C(20)

   Manufacturer - C(20)

   Vehicle type - C: Car = 1; Truck = 2

   Body type - C: Two doors = 1; Four doors = 2

   Engine size - C: Eight cylinder = 1; Six cylinder = 2;
                     Four cylinder = 3

   Air conditioner - C: Y = Yes; N = No

   AM/FM Radio - C: Y = Yes; N = No

   Provide the logic to write a program in the report format below.

SAMPLE REPORT FORMAT:

<pre>
                    SARAH'S SHINY NEW CARS
                     INVENTORY PROFILE

TOTAL CARS/TRUCKS IN INVENTORY: NNNN

TOTAL BY VEHICLE TYPE:
     CAR: NNNN   TRUCK: NNNN

TOTAL BY BODY TYPE:
     TWO DOOR: NNNN   FOUR DOOR: NNNN

TOTAL BY ENGINE SIZE:
     FOUR CYLINDER: NNNN   SIX CYLINDER: NNNN   EIGHT CYLINDER: NNNN

TOTAL WITH AIR CONDITIONER:
     YES: NNNN   NO: NNNN

TOTAL WITH AM/FM RADIO:
     YES: NNNN   NO: NNNN
</pre>

5. The population of Durango City is divided, with 3.2 million people living in the city, 2.4 million living in the suburbs, and 1.7 million living in rural areas. During the course of a ten-year period, the population will shift dramatically in the following ways:

   Percentage of pop. living in city will move to suburbs

   Percentage of pop. living in city will move to rural areas

   Percentage of pop. living in suburbs will move to city

   Percentage of pop. living in suburbs will move to rural areas

   Percentage of pop. living in rural areas will move to city

   Percentage of pop. living in rural areas will move to suburbs

Write a program to allow population shifts to be projected for any city based on the population of the city in three areas (city, suburbs, rural) and the six projected percentage shifts shown above.

SAMPLE REPORT FORMAT:


```
                    ANY CITY, USA
                 POPULATION MOVEMENT


        POPULATION BEFORE SHIFT:
            IN CITY:          N,NNN,NNN
            IN SUBURB:        N,NNN,NNN
            IN RURAL AREAS: N,NNN,NNN


        PERCENTAGES OF POPULATION MOVEMENT:
            LIVING IN CITY MOVE TO SUBURBS:          NNN.NN
            LIVING IN CITY MOVE TO RURAL AREAS:      NNN.NN
            LIVING IN SUBURBS MOVE TO CITY:          NNN.NN
            LIVING IN SUBURBS MOVE TO RURAL AREAS: NNN.NN
            LIVING IN RURAL AREAS MOVE TO SUBURBS: NNN.NN
            LIVING IN RURAL AREAS MOVE TO CITY:      NNN.NN


        POPULATION AFTER PERCENTAGE SHIFT:
            IN CITY:          N,NNN,NNN
            IN SUBURB:        N,NNN,NNN
            IN RURAL AREAS: N,NNN,NNN
```

6. Dr. Tommy Testtube wants you to write a program to calculate the density of any gas. The density of a gas can be calculated from the formula:

$$d = m / v$$

where m stands for mass of the gas and v for the volume. The volume of a gas is a constant at standard conditions of temperature and pressure. Assume standard conditions at a constant volume of 22.4 liters. Dr. Testtube wants to enter a variable number of gases (such as oxygen, methane, and neon) and their respective mass in grams and produce the following report.

SAMPLE REPORT FORMAT:

DR. TESTTUBE'S REPORT
CALCULATION OF THE DENSITY OF VARIOUS GASES

GAS	MASS	DENSITY
CCCCCCCCCCCCCCCCCCC	NNNN	NNNN.NN
CCCCCCCCCCCCCCCCCCC	NNNN	NNNN.NN
CCCCCCCCCCCCCCCCCCC	NNNN	NNNN.NN
CCCCCCCCCCCCCCCCCCC	NNNN	NNNN.NN
CCCCCCCCCCCCCCCCCCC	NNNN	NNNN.NN
CCCCCCCCCCCCCCCCCCC	NNNN	NNNN.NN

7. Archie Addison is the senior accountant for his company. Archie would like a program that calculates straight-line depreciation using this formula:

$$D = (P - S) / Y$$

where D is calculated yearly depreciation amount, P is original purchase price of the asset, S is salvage value of the asset at the end of depreciation period, and Y is the number of depreciation years.

Archie wants to enter the description of the asset (desk, typewriter, machinery, etc.), original purchase price, expected salvage value, and depreciation years for any number of assets. He also wants grand totals for the purchase prices of the assets and their calculated yearly depreciation amount.

SAMPLE REPORT FORMAT:

```
                    ABC MANUFACTURING INC.
               STRAIGHT-LINE DEPRECIATION REPORT

ITEM DESCRIPTION      PURCHASE      SALVAGE      DEPREC    YEARLY DEPREC
                      PRICE         VALUE        YEARS     AMOUNT

CCCCCCCCCCCCCCCCCCC   NNNNN.NN      NNNN.NN      NN        NNNNN.NN

CCCCCCCCCCCCCCCCCCC   NNNNN.NN      NNNN.NN      NN        NNNNN.NN

CCCCCCCCCCCCCCCCCCC   NNNNN.NN      NNNN.NN      NN        NNNNN.NN

CCCCCCCCCCCCCCCCCCC   NNNNN.NN      NNNN.NN      NN        NNNNN.NN

CCCCCCCCCCCCCCCCCCC   NNNNN.NN      NNNN.NN      NN        NNNNN.NN

CCCCCCCCCCCCCCCCCCC   NNNNN.NN      NNNN.NN      NN        NNNNN.NN

CCCCCCCCCCCCCCCCCCC   NNNNN.NN      NNNN.NN      NN        NNNNN.NN


GRAND TOTAL PURCHASE PRICE:         N,NNN,NNN.NN

GRAND TOTAL YEARLY DEPREC AMOUNT:   N,NNN,NNN.NN
```

REFERENCES

Kenneth Orr, *Structured Systems Development,* Yourdon Press, New York, 1977.

The Structure Chart

OBJECTIVES

After studying this chapter, you will be able to:

- Define the components of a structure chart
- Navigate through a structure chart
- Understand and recognize the rules and constraints applicable to the structure chart
- Represent the three program logic structures with the structure chart methodology
- List the advantages and disadvantages of structure charts
- Solve problems with the structure chart logic development tool

Introduction

The structure chart is a relatively new logic tool that employs some of the techniques inherent in the hierarchy chart. The logic tool objective is to provide flexible and maintainable programs. The main design strategy is to break the program down into functional components or modules. These modules contain the specific logic necessary to accomplish a goal or task. The individual using this tool should take special care to avoid packing too many functions in one module. One of the tool's strong points is that a solution to a program specification can be divided into hierarchical, top-down modules that show actual information that is passed throughout the chart.

Components

The structure chart is broken down into two or more levels. Each level consists of one or more modules with a single entry and exit point. The first level contains one module and is referred to as the *driver* or *supervisor* module. This module will invoke one or more submodules at level 2 (refer to Figure 8.1).

A submodule at level 2 can perform in the same manner as the driver module; it can call a submodule at a lower level. This process of communication between modules can continue to the level number necessary to satisfy the requirements of the program specification.

Normally, when control is transferred to a module, information is passed between the boss (calling) module and the subordinate (called) module. This is not a one-directional communication; information can be passed to the submodule from the boss or vice versa. The information transferred is of two types: data and control. To depict the transfer of information, two indicators (flags) are used. Data indicators exhibit the actual data variables that are passed between modules. A control indicator is used under different circumstances, such as when a repeat structure should end or if a field or record has been edited correctly. Figure 8.2a shows the two indicators and how they are represented. The direction of the arrow identifies from what module the information originated.

Each indicator should be labeled to adequately depict what data is actually being transferred between modules (Figure 8.2b).

One can see the limitation in labeling a flag: in most cases there will be more than one data value transferred. This is where the use of the data dictionary is appropriate. The data dictionary will group all of the data elements under one name (label) and provide a description of each individual data item. The description of each data item will include an appropriate name (which should easily identify the function of the variable) and the type and size of the variable. For example, Figure 8.3 displays the data dictionary entry for a label named PAYROLL.RECORD, which consists of three data elements.

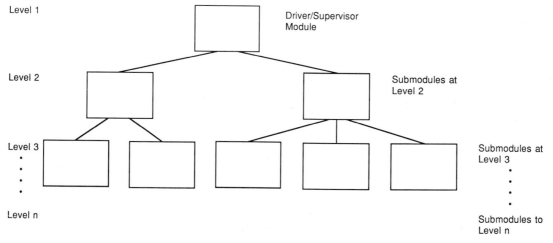

Figure 8.1 Structure Chart Level and Module Relationships

The name of each element is descriptive and two characters are used to signify whether the item consists of a character or numeric information. C represents one character (any key on the keyboard), and N depicts the numeric characters 0–9. The precision of the numeric data items is represented by the decimal point. In Figure 8.3, EMPLOYEE.NAME can store up to 20 characters, and HOURS.WORKED can store whole and partial hours worked.

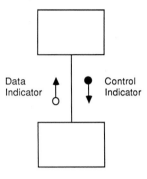

Figure 8.2a Module Data and Control Indicators

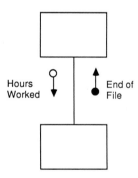

Figure 8.2b Module Data and Control Indicators with Descriptive Labels

```
PAYROLL.RECORD          <======      Data label or record name

     EMPLOYEE.NAME      —    CCCCCCCCCCCCCCCCCCCC or C(20)
     HOURS.WORKED       —    NN.N
     PAY.RATE           —    NN.NN
```

Figure 8.3 Sample Data Dictionary

Rules and Constraints

1. Most proponents of the structure chart espouse the theory that this tool will not display the physical order of execution of the modules. They emphasize that the modules represent the logical functions performed, but do not depict the physical order that occurs in the eventual program. This text takes a different approach. It is important to recognize that a structure chart is a logical model of a proposed solution to a program specification. To facilitate the conversion of the structure chart to a program, we feel that the physical order of execution of the modules must be considered in structure chart design. The techniques and solutions presented will assume that the modules will be physically executed in a specific order. The order of execution of the structure chart begins with the top module on level 1 and proceeds in top-down, left-to-right order. Figure 8.4 illustrates this order.

2. Each module should be labeled with an appropriate description of the exact function of the module. The driver module will normally be labeled to show the overall function of the entire structure chart, such as PAYROLL DRIVER, or INVENTORY DRIVER. The lower-level module description should contain an action verb denoting a concise summary of the module's activity (READ a record, CALCULATE interest formula, EDIT input record, etc.).

3. Every module identified must have information going into or coming from it, or both. Each module drawn must show some type of information flow.

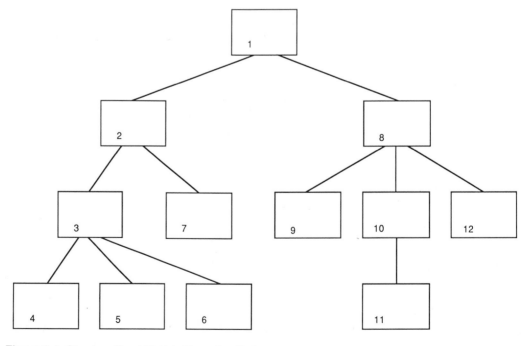

Figure 8.4 Structure Chart Module Execution Order

4. A big question to consider is when to combine modules and when to divide modules. If there is a problem in attempting to limit the naming of a module because more than one function is identified, then that module is a good candidate for division into two or more modules. The general rule to follow is: it is better to be too specific than too general, so if in doubt, create another module. On the other hand, if you have trouble naming a module because a strong function cannot be identified, that module should probably not exist independently but should be incorporated into another module.

5. A module's span of control is another consideration: what is the maximum number of subordinate modules that report to a boss module? A general rule of thumb is that one supervisor module should not control more than seven subordinate modules. If a program specification requires that one module in the proposed structure chart control more than seven submodules, reanalysis of the program specification should be considered.

6. If a module is invoked in more than one location in a structure chart, a special notation is used: a line drawn in the corner of the module that is repeated elsewhere; or an alternate method, a letter circled in the left-hand corner of the repeating module. Figure 8.5 illustrates the two notations used to represent a module that is shown in more than one place in a structure chart.

7. A structure chart by itself will not incite a deep level of meaning or understanding to the reader, and more importantly, a program could not be written with only the chart information. Included with a structure chart are two other items: a data dictionary and pseudocode for each module identified in the structure chart. The rules for data dictionary definition were discussed earlier. Pseudocode or structured English provides the level of detail needed to permit a program to be written. This text has devoted an entire chapter to pseudocode. Please refer to that chapter for more specific information.

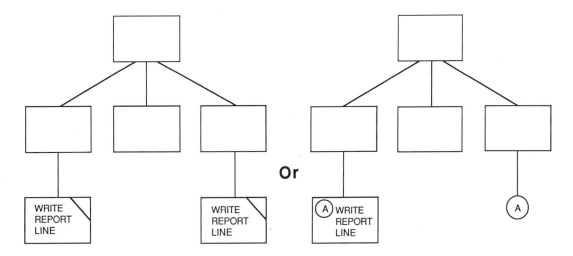

Figure 8.5 Representation of Modules Repeated in a Structure Chart

Program Logic Structures

To represent the sequential execution of processes, the structure chart follows a top-down, left-to-right order. (Refer to Figure 8.4.)

The structure chart uses two methods to portray the second logic structure, selection. A shaded diamond symbol on the communication line connecting modules signifies that the lower-level module is invoked conditionally. (Refer to Figure 8.6.) Module B will be called by module A only under conditions dictated by a control indicator.

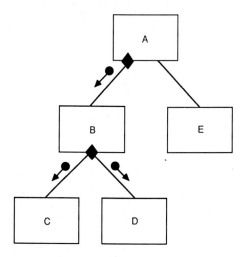

Figure 8.6 Selection Logic Representation with Diamond Symbol

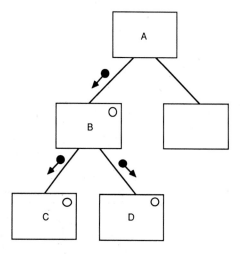

Figure 8.7 Selection Logic Representation with Circle Symbol

The same circumstance applies to modules C and D. These modules are called by module B under certain conditions. Figure 8.7 illustrates the same representation with a circle symbol. This symbol appears in the upper right-hand corner of a module to demonstrate that that module is invoked conditionally.

The last logic structure, repetition, can also be represented by two different approaches. A rounded arrow drawn underneath a module, or an asterisk in the upper right-hand corner of a module, specifies that activities or instructions within the module will be repeated until some condition occurs. This condition is revealed in the pseudocode provided with the module. Figures 8.8 and 8.9 illustrate the two methods. In both figures, activities within module B are conditionally repeated.

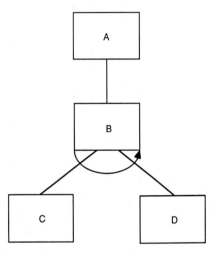

Figure 8.8 Repetition Logic Structure with Rounded Arrow

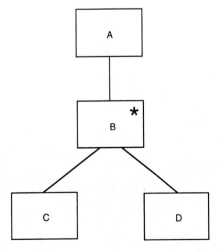

Figure 8.9 Repetition Logic Structure with Asterisk

Advantages and Disadvantages of Structure Charts

Some of the advantages of structure charts are:

- They provide an overview of the entire program specification in an easy-to-comprehend manner.

- A structure chart employs a very small number of symbols, which allows a beginner to become familiar with the technique quickly. This does not mean that one can become an expert overnight; the number of symbols are few, but the actual implementation of the symbols is more intricate than one first suspects.

- A great degree of flexibility in the design of the structure chart is available. It is easy to add, replace, or delete modules without disturbing other modules drawn.

- A structure chart promotes maintainability. Once a program has been written, another programmer can view this logic tool and determine the effects of modifying the program at a later time.

- Structure charts are an excellent means of program documentation. One can view a structure chart and perceive the basic functions accomplished in the program without making an actual reference to program code. The data transferred between modules is readily apparent. This is a valuable tool for programming managers and new programmers hired by an organization.

- Evidence of the versatility of a structure chart is the current popularity it is enjoying in the data processing community. Many data processing organizations are adopting this logic tool because it can easily represent simple or complex programs and is not programming-language dependent. Programs written in BASIC, FORTRAN, COBOL or some other high-level language can be smoothly derived from a structure chart.

Some of the disadvantages are:

- The detailed instructions cannot be shown in an individual module; the appropriate pseudocode for that module must be referenced.

- The top-down, hierarchical approach of structure charts may be difficult for programmers experienced in another logic tool to follow until they gain more experience with this tool.

Summary of Structure Chart Procedures

When solving a problem using the structure chart logic development tool, follow these steps:

1. Draw the driver or boss module and provide a descriptive label of the function.

2. Divide the problem into distinct modules and place these modules at a lower level to the driver module. Label each module with a succinct description of its function.

3. Determine the data that should be passed to and from the module. Place these data variables in the data dictionary.

4. Describe with pseudocode all of the activities that occur in each module.

5. Verify that all problem requirements are satisfied. If not, place a module at a lower level and establish a boss-subordinate relationship between the new module and a module at a higher level. Provide this new module with a descriptive label. Repeat steps 3–5 until the problem requirements are achieved.

PROBLEM SOLUTIONS

The rest of the chapter contains the solutions to the problems introduced in Chapter 1 using the structure chart logic development tool. Each solution is divided into five components:

1. Restatement of the problem

2. Structure chart

3. Solution narrative

4. Data dictionary

5. Module pseudocode

To aid the reader, some standard naming conventions are used. The pseudocode has been divided into the modules identified on the structure chart. The CALL statement is used to show when one module is invoking a lower-level module. All module names referenced in the pseudocode statements are underlined to distinguish them from variable or record names. Most of the solutions have a WRITE REPORT LINE module containing a conditional statement that refers to NEW PAGE. This statement handles the printing of the report headings (on a new page) identified in the sample report format for each problem. Enjoy yourself!

▶ Problem 1—Lease Versus Buy ◀

Ajax Manufacturing Company has the option to purchase outright or lease (with an option to buy at lease-end) a computer system to aid in its business operations. If Ajax purchases the system for $10,000, it will finance the full amount for four years at a 10% interest rate.

> **NOTE:** Simple Interest (I) = Principal (P) × Rate (R) × Time Period (T).

If Ajax leases the equipment for four years and decides to purchase at lease-end, the monthly cost will be $250 with a final payment of $3000. Which option should Ajax choose in order to minimize the total cost of the computer system? The problem solution should satisfy varying lease versus buy input information.

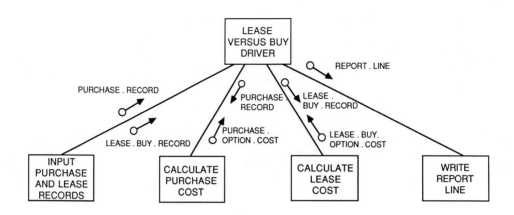

Figure S8.1 Problem 1 Structure Chart Solution

The solution to this problem entails two levels and five modules (refer to Figure S8.1). To view the detail statements within each module, examine the module pseudocode section.

The driver module calls four lower-level modules: INPUT PURCHASE AND LEASE RECORDS, CALCULATE PURCHASE COST, CALCULATE LEASE COST, and WRITE REPORT LINE. In the INPUT PURCHASE AND LEASE RECORDS module, the PURCHASE.RECORD and LEASE.BUY.RECORDs are read and the LENGTH.OF.LEASE.MONTHS is calculated. The CALCULATE PURCHASE COST and CALCULATE LEASE COST modules perform their functions based on data read from the INPUT module. WRITE REPORT LINE receives COST variables, compares the two variables, and makes a recommendation on the option.

```
<<DATA DICTIONARY>>

PURCHASE.RECORD                           REPORT.LINE
    PURCHASE.PRICE      NNNNN.NN              PURCHASE.OPTION.COST    NNNNN.NN
    INTEREST.RATE       N.NN                  LEASE.BUY.OPTION.COST   NNNNN.NN
    FINANCED.YEARS      NN

LEASE.BUY.RECORD
    MTHLY.LEASE.COST            NNN.NN
    LENGTH.OF.LEASE.MONTHS      NN
    FINAL.PAYMENT               NNNN.NN
```

```
<<MODULE PSEUDOCODE>>

LEASE VS. BUY DRIVER
    CALL INPUT PURCHASE AND LEASE RECORDS
    CALL CALCULATE PURCHASE COST
    CALL CALCULATE LEASE COST
    CALL WRITE REPORT LINE


INPUT PURCHASE AND LEASE RECORDS
    INPUT PURCHASE.RECORD
    INPUT LEASE.BUY.RECORD)
    LENGTH.OF.LEASE.MONTHS = FINANCED.YEARS * 12


CALCULATE PURCHASE COST
    PURCHASE.OPTION.COST = PURCHASE.PRICE + (PURCHASE.PRICE *
                          INTEREST.RATE * FINANCED.YEARS)


CALCULATE LEASE COST
    LEASE.BUY.OPTION.COST = MTHLY.LEASE.COST * LENGTH.OF.LEASE.MONTHS
                          + FINAL.PAYMENT


WRITE REPORT LINE
    WRITE REPORT HEADINGS
    FORMAT REPORT.LINE
    WRITE REPORT.LINE
    IF PURCHASE.OPTION.COST < LEASE.BUY.OPTION.COST
        FORMAT REPORT.LINE WITH PURCHASE.OPTION.COST
    ELSE
        FORMAT REPORT.LINE WITH LEASE.BUY.OPTION.COST
    ENDIF
    WRITE REPORT.LINE WITH RECOMMENDATION
```

▶ Problem 2—Payroll ◀

Easymoney Inc. desires to generate their current manual payroll via computer. The information collected every payroll period includes the employee social security number, pay rate, hours worked, and total other deductions. The payroll department would like a report listing these items: employee social security number, hours worked, pay rate, gross pay, FICA withheld (6.13% of gross pay), federal tax withheld (20% of gross pay), total other deductions, and net pay.

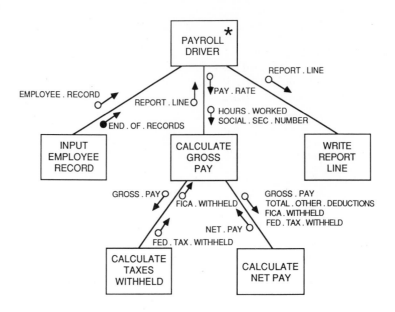

Figure S8.2 Problem 2 Structure Chart Solution

The solution consists of six modules distributed across three levels (see Figure S8.2). Notice the asterisk in the PAYROLL DRIVER module. This means that certain activities within that module will be repeated. Look at the PAYROLL DRIVER module pseudocode. There is a WHILE repetition loop defined. As long as the variable END.OF.RECORDS is equal to NO, this loop will be repeated. END.OF.RECORDS is set to YES in the INPUT EMPLOYEE RECORD module when the last record has been read.

The three modules on the second level—INPUT EMPLOYEE RECORD, CALCULATE GROSS PAY, WRITE REPORT LINE—are all invoked by the driver module. The CALCU- LATE GROSS PAY module computes GROSS.PAY and then calls the two modules at the third level, CALCULATE TAXES WITHHELD and CALCULATE NET PAY. CALCULATE TAXES WITHHELD cannot be called until GROSS.PAY has been derived. CALCULATE NET PAY requires GROSS.PAY and the withholding variables before it can be executed. WRITE REPORT LINE checks to see if the previous REPORT.LINE printed has reached the bottom of the page. If so, report headings are written at the top of a new page, and the next REPORT.LINE is written.

<<DATA DICTIONARY>>

EMPLOYEE.RECORD
```
    SOCIAL.SEC.NUMBER          N(9)
    PAY.RATE                   NN.NN
    HOURS.WORKED               NN.N
    TOTAL.OTHER.DEDUCTIONS     NNNN.NN
```

REPORT.LINE
```
    SOCIAL.SEC.NUMBER          N(9)
    HOURS.WORKED               NN.N
    PAY.RATE                   NN.NN
    GROSS.PAY                  NNNN.NN
    FICA.WITHHELD              NNN.NN
    FED.TAX.WITHHELD           NNNN.NN
    TOTAL.OTHER.DEDUCTIONS     NNNN.NN
    NET.PAY                    NNNN.NN
```

MISCELLANEOUS VARIABLES
```
    END.OF.RECORDS             CCC
    VALID.EMPLOYEE.RECORD      CCC
```

- -

<<MODULE PSEUDOCODE>>

PAYROLL DRIVER
```
    END.OF.RECORDS = 'NO'
    CALL INPUT EMPLOYEE RECORD
    WHILE END.OF.RECORDS = 'NO'
       BEGIN
            CALL CALCULATE GROSS PAY
            CALL WRITE REPORT LINE
            CALL INPUT EMPLOYEE RECORD
    END WHILE LOOP
```

INPUT EMPLOYEE RECORD
```
    READ EMPLOYEE.RECORD
    IF LAST EMPLOYEE.RECORD THEN
        END.OF.RECORDS = 'YES'
```

CALCULATE GROSS PAY
```
    GROSS.PAY = PAY.RATE * HOURS.WORKED)
    CALL CALCULATE TAXES WITHHELD
    CALL CALCULATE NET PAY
```

```
CALCULATE TAXES WITHHELD
  FICA.WITHHELD = GROSS.PAY * .0613
  FED.TAX.WITHHELD = GROSS.PAY * .20


CALCULATE NET PAY
  NET.PAY = GROSS.PAY - FICA.WITHHELD - FED.TAX.WITHHELD -
            TOTAL.OTHER.DEDUCTIONS


WRITE REPORT LINE
  IF NEW PAGE
     WRITE REPORT HEADINGS
  ENDIF
  FORMAT REPORT.LINE
  WRITE REPORT.LINE
```

► Problem 3—Health and Diet ◄

Bedford Waistwatchers Association requests that a program be written to motivate members to stay on their diet and show the cost savings that can result from a change in diet. One of the staple diet items recommended is yogurt. If a member follows the Association diet strictly, a large amount of yogurt can be consumed over a short period of time. The cost effectiveness of buying yogurt or making yogurt at home should be evaluated. If a monetary savings can be realized by making yogurt at home versus buying it at the store, how many cups of yogurt must be produced to achieve this savings? The data needed to provide an analysis is store cost of yogurt per cup, cost of yogurt maker if made at home, cost of home ingredients per cup, and number of cups. An analysis should show the home cost, store cost, and savings or loss per cup.

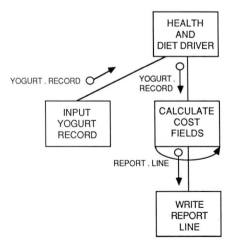

Figure S8.3 Problem 3 Structure Chart Solution

This solution consists of four modules dispersed among three levels (see Figure S8.3). Refer to the individual module pseudocode section for more detail. The HEALTH AND DIET DRIVER invokes two modules at the second level, INPUT YOGURT RECORD and CALCU-LATE COST FIELDS. INPUT YOGURT RECORD provides the input values that govern the execution of the remainder of the solution. CALCULATE COST FIELDS contains a WHILE loop that is repeated a variable number of times. (Notice how this is represented with the curved arrow drawn under the CALCULATE COST FIELDS module.) While the incremented CUP.NUMBER (one is added to CUP. NUMBER each time this loop is executed) is less than the entered NUMBER.OF.CUPS variable (from INPUT YOGURT RECORD module), this loop will continue. Within this WHILE loop, the cost and savings variables are manipulated to produce the information written on the REPORT.LINE. The only module on level three is WRITE REPORT LINE which is called within the WHILE loop. This module checks for an end-of-page condition. (This normally occurs when REPORT.LINE has been written past line 50 on the current page. A typical report page allows a maximum of 56 lines.) If TRUE, headings are generated on the top of a new page and the next REPORT.LINE is written.

<<DATA DICTIONARY>>

YOGURT.RECORD		REPORT.LINE	
STORE.COST.YOGURT.PER.CUP	NN.NN	CUP.NUMBER	NN
COST.YOGURT.MAKER	NN.NN	CALC.HOME.COST	NNN.NN
HOME.COST.INGREDIENTS.PER.CUP	NN.NN	CALC.STORE.COST	NNN.NN
NUMBER.OF.CUPS	NN	CALC.SAVINGS.OR.LOSS	NNN.NN

<<MODULE PSEUDOCODE>>

```
HEALTH AND DIET DRIVER
    CALL INPUT YOGURT RECORD
    CALL CALCULATE COST FIELDS


INPUT YOGURT RECORD
    INPUT STORE.COST.YOGURT.PER.CUP
    INPUT COST.YOGURT.MAKER
    INPUT HOME.COST.INGREDIENTS.PER.CUP
    INPUT NUMBER.OF.CUPS


CALCULATE COST FIELDS
    CUP.NUMBER = 1
    WHILE CUP.NUMBER <= NUMBER.OF.CUPS
      BEGIN
```

```
CALC.HOME.COST = (HOME.COST.INGREDIENTS.PER.CUP * CUP.NUMBER)
                   + COST.YOGURT.MAKER
CALC.STORE.COST = STORE.COST.YOGURT.PER.CUP * CUP.NUMBER
CALC.SAVINGS.OR.LOSS = CALC.STORE.COST - CALC.HOME.COST
CALL WRITE REPORT LINE
CUP.NUMBER = CUP.NUMBER + 1
END OF WHILE LOOP


WRITE REPORT LINE
   IF NEW PAGE
      WRITE REPORT HEADINGS
   ENDIF
   FORMAT REPORT.LINE
   WRITE REPORT.LINE
```

► Problem 4—Daily Sales ◄

Vidal Blass is the owner of Obnoxious Telephone Sales. Vidal has had up to 20 employees solicit sales via telephone on a specific day. Vidal would like to produce a sales summary report at the end of each business day to determine which salespeople generate the most revenue. Employees make a phone sale, write the sales information down on a receipt with their name and the total sale, and place the receipt in a bin shared by all of the employees. At the end of the day, all of the receipts are gathered and the summary report produced by entering the name and sales amount from each receipt. The first activity the computer will perform is to sort all input records in name order. (Assume that no two salespeople have the same name.) The sales summary will list the total sales by each name and the grand total sales for the day's business activities.

This solution consists of six modules segmented into four levels. DAILY SALES DRIVER calls three modules at the second level: INITIALIZATION ACTIVITIES, CONTROL BREAK PROCESSING, and PRINT FINAL TOTAL. INITIALIZATION ACTIVITIES is executed one time at the beginning of the solution. CONTROL BREAK PROCESSING is repeated until all records have been read. This same module invokes two lower level modules: CHECK FOR CONTROL BREAK and READ SALESPERSON RECORD.

Notice an alternative solution method: the CONTROL BREAK PROCESSING module could have been eliminated. The two modules on the third level moved to the second level to be invoked by the DAILY SALES DRIVER module. The ultimate result would be the same.

The CHECK FOR CONTROL BREAK module compares SALESPERSON.NAME to PREVIOUS.SALESPERSON.NAME. If there is a difference, control break processing is performed and the only module on the fourth level, WRITE REPORT LINE, is called.

The last module is PRINT FINAL TOTAL on the second level. It is executed one time after the END.OF.FILE variable is changed to "YES" in the READ SALESPERSON RECORD module.

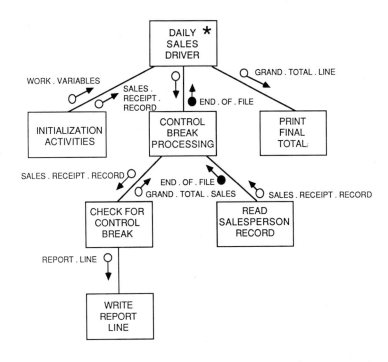

Figure S8.4 Problem 4 Structure Chart Solution

<<DATA DICTIONARY>>

SALES.RECEIPT.RECORD
   SALESPERSON.NAME   C(20)
   AMT.OF.SALE   NNN.NN

REPORT.LINE
   SALESPERSON.NAME   C(20)
   TOTAL.SALES   NNNN.NN

GRAND.TOTAL.LINE
   GRAND.TOTAL.SALES   N(5).NN

WORK.VARIABLES
   END.OF.FILE   CCC
   LINE.CTR   NN
   PREVIOUS.SALESPERSON.NAME C(20)

```
<<MODULE PSEUDOCODE>>

DAILY SALES DRIVER
    CALL INITIALIZATION ACTIVITIES
    WHILE END.OF.FILE = "NO"
       CALL CONTROL BREAK PROCESSING
    END WHILE LOOP
    FORMAT REPORT.LINE
    WRITE REPORT.LINE
    CALL PRINT FINAL TOTAL


INITIALIZATION ACTIVITIES
    END.OF.FILE = "NO"
    TOTAL.SALES = 0
    GRAND.TOTAL.SALES = 0
    LINE.CTR = 55
    READ SALES.RECEIPT.RECORD
    PREVIOUS.SALESPERSON.NAME = SALESPERSON.NAME


CONTROL BREAK PROCESSING
    CALL CHECK FOR CONTROL BREAK
    CALL READ SALESPERSON RECORD


READ SALESPERSON RECORD
    READ SALES.RECEIPT.RECORD
    IF LAST RECORD THEN
       END.OF.FILE = "YES"
    ENDIF


CHECK FOR CONTROL BREAK
    IF SALESPERSON.NAME = PREVIOUS.SALESPERSON.NAME THEN
       TOTAL.SALES = TOTAL.SALES + AMT.OF.SALE
    ELSE
       CALL WRITE REPORT LINE
       TOTAL.SALES = AMT.OF.SALE
       PREVIOUS.SALESPERSON.NAME = SALESPERSON.NAME
    ENDIF
    GRAND.TOTAL.SALES = GRAND.TOTAL.SALES + AMT.OF.SALE


WRITE REPORT LINE
    FORMAT REPORT.LINE
    IF LINE.CTR > 50 THEN
       WRITE REPORT HEADINGS ON NEW PAGE
       LINE.CTR = 5
```

```
ENDIF
WRITE REPORT.LINE
LINE.CTR = LINE.CTR + 2
```

PRINT FINAL TOTAL
```
    FORMAT GRAND.TOTAL.LINE
    WRITE GRAND.TOTAL.LINE
```

Problem 5—House Construction

Well-Bilt Homes Inc. would like you to design a program which enables builders to calculate home building costs based on prospective room sizes. This program is interactive; it allows the user to input the number of rooms desired and the individual room dimensions (length and width only). The building cost per square foot is based on the following:

1000 square feet or less	$60 per square foot
1001–2000 square feet	$50 per square foot
More than 2000 square feet	$40 per square foot

Develop the logic to compute the building cost of the house.

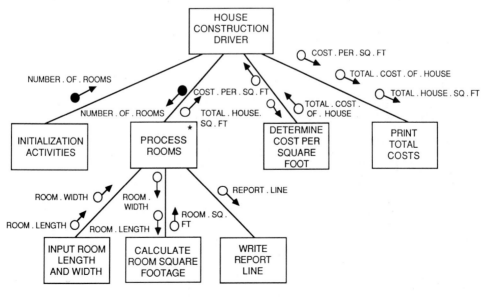

Figure S8.5 Problem 5 Structure Chart Solution

This solution contains eight modules positioned at three levels as illustrated in Figure S8.5. The HOUSE CONSTRUCTION DRIVER calls four modules at the second level. INITIALIZATION ACTIVITIES prints the report headings and receives the NUMBER.OF.ROOMS. PROCESS ROOMS contains a loop that repeats the number of times specified by the value stored in NUMBER.OF.ROOMS. This loop calls three modules at the third level and each module performs one of these activities: input room length and width, compute room square footage, write the room square footage calculation. After each room's square footage has been calculated, that value is added into the TOTAL.HOUSE.SQ.FT variable. DETERMINE COST PER SQUARE FOOT module looks at the value stored in the TOTAL.HOUSE.SQ.FT variable to determine the cost charged per square foot for the house. The total cost of the house is derived and these variables are passed to the PRINT TOTAL COSTS module to finish the report.

```
<<DATA DICTIONARY>>

NUMBER.OF.ROOMS        NN           REPORT.LINE
ROOM.LENGTH            NN              ROOM.LENGTH       NN
ROOM.WIDTH             NN              ROOM.WIDTH        NN
TOTAL.HOUSE.SQ.FT      N(5)            ROOM.SQ.FT        NNNN
COST.PER.SQ.FOOT       NNN.NN
TOTAL.COST.OF.HOUSE    N(6).NN

----------------------------------------------------------------------

<<MODULE PSEUDOCODE>>

HOUSE CONSTRUCTION DRIVER
    CALL INITIALIZATION ACTIVITIES
    CALL PROCESS ROOMS
    CALL DETERMINE COST PER SQUARE FOOT
    CALL PRINT TOTAL COSTS


INITIALIZATION ACTIVITIES
    INPUT NUMBER.OF.ROOMS
    TOTAL.HOUSE.SQ.FT = 0
    PRINT HEADINGS
    PRINT NUMBER.OF.ROOMS LINE
    PRINT COLUMN HEADINGS
```

```
PROCESS ROOMS
   REPEAT NUMBER.OF.ROOMS TIMES
      CALL INPUT ROOM LENGTH AND WIDTH
      CALL CALCULATE ROOM SQUARE FOOTAGE
      CALL WRITE REPORT LINE
      TOTAL.HOUSE.SQ.FT = TOTAL.HOUSE.SQ.FT + ROOM.SQ.FT
   END REPEAT LOOP


INPUT ROOM LENGTH AND WIDTH
   INPUT ROOM.LENGTH AND ROOM.WIDTH


CALCULATE ROOM SQUARE FOOTAGE
   ROOM.SQ.FT = ROOM.LENGTH * ROOM.WIDTH


WRITE REPORT LINE
   FORMAT REPORT.LINE
   WRITE REPORT.LINE


DETERMINE COST PER SQUARE FOOT
   IF TOTAL.HOUSE.SQ.FT <= 1000 THEN
      COST.PER.SQ.FT = 60
   ELSE
      IF TOTAL.HOUSE.SQ.FT > 1001 AND <= 2000 THEN
         COST.PER.SQ.FT = 50
      ELSE
         COST.PER.SQ.FT = 40
   ENDIF
   TOTAL.COST.OF.HOUSE = TOTAL.HOUSE.SQ.FT * COST.PER.SQ.FOOT


PRINT TOTAL COSTS
   PRINT TOTAL.HOUSE.SQ.FT LINE
   PRINT COST.PER.SQ.FT LINE
   PRINT TOTAL.COST.OF.HOUSE LINE
```

▶ Problem 6—Personnel Statistics ◀

The chairman of the board of Eldorado Enterprises Inc. has requested a report from the Personnel Department that will show various types of information about the company's work force. This report should provide the following:

1. The total number of males and females (SEX CODE = M for males, F for females)

2. The total number of employees by the following age categories (BIRTHDAY YEAR)
   a. less than 21

b. 21–30
c. 31–40
d. 41–50
e. 51–60
f. 61–70
g. over 70

3. The total number of people who have been with the company for 10 years or more (SENIORITY CODE = 3, 4, or 5)

4. The total number of engineers (OCCUPATION CODE = 7) in the company

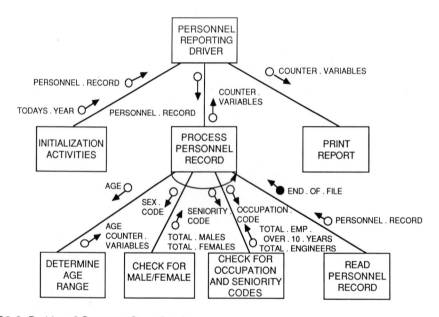

Figure S8.6 Problem 6 Structure Chart Solution

The personnel reporting solution is comprised of eight modules distributed across three levels as shown in Figure S8.6. The PERSONNEL REPORTING DRIVER module activates three modules at the second level. INITIALIZATION ACTIVITIES sets all counter variables to zero and reads in the current year and first PERSONNEL.RECORD. The PROCESS PERSONNEL RECORD module contains a loop that continues to execute until all records are read (END.OF.FILE = "YES"). Within this loop, the age of each employee is calculated and the four modules at the third level are invoked.

DETERMINE AGE RANGE compares AGE to the breakdown ranges (less than 21, 21–30, etc.) and adds one to the proper variable. The CHECK FOR MALE/FEMALE module tests SEX.CODE variable for "M" or "F" and updates the appropriate counter variable. CHECK FOR OCCUPATION AND SENIORITY CODES module looks at OCCUPATION.CODE and

SENIORITY.CODE for specific comparison values and increments the correct counter variable. If SENIORITY.CODE is 3, 4, or 5, that person has been with the company for more than 10 years. If OCCUPATION.CODE is equal to 7, that employee is an engineer. READ PERSONNEL RECORD accepts the next PERSONNEL.RECORD and checks for end-of-file condition. When end-of-file condition is TRUE, END.OF.FILE is set to "YES."

After the entire file has been processed, the counter variables are passed to the PRINT REPORT module to complete the report.

```
<<DATA DICTIONARY>>
```

PERSONNEL.RECORD		COUNTER.VARIABLES	
SEX.CODE	C	TOTAL.MALES	N(5)
BIRTHDAY.YEAR	NN	TOTAL.FEMALES	N(5)
SENIORITY.CODE	N	MF.LESS.21.CTR	N(4)
OCCUPATION.CODE	N	MF.21-30.CTR	N(4)
		MF.31-40.CTR	N(4)
		MF.41-50.CTR	N(4)
OTHER.VARIABLES		MF.51-60.CTR	N(4)
TODAYS.YEAR	NN	MF.61-70.CTR	N(4)
END.OF.FILE	CCC	MF.OVER.70.CTR	N(4)
AGE	NN	TOTAL.EMP.OVER.10.YEARS	N(4)
		TOTAL.ENGINEERS	N(4)

```
<<MODULE PSEUDOCODE>>

PERSONNEL REPORTING DRIVER
    CALL INITIALIZATION ACTIVITIES
    CALL PROCESS PERSONNEL RECORD
    CALL PRINT REPORT


INITIALIZATION ACTIVITIES
    END.OF.FILE = "NO"
    ASSIGN ALL COUNTER VARIABLES THE VALUE ZERO
    READ TODAYS.YEAR
    READ PERSONNEL.RECORD


PROCESS PERSONNEL RECORD
    WHILE END.OF.FILE = "NO"
        AGE = TODAYS.YEAR - BIRTHDAY.YEAR
        CALL DETERMINE AGE RANGE
        CALL CHECK FOR MALE/FEMALE
        CALL CHECK FOR OCCUPATION AND SENIORITY CODES
        CALL READ PERSONNEL RECORD
    END WHILE LOOP
```

```
DETERMINE AGE RANGE
   IF AGE < 21 THEN
      ADD 1 TO MF.LESS.21.CTR
   ELSE
     IF AGE <= 30 THEN
        ADD 1 TO MF.21-30.CTR
     ELSE
       IF AGE <= 40 THEN
          ADD 1 TO MF.31-40.CTR
       ELSE
         IF AGE <= 50 THEN
            ADD 1 TO MF.41-50.CTR
         ELSE
           IF AGE <= 60 THEN
              ADD 1 TO MF.51-60.CTR
           ELSE
             IF AGE <= 70 THEN
                ADD 1 TO MF.61-70.CTR
             ELSE
                ADD 1 TO MF.OVER.70.CTR
   ENDIF


CHECK FOR MALE/FEMALE
   IF SEX.CODE = "M" THEN
      ADD 1 TO TOTAL.MALES
   ENDIF
   IF SEX.CODE = "F" THEN
      ADD 1 TO TOTAL.FEMALES
   ENDIF


CHECK FOR OCCUPATION AND SENIORITY CODES
   IF SENIORITY.CODE = 3 OR 4 OR 5 THEN
      ADD 1 TO TOTAL.EMP.OVER.10.YEARS
   ENDIF
   IF OCCUPATION.CODE = 7 THEN
      ADD 1 TO TOTAL.ENGINEERS
   ENDIF


READ PERSONNEL RECORD
   READ PERSONNEL.RECORD
   IF LAST RECORD READ THEN
      END.OF.FILE = "YES"
   ENDIF
```

```
PRINT REPORT
   PRINT REPORT HEADINGS
   PRINT TOTAL.MALES LINE
   PRINT TOTAL.FEMALES LINE
   PRINT MALES AND FEMALES BY AGE BREAKDOWN LINES
   PRINT TOTAL.EMP.OVER.10.YEARS LINE
   PRINT TOTAL.ENGINEERS LINE
```

Structure Chart Walk-Through

This section illustrates how to walk through a structure chart solution. Arbitrary values are inserted into the variables defined in the data dictionary for problems 5 and 6. Refer to the completed problem solutions in the previous section. Each module name is underlined and the data value for each variable within the module is shown. Lower-level modules invoked by a higher-level module are indented within the higher-level module. Please study the walk-through for problem 5.

► Problem 5—House Construction ◄

INITIALIZATION ACTIVITIES:
NUMBER.OF.ROOMS = 4
TOTAL.HOUSE.SQ.FT = 0
The report headings are printed.

PROCESS ROOMS:
The PROCESS ROOMS module calls three lower-level modules NUMBER.OF.ROOMS (4) times.

INPUT ROOM LENGTH AND ROOM WIDTH:
ROOM.LENGTH = 15
ROOM.WIDTH = 10

CALCULATE ROOM SQUARE FOOTAGE:
ROOM.SQ.FT = 150
(15 * 10)

WRITE REPORT LINE:
The REPORT.LINE is formatted and printed for
ROOM.LENGTH, ROOM.WIDTH, AND ROOM.SQ.FT

TOTAL.HOUSE.SQ.FT = 150
(0 + 150)

INPUT ROOM LENGTH AND ROOM WIDTH:
    ROOM.LENGTH = 10
    ROOM.WIDTH = 8

CALCULATE ROOM SQUARE FOOTAGE:
    ROOM.SQ.FT = 80
    (10 * 8)

WRITE REPORT LINE:
    The REPORT.LINE is formatted and printed for
      ROOM.LENGTH, ROOM.WIDTH, AND ROOM.SQ.FT

TOTAL.HOUSE.SQ.FT = 230
(150 + 80)

INPUT ROOM LENGTH AND ROOM WIDTH:
    ROOM.LENGTH = 20
    ROOM.WIDTH = 10

CALCULATE ROOM SQUARE FOOTAGE:
    ROOM.SQ.FT = 200
    (20 * 10)

WRITE REPORT LINE:
    The REPORT.LINE is formatted and printed for
      ROOM.LENGTH, ROOM.WIDTH, AND ROOM.SQ.FT

TOTAL.HOUSE.SQ.FT = 430
(230 + 200)

INPUT ROOM LENGTH AND ROOM WIDTH:
    ROOM.LENGTH = 15
    ROOM.WIDTH = 15

CALCULATE ROOM SQUARE FOOTAGE:
    ROOM.SQ.FT = 225
    (15 * 15)

WRITE REPORT LINE:
    The REPORT.LINE is formatted and printed for ROOM.LENGTH,
      ROOM.WIDTH, AND ROOM.SQ.FT

TOTAL.HOUSE.SQ.FT = 655
(430 + 225)

DETERMINE COST PER SQUARE FOOT:
The TOTAL.HOUSE.SQ.FT (655) is less than 1000 so
   COST.PER.SQ.FT = 60

TOTAL.COST.OF.HOUSE = 39,300
(655 * 60)

PRINT TOTAL COSTS
The values for TOTAL.HOUSE.SQ.FT, COST.PER.SQ.FT, and
TOTAL.COST.OF HOUSE are printed.

► Problem 6—Personnel Statistics ◄

INITIALIZATION ACTIVITIES:
END.OF.FILE = "NO"
ALL COUNTER.VARIABLES ARE ASSIGNED THE VALUE ZERO
TODAYS.YEAR = 86
SEX.CODE = "M"
BIRTHDAY.YEAR = 56
SENIORITY.CODE = 6
OCCUPATION.CODE = 7

PROCESS PERSONNEL RECORD:
AGE = 30
(86 − 56)

DETERMINE AGE RANGE:
AGE is within the 21 to 30 range so:
   MF.21–30.CTR = 1
   (0 + 1)

CHECK FOR MALE/FEMALE:
SEX.CODE is equal to "M" so;
   TOTAL.MALES = 1
   (0 + 1)

CHECK FOR OCCUPATION AND SENIORITY CODES:
SENIORITY.CODE is equal to 6 so:
   no action is taken

OCCUPATION.CODE is equal to 7 so:
   TOTAL.ENGINEERS = 1
   (0 + 1)

READ PERSONNEL RECORD:
SEX.CODE = "M"
BIRTHDAY.YEAR = 40
SENIORITY.CODE = 3
OCCUPATION.CODE = 9

This is not the last record within the file, so the modules within PROCESS PERSONNEL RECORD are repeated.

PROCESS PERSONNEL RECORD:
AGE = 46
(86 − 40)

DETERMINE AGE RANGE:
AGE is within the 41 to 50 range so:
MF.41−50.CTR = 1
(0 + 1)

CHECK FOR MALE/FEMALE:
SEX.CODE is equal to "M" so:
TOTAL.MALES = 2
(1 + 1)

CHECK FOR OCCUPATION AND SENIORITY CODES:
SENIORITY.CODE is equal to 3 so:
TOTAL.EMP.OVER.10.YEARS = 1
(0 + 1)

OCCUPATION.CODE is equal to 9 so:
No action

READ PERSONNEL RECORD:
SEX.CODE = "F"
BIRTHDAY.YEAR = 25
SENIORITY.CODE = 5
OCCUPATION.CODE = 7

Do you get the idea of what is accomplished in a structure chart walk-through? The modules in PROCESS PERSONNEL RECORD would repeat execution until the last record is read (END.OF.FILE = "YES"). After the completion of this repetition, the PRINT REPORT module is invoked, completing the solution.

This concludes the section on structure chart walk-through. This technique should be used for each structure chart solution designed. Logic errors are easily identified when "live" data is introduced to a solution.

SUMMARY

At this time, you should be able to solve a problem using the structure chart methodology. The components of a structure chart consist of two or more levels. Each level can contain one or more modules. The first level contains one module which is referred to as the driver. The driver module controls the execution order of the remaining modules in the structure chart. These components must adhere to the following rules:

- Each module must have a descriptive label referring to its function.

- Every module identified must have information going into or coming from it, or both.

- The data variables passed to and from each module must be defined in the data dictionary.

- Each module must be accompanied by a pseudocode description specifying the detailed activities occurring in the module.

The advantages of the structure chart as a logic development tool are:

- It provides an overview of the solution in a manner that is easy to comprehend.

- It uses very few symbols.

- It has flexibility: it is easy to add, replace, or delete modules.

- It is maintainable: a programmer can view this logic tool and determine the effects of modifying the program at a later time.

- It provides excellent program documentation; one can view a structure chart and perceive the basic functions accomplished in the program without actual reference to program code.

The disadvantages are:

- The detailed instructions cannot be shown in an individual module; the appropriate pseudocode for that module must be viewed.

- The top-down, hierarchical approach may be difficult to comprehend initially.

The structure chart is a fairly new logic development tool for the computer industry. This technique is gaining acceptance by more information systems departments nationwide.

REVIEW QUESTIONS

MULTIPLE CHOICE

1. A control indicator passed to or from a module could be used as a
   a. flag variable to specify when a loop should stop being repeated.
   b. signal variable for an end-of-file condition.
   c. variable denoting the results of a data editing module (edit results were successful or not successful).
   d. all of the above.

2. The physical execution of the module within a structure chart is important. That order is in
   a. left-to-right, top-down order
   b. right-to-left, top-down order
   c. bottom-up, left-to-right order
   d. top-down, left-to-right order

3. Which of the following statements is false?
   a. Every structure chart must include a driver module.
   b. Some modules do not require information to be passed to or from it.
   c. All modules should contain a descriptive label.
   d. A module can have one or more modules reporting to it.

4. Which of the following is an advantage of using a structure chart?
   a. Structure charts are easy to comprehend and understand.
   b. Structure charts are relatively simple to maintain.
   c. Structure charts are an excellent program documentation method.
   d. All of the above are advantages.

5. If a module is invoked in more than one location in a structure chart, the special notation used is
   a. an asterisk drawn in the corner of the repeating module
   b. a line drawn in the corner of the repeating module
   c. a letter circled in the left-hand corner of the repeating module
   d. both b and c

FILL IN THE BLANK

1. The structure chart employs some techniques used in the _____ chart.

2. The structure chart is broken down into components called _____.

3. Structure charts are read in _____, left-to-right order.

4. The two types of information passed between modules are depicted with _____ and _____ indicators.

5. All data variables should be defined in the _____.

SHORT ANSWER

1. Draw a three-level structure chart with at least eight modules.

2. Explain the concept of module span of control and the guidelines to follow for the concept.

3. Explain how a structure chart represents the three program logic structures (use a diagram).

4. Discuss the relationship between structure chart modules and pseudocode.

5. In what ways does the structure chart differ from the hierarchy chart?

EXERCISES

1. Against the advice of her investment counselor (who believes the fad is over), Valerie is considering opening a video game parlor. Valerie wants you to design a computer program that will provide break-even analysis comparisons for different input factors. Design the structure chart logic necessary to assist Valerie in deciding if Valerie's Vivacious Video Games should become a reality. The input information includes:

Number of video game machines

Estimated number of quarters per hour for each machine

Number of hours the parlor is open each week

Estimated monthly overhead expenses

```
SAMPLE REPORT FORMAT:

              VALERIE'S VIVACIOUS VIDEO GAMES
                    BREAK-EVEN ANALYSIS

NUMBER OF VIDEO GAME MACHINES:   NN
ESTIMATED QUARTERS RECEIVED PER HOUR PER MACHINE:   NNN
ESTIMATED NUMBER OF HOURS OPEN PER WEEK:  NN
ESTIMATED MONTHLY OVERHEAD EXPENSES:   NNNN.NN


                    CALCULATED VALUES

ESTIMATED MONTHLY REVENUE:   $NNNN.NN
ESTIMATED MONTHLY EXPENSES:  $NNNN.NN

ESTIMATED YEARLY REVENUE:   $NNNNN.NN
ESTIMATED YEARLY EXPENSES:  $NNNNN.NN

ESTIMATED YEARLY GAIN/LOSS:   $NNNNN.NN
```

2. Frederick owns a company that specializes in building fences for houses in residential areas. Frederick spends approximately one-third of each working day providing job estimates. He would like to automate this procedure with a computer to furnish more timely and competitive estimates. Given the following information, develop a structure chart solution to assist Frederick in solving his dilemma.

Input:

Type of fence material (Cedar, Redwood, Spruce)

Estimated number of feet to enclose area

Number of entrance gates

Additional information:

1. There is one pole for every eight feet of fence.

2. There are twenty-eight pickets for every eight feet of fence.

3. The cost of two eight-foot sections of 1″ by 3″ wood used to connect the poles and nail the pickets to is $4.

4. Cost per pole is $3.75 (which includes concrete to secure pole).

5. Cost per picket:

   Cedar—$.95

   Redwood—$.80

   Spruce—$.70

6. Cost per gate:

   Cedar—$300

   Redwood—$220

   Spruce—$180

7. Labor cost per eight feet of fence is $2.50.

SAMPLE REPORT FORMAT:

```
                 FREDERICK'S FASHIONABLE FENCE COMPANY
                        FENCE COST ESTIMATE

TYPE OF FENCE:   CCCCCCCCC
ESTIMATED FEET TO ENCLOSE AREA:   NNNNN
NUMBER OF GATES:   NN
```

```
                         CALCULATED MATERIALS

        NUMBER OF POLES:   NNN
        NUMBER OF EIGHT FOOT 1" BY 3" WOOD BOARDS (IN PAIRS):   NNN
        NUMBER OF INDIVIDUAL PICKETS:   NNNNN



        MATERIALS COST:    $NNNN.NN
        LABOR COST:        $NNNN.NN
        TOTAL COST:        $NNNN.NN
```

3. You were elected official statistician for the Riverdale City Little Squirts Baseball League. There are six teams in the league and you are given this information on each player: team name, player name, hits, at bats, runs batted in (RBI), and runs scored. Assume this input information is sorted by team name and player name. Write the logic necessary to produce the following report. (Hint: Batting average is calculated by dividing at bats into hits. This solution requires control break logic.)

```
        RIVERDALE CITY LITTLE SQUIRTS BASEBALL LEAGUE
               INDIVIDUAL TEAM STATISTICS


TEAM: CCCCCCCCCCCCCCCCCCCC

PLAYER NAME              HITS       AT BATS     BATTING    RBI     RUNS
                                                AVG                SCORED

CCCCCCCCCCCCCCCCCCCCC    NN          NN         N.NNN      NN      NN
         .               .           .          .          .       .
         .               .           .          .          .       .
CCCCCCCCCCCCCCCCCCCCC    NN          NN         N.NNN      NN      NN

TEAM TOTALS:            NNN         NNN          .NNN      NNN     NNN

   .                    .           .          .          .       .
   .                    .           .          .          .       .
   .                    .           .          .          .       .
   .                    .           .          .          .       .
   .                    .           .          .          .       .
```

```
TEAM:  CCCCCCCCCCCCCCCCCCCC

PLAYER NAME              HITS         AT BATS       BATTING      RBI       RUNS
                                                    AVG                    SCORED

CCCCCCCCCCCCCCCCCCCC     NN           NN            N.NNN        NN        NN
            .             .            .             .            .         .
            .             .            .             .            .         .

CCCCCCCCCCCCCCCCCCCC     NN           NN            N.NNN        NN        NN

TEAM  TOTALS:            NNN          NNN           .NNN         NNN       NNN


LEAGUE  TOTALS:          NNNN         NNNN          .NNN         NNNN      NNNN
```

4. Patricia's Political Pollers desires a computer program to aid in the collection of demographic data during exit interviews with voters on election day. The input data for each voter includes sex, age, political party (Republican, Democrat, Other), and yearly salary. Design the logic necessary to convert this input (there can be any number of input records) to the following one-page summary report.

SAMPLE REPORT FORMAT:

```
                PATRICIA'S POLITICAL POLLERS
             VOTER SURVEY FOR _____ ELECTION

      NUMBER OF MALES:      NNNN

      AGE UNDER 40:        NNNN
      AGE 40 AND OVER:     NNNN

      NUMBER OF REPUBLICANS: NNNN
      NUMBER OF DEMOCRATS:   NNNN
      NUMBER OF OTHERS:      NNNN

      AVERAGE MALE YEARLY SALARY:   $NNNNNN.NN

      NUMBER OF FEMALES:    NNNN

      AGE UNDER 40:        NNNN
      AGE 40 AND OVER:     NNNN

      NUMBER OF REPUBLICANS: NNNN
      NUMBER OF DEMOCRATS:   NNNN
      NUMBER OF OTHERS:      NNNN

      AVERAGE FEMALE YEARLY SALARY: $NNNNNN.NN
```

5. A factor of a number is a number that is divisible into that number. The factors of a number are numbers that, when multiplied together, yield that number. Factors always include one and the number itself. For example, the factors of ten are 1, 2, 5, and 10. To determine if a number is a factor of another number, you simply divide. If there is no remainder, the number is a factor; otherwise, the number is not a factor.

Is 12 a factor of 64? No, because there is a remainder of 4. Develop a solution to find the set of factors of any number up to 999.

SAMPLE REPORT FORMAT:

```
     INPUT NUMBER: NNN

     FACTORS OF NNN ARE:   NNN NNN NNN . . . NNN
```

6. The manager of Hooperstown Holiday Hotel wants you to write a program to assist her in setting weekly budget goals based on the estimated number of rooms rented. The hotel has 100 single rooms, 100 double rooms, and 50 suites. The daily room rate is $70 for a single, $100 for a double, and $150 for a suite. The manager enters as input weekly payroll expenses, weekly fixed operating expenses, and the percentage of weekly profit desired based on the weekly expenses. The output will include estimated weekly revenue, weekly profit, and number of rooms rented (with single and double rooms approximately equal and suites roughly one-half the single and double room values).

SAMPLE REPORT FORMAT:

```
                  HOOPERSTOWN HOLIDAY HOTEL
               WEEKLY BUDGET ESTIMATION REPORT

     INPUT:
          PAYROLL EXPENSES:             NN,NNN.NN
          FIXED OPERATING EXPENSES:     NN,NNN.NN
          PCT OF WEEKLY PROFIT DESIRED: N.NN


     CALCULATED RESULTS:
          REVENUE:                 NN,NNN.NN
          EXPENSES:                NN,NNN.NN
                                   ------------
          PROFIT:                  NN,NNN.NN


     NUMBER OF ROOMS RENTED:
          SINGLE -- NNN
          DOUBLE -- NNN
          SUITE  -- NN
```

7. Your business must reduce its monthly long distance telephone bill. After studying the trends of the company's long distance calls for three months, the six most popular locations were identified with their appropriate rates:

Location	Cost For First Three Minutes	Cost Each Additional Minutes
Chicago	$1.50	$.15
Los Angeles	$1.80	$.20
Philadelphia	$2.00	$.25
San Jose	$1.60	$.20
Washington, D.C.	$1.90	$.25
Other	$1.00	$.10

Before placing a long distance call, each employee will enter the estimated minutes for the call and the location he or she is calling. This will provide the employee with an estimate of the call before it has been placed and constantly remind employees of the long distance phone costs. The ultimate objective is to encourage all employees not to make a long distance call unless it is absolutely necessary. Develop the logic necessary to solve this problem.

> **NOTE:** This problem encourages the use of an array. You may need to refer to Appendix A.

SAMPLE REPORT FORMAT:

```
            LONG DISTANCE PHONE ESTIMATE


      ESTIMATED MINUTES:   NN
      LOCATION CALLING:    CCCCCCCCCCCCCCC

      COST OF CALL:        $NN.NN
```

8. The state Department of Public Safety requests a program to monitor traffic violators and suspend their license if necessary. The input values are:

Driver Name

Current Points

Offense

The possible violations with the fine amount and point penalty are:

Violation	Point Value	Fine Amount
DD—Drunk Driving	9	$400
RR—Running a Red Light	3	30
SP—Speeding	5	75
RD—Reckless Driving	4	50

If the current points plus the point penalty for the current offense is greater than 10, suspend the driver's license. The fine amount is derived from the current offense. Determine the logic that will solve this problem.

SAMPLE REPORT FORMAT:

TRAFFIC FINES

DRIVER NAME	PREVIOUS POINTS	OFFENSE	CURRENT POINTS	FINE AMOUNT	SUSPENDED
JOE JONES	5	DD	14	$ 400	YES
.	.	.	.	.	.
.	.	.	.	.	.
.	.	.	.	.	.
JIM SMITH	0	RR	3	$ 30	NO

9. Solve problem 8, but use an array(s) to store violation, point value, and fine amount. To review arrays, refer to Appendix A.

REFERENCES
Edward Yourdon and Larry Constantine, *Structured Design Fundamentals of a Discipline of Computer Program and Systems Design*, Yourdon Press, New York, 1978.

Arrays

The purposes of this appendix are:

- To define what an array is

- To discuss some typical uses of arrays through some illustrative examples

An array is the term used to refer to a set of contiguous computer memory locations that collectively represent a group of data variables. Most business programmers refer to an array as a table. Arrays are defined in programming languages using special statements. These statements will not be discussed in this appendix.

Perhaps the best way to describe an array is with a picture. Figure A.1 depicts an array A with ten memory locations. The individual memory locations within an array are called cells, elements, or entries. The important thing to note about these locations is that they each represent a unique data variable which can be used to store a single data value.

You are probably wondering at this point how you reference or access individual cells within an array. This is done through the use of something called a subscript. A subscript is a number which identifies a specific location or element within an array. The notation most commonly used to refer to an array element is shown in Figure A.2. Notice in Figure A.2 that the subscript is enclosed within parentheses. The letter or group of letters to the left of the opening parenthesis is the array name. Collectively, all cells or elements within the array are referred to by the array name, which in this case is A.

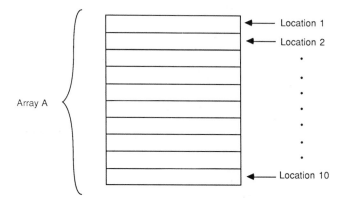

Figure A.1 Pictorial Representation of an Array

Figure A.2 Array Notation—Non-Variable Subscript

Another method of notation for referencing array elements is shown in Figure A.3. Under this notation, the subscript is a variable that must contain an integer value that points to a specific cell or entry in the array. For instance, in the array described in Figure A.3, if I contained a value of 3, then BB(I) would be referring to BB(3). This means that you would be working with a variable called BB(3) that is the third cell in the array BB.

Please note that in some programming languages, the first cell in the array is referenced by using a subscript of 0 (zero) instead of 1. In these languages, the notation shown in Figure A.4 would be used to access the first entry in an array named C. (Rely on your instructor for guidance concerning this characteristic of arrays for your particular course.)

By definition, an array whose elements are referenced by using a single subscript is called a one-dimensional array.

Figure A.3 Array Notation—Variable Subscript

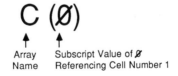

Figure A.4 First Cell in an Array in Some Programming Languages

Sample Problem #1

Load a 10-position array called NUM with the first 10 positive integers.

The most straightforward method for doing this problem would be to set up the statements shown in Figure A.5. The statements shown in Figure A.5 identify ten different variables, NUM(1), NUM(2),. . ., NUM(10) and store ten different values, 1, 2,. . ., 10 into the individual cells of the array.

An alternative method for loading the array NUM with the values 1 through 10 is shown in Figure A.6.

The results of this solution are identical to the results of the first solution. However, the second solution uses a variable subscript and requires fewer statements. Both solutions are equally valid and are shown here to illustrate alternative ways of manipulating array items.

```
NUM (1) = 1
NUM (2) = 2
NUM (3) = 3
      .       .
      .       .
      .       .
NUM (10) = 10
```

Figure A.5 Solution 1 to Sample Problem 1

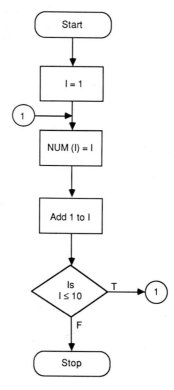

Figure A.6 Solution 2 to Sample Problem 2

Two-Dimensional Arrays

A two-dimensional array is like a one-dimensional array with the exception that cells within the array are referenced using two subscripts instead of one. A two-dimensional array D is shown in Figure A.7. Notice that the drawing in Figure A.7 has nine cells which can be addressed using the notation shown in Figure A.8.

Array D is called a two-dimensional, 3 by 3 (or 3 × 3) array because it has two subscripts denoting three rows and three columns. By convention, the first subscript within the parentheses designates the row location and the second subscript designates the column location of the cell being referenced.

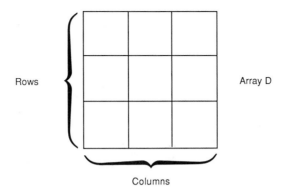

Rows

Array D

Columns

Figure A.7 Two-Dimensional Array

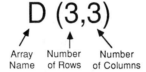

$$D\ (3,3)$$

Array   Number   Number
Name   of Rows   of Columns

Figure A.8 Two-Dimensional Array With 3 Rows and 3 Columns

	Size 1	Size 2	Size 3
Product 1	7.00	11.00	17.00
Product 2	6.00	9.00	15.00
Product 3	5.00	8.00	11.00

Array PRICE

Figure A.9 A Two-Dimensional Pricing Array

Again, to re-emphasize the point, each one of the cells in the two-dimensional array represents a unique data variable which can be used to store a single data value.

A logical question at this point would be to ask what a two-dimensional table would be used for. Please look at Figure A.9. This array presents the costs for a set of products that come in various sizes. Notice that the rows of the array reference the various products that are available. The columns reference the various sizes that are available for each product. The intersection of the rows and columns, that is, the cells of the array, represent the cost of a particular product in a particular size. For instance, PRICE (2,3) contains the value 15.00 which says that the cost of Product 2 in Size 3 is $15.00.

```
IF PRICE (1, 2) > 10
    PRINT "PRODUCT 1."
IF PRICE (2, 2) > 10
    PRINT "PRODUCT 2."
IF PRICE (3, 2) > 10
    PRINT "PRODUCT 3."
```

```
J = 1
WHILE J < = 3
    IF PRICE (J, 2) > 10
        PRINT "PRODUCT" J.
    J = J + 1
END WHILE LOOP
```

Figure A.10 Solution 1 to Sample Problem 2

Figure A.11 Solution 2 to Sample Problem 2

Sample Problem #2

In the array shown in Figure A.9, find all products in Size 2 that cost more than $10.00.

In this problem, we know that we will only be looking at products in the Size 2 category. This fact tells us that we will only need to look at values in the array that are in column 2. Therefore, the logic statements required to solve this problem are shown in Figure A.10.

An alternative method for solving this problem is shown in Figure A.11.

The results of this solution are identical to the results of the first solution. The difference between the two solutions is that the second uses a variable subscript for the product number and can easily be modified to handle any number of products. Both solutions are equally valid and are shown to illustrate alternative ways of manipulating two-dimensional array items.

Three-Dimensional Arrays

A three-dimensional array is similar to a two-dimensional array except that its cells are referenced using three subscripts instead of two. Please refer to Figure A.12, a drawing of a three-dimensional array R.

A very good visual representation of a three-dimensional array is a Rubik's cube. The cube has the three dimensions of height, width, and depth, and each individual piece of the cube can be referenced by specifying a value for each of the associated dimensions.

Refer back to the array shown in Figure A.12. Notice that the array has three cells along its height dimension, three along its width dimensions, and three along its depth dimension. This particular array would be called a 3 × 3 × 3 array because it has 3 units or cells along each dimension of the array. This array is shown to be a 3 × 3 × 3 with the notation R(3,3,3). By convention, the first subscript represents the row dimension, the second represents the column dimension, and the third represents the depth dimension (which is also referred to as a file dimension).

Again, it should be emphasized, as it was for one- and two-dimensional arrays, that each one of the cells in the three-dimensional array represents a unique data variable which can be used to store a single data value. Now, let's build on the two-dimensional pricing array in Figure A.9 by extending the array by one dimension for color. Please refer to Figure A.13.

As before, this array presents the costs for a set of products that come in various sizes and colors. Notice that the rows of the array reference various products that are available, the columns reference the various sizes, and the files reference the various colors. Again, the intersection of the rows, columns, and files (the cells of the array) represent the cost of a

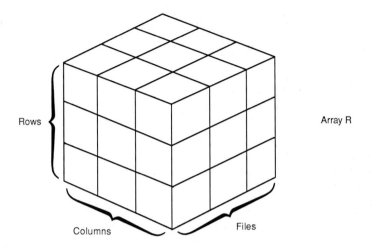

Figure A.12 Three-Dimensional Array

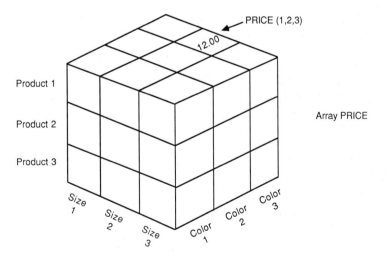

Figure A.13 A Three-Dimensional Pricing Array

particular product in a particular size and in a particular color. For instance, PRICE (1,2,3) contains the value of $12.00 which says that the cost of Product 1 in Size 2 and Color 3 is $12.00.

At this point, we will not attempt to discuss arrays exceeding three dimensions. It should be noted that in mathematics, an array can assume an infinite number of dimensions and would be called an n-dimensional array. In programming, the practical limit on the number of dimensions available to the programmer for an array is dictated by the rules and constraints of the language being used. In most programming languages, the practical limit is three dimensions. However, this limit is by no means universal.

It is important to remember that arrays provide a convenient facility in programming operations for many looping and accumulation processes. In many cases, arrays make the storing and referencing of groups of similar data in a computer's memory area much more efficient and easy to use in achieving the desired output results.

Array Problem

A local radio station requests a program that will read in the daily temperatures from the previous year (365 values) and produce the following report:

XYZ RADIO STATION
TEMPERATURE RANGE ANALYSIS FOR YEAR: XXXX

RANGE			NUMBER
−10	TO	0	NN
1	TO	10	NN
11	TO	20	NN
21	TO	30	NN
31	TO	40	NN
41	TO	50	NN
51	TO	60	NN
61	TO	70	NN
71	TO	80	NN
81	TO	90	NN
91	TO	100	NN
101	TO	110	NN

Using an array to store the count of the temperature range values, write the logic necessary to produce this report.

Flowchart Solution

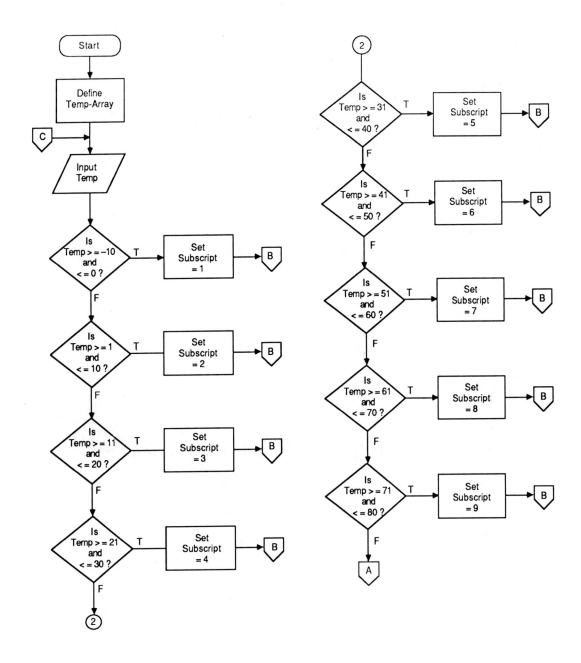

(continued)

(continued)

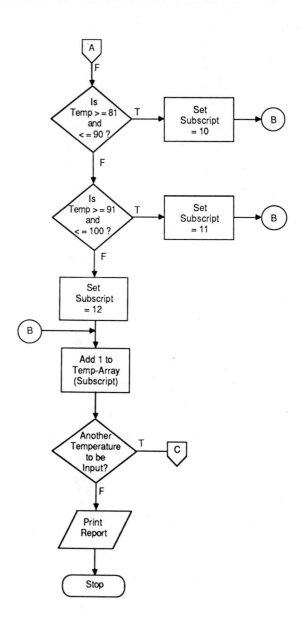

Pseudocode Solution

1. Define a 12-cell array (TEMP-ARRAY) to hold daily temperature ranges.
2. Input a daily temperature (TEMP).
3. If TEMP $> = -10$ and $< = 0$
   set subscript $= 1$.
4. If TEMP $> = 1$ and $< = 10$
   set subscript $= 2$.
5. If TEMP $> = 11$ and $< = 20$
   set subscript $= 3$.
6. If TEMP $> = 21$ and $< = 30$
   set subscript $= 4$.
7. If TEMP $> = 31$ and $< = 40$
   set subscript $= 5$.
8. If TEMP $> = 41$ and $< = 50$
   set subscript $= 6$.
9. If TEMP $> = 51$ and $< = 60$
   set subscript $= 7$.
10. If TEMP $> = 61$ and $< = 70$
    set subscript $= 8$.
11. If TEMP $> = 71$ and $< = 80$
    set subscript $= 9$.
12. If TEMP $> = 81$ and $< = 90$
    set subscript $= 10$.
13. If TEMP $> = 91$ and $< = 100$
    set subscript $= 11$.
14. If TEMP $> = 101$ and $< = 110$
    set subscript $= 12$.
15. Add 1 to TEMP-ARRAY (subscript).
16. Perform step 2 through step 15 until all temperatures have been processed.
17. Print a report showing the various ranges and the total number of temperatures occurring in each range.
18. Stop processing.

Hierarchy Chart Solution

TEMPERATURE ARRAY DRIVER
1. Define a 12-cell array (TEMP-ARRAY) to hold daily temperature ranges.
2. Input a daily temperature (TEMP).
3. Determine temperature range category and accumulate.
4. Perform step 2 and step 3 until all temperatures have been processed.
5. Generate a temperature range analysis report.
6. Stop processing.

INPUT DAILY TEMPERATURE
1. Input a daily temperature (TEMP).

DETERMINE A TEMPERATURE RANGE CATEGORY AND ACCUMULATE
1. If TEMP $> = -10$ and $< = 0$
     set subscript = 1.
2. If TEMP $> = 1$ and $< = 10$
     set subscript = 2.
3. If TEMP $> = 11$ and $< = 20$
     set subscript = 3.
4. If TEMP $> = 21$ and $< = 30$
     set subscript = 4.
5. If TEMP $> = 31$ and $< = 40$
     set subscript = 5.
6. If TEMP $> = 41$ and $< = 50$
     set subscript = 6.
7. If TEMP $> = 51$ and $< = 60$
     set subscript = 7.
8. If TEMP $> = 61$ and $< = 70$
     set subscript = 8.
9. If TEMP $> = 71$ and $< = 80$
     set subscript = 9.
10. If TEMP $> = 81$ and $< = 90$
     set subscript = 10.
11. If TEMP $> = 91$ and $< = 100$
     set subscript = 11.
12. If TEMP $> = 101$ and $< = 110$
     set subscript = 12.
13. Add 1 to TEMP-ARRAY (subscript).

GENERATE TEMPERATURE RANGE ANALYSIS REPORT
1. Write a report showing the twelve temperature ranges and the total number of temperatures occurring in each range.

(continued)

(continued)

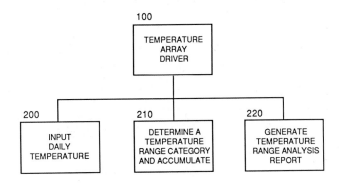

IPO Chart Solution

OUTPUT COLUMN

1. TEMPERATURE RANGE ANALYSIS REPORT.

INPUT COLUMN

1. Daily Temperature (TEMP).

PROCESS COLUMN

1. Define a 12-cell array (TEMP-ARRAY).
2. Input a daily temperature (TEMP).
3. Check for appropriate temperature range.
   If TEMP $> = -10$ and $< = 0$
     set subscript $= 1$.
   If TEMP $> = 1$ and $< = 10$
     set subscript $= 2$.
   If TEMP $> = 11$ and $< = 20$
     set subscript $= 3$.
   If TEMP $> = 21$ and $< = 30$
     set subscript $= 4$.
   If TEMP $> = 31$ and $< = 40$
     set subscript $= 5$.
   If TEMP $> = 41$ and $< = 50$
     set subscript $= 6$.
   If TEMP $> = 51$ and $< = 60$
     set subscript $= 7$.
   If TEMP $> = 61$ and $< = 70$
     set subscript $= 8$.
   If TEMP $> = 71$ and $< = 80$
     set subscript $= 9$.
   If TEMP $> = 81$ and $< = 90$
     set subscript $= 10$.
   If TEMP $> = 91$ and $< = 100$
     set subscript $= 11$.
   If TEMP $> = 101$ and $< = 110$
     set subscript $= 12$.
4. Accumulate appropriate temperature range. — Add 1 to TEMP-ARRAY (subscript).
5. Perform step 2 through step 4 until all temperatures have been processed.
6. Print a report showing the various ranges and the total number of temperatures occurring in each range.
7. Stop processing.

Structure Chart Solution

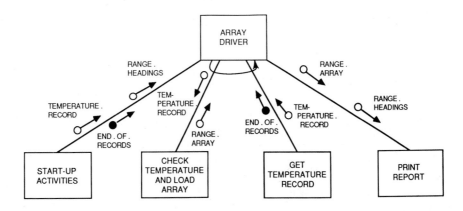

```
<<DATA DICTIONARY>>
```

```
TEMPERATURE.RECORD                                 MISCELLANEOUS.VARIABLES
   DAILY.TEMP                    NNN                   END.OF.RECORDS          CCC
                                                       SUB                     NN


RANGE.ARRAY OCCURS 12 TIMES        NN
RANGE.HEADINGS OCCURS 12 TIMES     C(12)
```

```
<<MODULE PSEUDOCODE>>
```

```
ARRAY DRIVER
   CALL STARTUP ACTIVITIES
   WHILE END.OF.RECORDS = "NO"
      CALL CHECK TEMP AND LOAD ARRAY
      CALL GET TEMPERATURE RECORD
   END WHILE LOOP
   CALL PRINT REPORT

STARTUP ACTIVITIES
   END.OF.RECORDS = "NO"

   OPEN TEMPERATURE FILE

   READ FIRST TEMPERATURE FILE RECORD
   IF END OF FILE THEN
      END.OF.RECORDS = "YES"

   LOAD LITERAL VALUES (-10 TO 0, 1 TO 10, ETC.) INTO SEPARATE
      ELEMENTS OF RANGE.HEADINGS ARRAY
```

(continued)

(continued)

```
CHECK TEMP AND LOAD ARRAY
    IF DAILY.TEMP >= -10 AND <= 0 THEN
        SUB = 1
    IF DAILY.TEMP >= 1 AND <= 10 THEN
        SUB = 2
    IF DAILY.TEMP >= 11 AND <= 20 THEN
        SUB = 3
    IF DAILY.TEMP >= 21 AND <= 30 THEN
        SUB = 4
    IF DAILY.TEMP >= 31 AND <= 40 THEN
        SUB = 5
    IF DAILY.TEMP >= 41 AND <= 50 THEN
        SUB = 6
    IF DAILY.TEMP >= 51 AND <= 60 THEN
        SUB = 7
    IF DAILY.TEMP >= 61 AND <= 70 THEN
        SUB = 8
    IF DAILY.TEMP >= 71 AND <= 80 THEN
        SUB = 9
    IF DAILY.TEMP >= 81 AND <= 90 THEN
        SUB = 10
    IF DAILY.TEMP >= 91 AND <= 100 THEN
        SUB = 11
    IF DAILY.TEMP >= 101 AND <= 110 THEN
        SUB = 12

    RANGE.ARRAY [SUB] = RANGE.ARRAY [SUB] + 1


GET TEMPERATURE RECORD
    READ TEMPERATURE FILE
    IF END OF FILE
        MOVE "YES" TO END.OF.RECORDS


PRINT REPORT
    PRINT HEADINGS

    FOR SUB = 1 TO 12
        PRINT RANGE.HEADINGS [SUB], RANGE.ARRAY [SUB]
    END OF FOR LOOP
```

Nassi-Shneiderman Chart Solution

```
<<DATA DICTIONARY>>

TEMPERATURE.RECORD                              MISCELLANEOUS.VARIABLES
    DAILY.TEMP                    NNN               END.OF.RECORDS         CCC
                                                    SUB                    NN


RANGE.ARRAY OCCURS 12 TIMES       NN
RANGE.HEADINGS OCCURS 12 TIMES    C(12)
```

END . OF . RECORDS = " NO "
OPEN TEMPERATURE FILE
READ FIRST TEMPERATURE FILE RECORD

END OF FILE	
True	False
END . OF . RECORDS = " YES "	NO ACTION

LOAD LITERAL VALUES (−10 TO 0, 1 TO 10, ETC.) INTO SEPARATE ELEMENTS OF RANGE . HEADINGS ARRAY

END . OF . RECORDS = " NO "

DAILY . TEMP >= −10 AND <= 0	
True	False
SUB = 1	NO ACTION

(continued)

(continued)

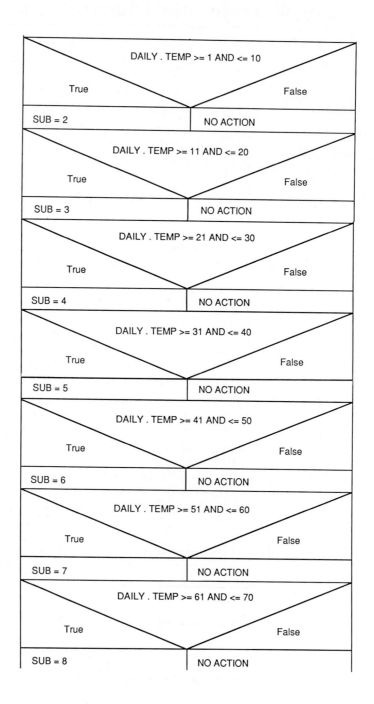

(continued)

(continued)

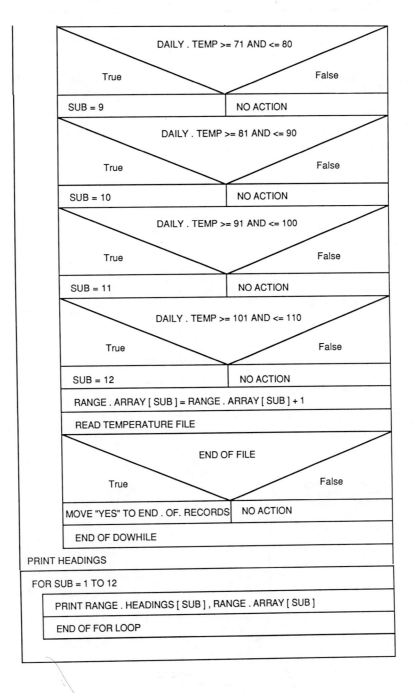

PRINT HEADINGS

FOR SUB = 1 TO 12

PRINT RANGE . HEADINGS [SUB] , RANGE . ARRAY [SUB]

END OF FOR LOOP

Warnier-Orr Diagram Solution

```
<<DATA DICTIONARY>>
```

```
TEMPERATURE.RECORD                           MISCELLANEOUS.VARIABLES
    DAILY.TEMP              NNN                   END.OF.RECORDS          CCC
                                                  SUB                     NN


RANGE.ARRAY OCCURS 12 TIMES      NN
RANGE.HEADINGS OCCURS 12 TIMES   C(12)
```

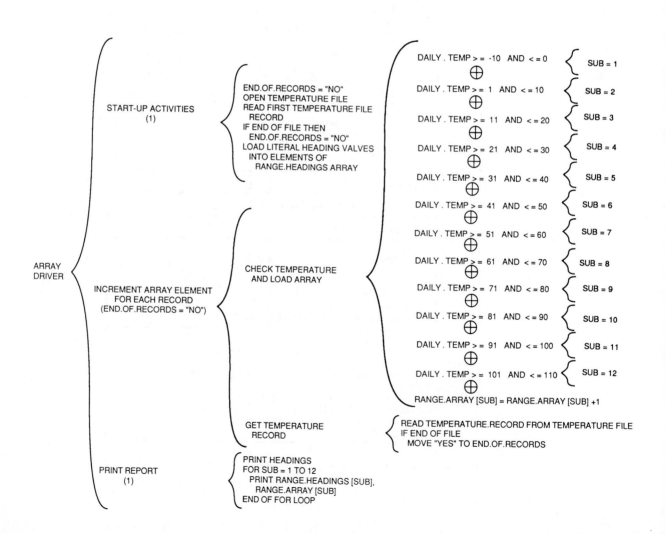

EXERCISES

1. Develop the logic required to load successive cells of an array with the following values: 2,4,6,8,. . ., 20.

2. Develop the logic required to sum the values stored in all elements of array TOTAL (2,2,3).

3. Develop the logic required to load product costs into a two-dimensional table for a product line that comes in four variations with each variation having a possibility of three colors.

4. Develop the logic required to find the largest data value stored in ARRAY1 (3,4,2).

5. Develop the logic required to sum the squares of all data values stored in SQUARE (15).

File Updating

The purposes of this appendix are:

- To define the term file updating
- To discuss how file updating occurs in data processing

Definition of File Updating

File updating is the term used to define the process of:

- Adding data to an existing file
- Changing data on an existing file
- Deleting data from an existing file

The above three processes, adding, changing, and deleting data, are known collectively as the file updating process and apply to all types of data files. Let's briefly discuss each of the three processes to gain an understanding of what the three terms really mean as far as file operations are concerned.

Adding Data

As the term implies, this file updating process is the one by which new or additional data gets added to a file. Typically, this process means that new records are being added in a certain order to an existing file based on the specific characteristics of the file being processed.

Changing Data

This file updating process changes data in existing records in the file. This means that the record to be changed in the file must be located so that the appropriate field(s) can be modified to reflect the new desired values for these fields.

Deleting Data

This file updating process is the one by which data records are physically removed from a file. Just as in the changing data file updating process, the appropriate record to be deleted must be located on the file so that it can be removed from the file.

Before discussing how each of these file updating processes are accomplished for a data file, we need to spend some time discussing a topic called file organization because a file's organization has a great deal of impact on how file updating occurs.

File Organizations

There are five different types of file organizations that are used in today's business data processing environment:

- sequential

- indexed

- relative

- direct

- data base

Let's discuss briefly what each of these file organizations are.

Sequential

In a file that is sequentially organized, the records are stored on the file in the physical sequence in which they were written to the file, one record right after another. This means that records on this file can only be accessed one at a time in the same order that they were written to the file. Hence, the file is said to be a sequential file and records on the file can only be accessed sequentially and never randomly.

Indexed

An indexed file is a file in which records can be accessed either sequentially or randomly. If the file is accessed sequentially, the records are retrieved just as if the file were a sequential file. If the file is accessed randomly, a key field is used to search an index that points to a specific record in the file based on its key field. When this occurs, only the specified record is retrieved from the file based on the key value stored in the index for the file.

At this point, a definition of a key field should be provided. A key field is a designated field within a file that is used to access individual records from a particular file. In a sequential file, the key field is used to order the file by specifying the sequence in which records are physically written to the file. This order is either in ascending or descending sequence, based on the values stored in the key field. Whether the order is either ascending or descending is at the discretion of the creator of the file. The concept of a key field is important to all types of file organizations.

Relative

A file that is organized in relative fashion is also a file in which the records can be accessed either sequentially or randomly. Just as for an indexed file, if a relative file is accessed sequentially, the records are retrieved as if the file were a sequential file. If the file is accessed randomly, records are retrieved from the file based on their relative position within the file, not according to any key field value. What this means is if the first record of the file is desired, then record number 1 is specified. Again, if the one hundredth record stored on the file is wanted, then record number 100 is specified for the random access to take place. Also, in random access mode, each record is retrieved directly without accessing any other records on the file.

Direct

A direct file is a file in which each record on the file is stored at a specific location on a physical storage device. The location where the record is stored is determined by a software program which uses an algorithm to calculate the actual storage location on the device. The same algorithm is used to store records on and retrieve records from the file. For this reason, a direct file is always accessed randomly using the key field in the algorithm to determine the location of the desired record.

Data Base

Some readers may not agree that a data base is a file organization methodology. However, it is included here because it represents a method for storing and retrieving data that is commonly used throughout the business data processing environment today. A data base typically uses a vendor-supplier schema or mechanism for organizing, storing, and retrieving data. The mechanism typically uses a key field or fields for storing records, parts of records, segments, or whatever term a vendor may use for storing units of logically related data. Just as for any of the other file organization methods, a data base has need for file updating processes so that its data can be added to, changed, or deleted as appropriate.

File Updating

An important point which should be made from our discussion of the various file organizations is that files are updated based on two different accessing modes. These modes are either sequential or random. It should be noted that a file organized sequentially can only be updated in sequential mode. The other file organizations can generally use either of the two modes. Therefore, the remainder of the topic of file updating will be discussed from the prospective of the two accessing modes: sequential and random.

Sequential Mode

This section discusses how a file is updated in sequential mode regardless of the file organization for the particular file being updated. The file updating process in sequential mode typically involves three files: one is the "old master file" or file whose records will be

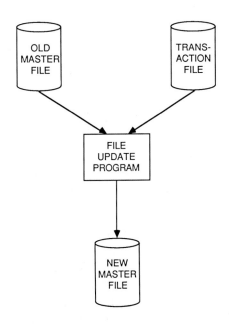

Figure B.1 Sequential File Updating Process

updated; the second file is the "transaction file" or file whose records contain the actual data adds, changes, or deletes that are to be applied against the master file; and the third file is the "new master file" or file which has been updated with the new data. Figure B.1 illustrates the files involved in sequential file updating.

In order for file updating to occur in sequential mode, the following requirements must be met:

1. The records contained in the master file must be in sequential order based on a key field (master key) that is contained in each record with no duplicate key fields.

2. The records contained in the transaction file must be in sequential order based on the same key field (transaction key) as the key field of the master file with no duplicate key fields.

3. Each record contained in the transaction file must have a transaction code that identifies the record as being an add transaction, a change transaction, or a delete transaction.

Given that the three previous requirements have been met, the following logic is involved in implementing the file update.

The basic logic required in performing a sequential file update is to read a record from the transaction file and then read records from the old master file until a record from the old master file has a key field that matches the key field from the incoming transaction record. When the match is made, the record from the old master file is updated and is written out to the new master file. This processing continues until all transactions from the transaction file have been read and the corresponding records on the old master file have been updated and written to the new master file.

In comparing the master key from the old master file record to the transaction key from the transaction file record, one of the following three conditions will result:

1. The transaction key is greater than the master key

2. The master key is greater than the transaction key

3. The transaction key is equal to the master key

Each of these three conditions is a separate case with follow-up requirements.

Case 1: Transaction Key > Master Key
1. Write a new master record from the most recently read old master record.

2. Read the next record from the old master file.

Case 2: Master Key > Transaction Key
1. If the transaction code = "A" (for ADD),
     write a new master record from the transaction record
   else
     write an error message for an invalid transaction
     record.
2. Read the next record from the transaction file.

Case 3: Transaction Key = Master Key
1. If the transaction code = "C" (for CHANGE)
     change the appropriate data on the old master record
     write a new master record from the just updated old
         master record
     read the next record from the old master file
     read the next record from the transaction file.
2. If the transaction code = "D" (for DELETE)
     read the next record from the old master file
     read the next record from the transaction file.
3. If the transaction code = "A" (for ADD)
     write an error message for trying to add a new
         record that is already on the old master file
     read the next record from the old master file
     read the next record from the transaction file.

These three cases will occur over and over again as transaction records and old master file records are read and the key field comparisons are made. When all transaction records have been read and applied against the corresponding old master file records, any remaining old master file records will be read and written to the new master file until no more old master file records remain. After this processing is complete, the new master file now becomes the old master file for the next scheduled file updating cycle. The previous old master file and transaction file can be saved or discarded depending on the wishes of the user.

It is important to note that the requirements and case logic which have been presented in this section are valid for any of the file organizations that have been discussed in this appendix.

Random Mode

The file organization for a particular file being updated in random mode determines the methodology used in the physical update to the master file. The file updating process in random mode typically is done in one of two ways. The first way is similar to sequential file updating in which a transaction file is read for required updates that are made against the master file in random order. The second way is through the use of a computer terminal where a user enters update transactions on-line to a master file, again in a random fashion. The two ways are illustrated in Figures B.2 and B.3.

The records coming in from the transaction file or the entries coming in from the computer terminal are not required to be in any order based on a key field. Neither is there a requirement for the master file to be in order by a key field. This is a very important difference between the way sequential file updating and random file updating takes place. Another basic difference between sequential and random file updating is the fact that two (old and new) physical master files are used to update sequential files while only one master file is used to update a random file.

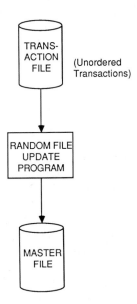

Figure B.2 Random Updates from a Transaction File to a Master File

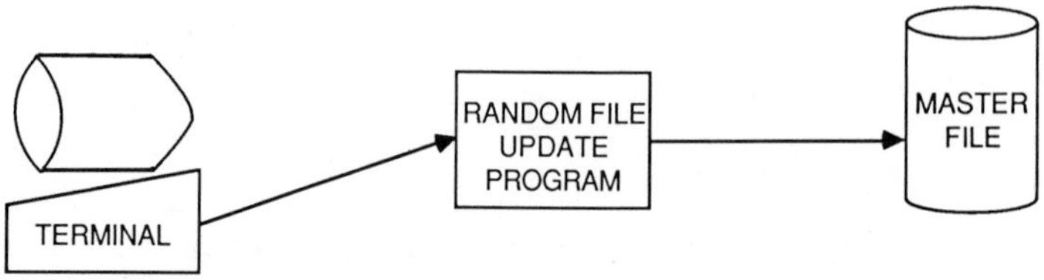

Figure B.3 Random Updates from a Computer Terminal to a Master File

The following is a discussion of each of the file organization methods that support random file updating.

Case 1: Indexed File
The key field from the input transaction is used to search an index that points to a specific record in the master file.

1. If the transaction code is an "A" and a match is not found in the index, a new index entry is made and the transaction record is written to the master file as a new master record.

2. If the transaction code is a "C" and a match is found, the changes from the transaction record are written to the master record.

3. If the transaction code is a "D" and a match is found, the master record is deleted from the file and the index entry is removed from the index.

Case 2: Relative File
A relative record number must be specified on the input transaction to be used to locate the desired record from the file.

1. If the transaction code is an "A", the relative record number of the highest numbered record in the file is incremented by 1, and the transaction record is written to the file with this new relative record number.

2. Same as Case 1, item 2.

3. If the transaction code is a "D" and a match is found, the master record is deleted from the file as well as the relative record number.

Case 3: Direct File
The key field specified on the input transaction is given to the algorithm that computes the physical location of the record to be updated. The physical location of the record to be updated or added is then accessed.

1. If the transaction code is an "A", and a record is not found at the particular location, a new master record is written at this location.

2. Same as Case 1, item 2.

3. If the transaction code is a "D" and a match is found, the master record is deleted from the file at this physical location.

Case 4: Data Base

For all practical purposes and for most data-base management systems, the random updating of a data base works very much like the scenario presented for direct files in Case 3. From a conceptual standpoint, the file updating that occurs for a data base is exactly the same as the file updating that occurs for direct files. Therefore, the same logic for items 1, 2, and 3 under Case 3 are also applicable for Case 4.

The concepts presented in this appendix explain the basic principles for performing file updates to various types of files. The actual programming statements required to implement these concepts will vary greatly from programming language to programming language and from hardware to hardware. However, the concepts are valid as presented for any language and any hardware system.

File Updating Problem

Cary's Custom Label Distributor keeps a master file of all customers ordering labels within the last two years. Each record on the file contains these fields:
  Customer number
  Customer name
  Customer address
  Contact person
  Phone number
  Last order date
  Number of labels ordered

The master file is updated daily. Cary uses a listing of the master file to perform one of three activities:
  1) Add (A)—A new customer places an order
  2) Change (C)—A current customer places a label order
  3) Delete (D)—The customer has not placed an order in two years

These three activities are implemented in a transaction file with these fields:
  Process code (A, C, or D)
  Customer number
  Customer name
  Customer address
  Contact person
  Phone number
  Last order date
  Number of labels ordered
  Type of labels ordered

For an (A)dd record all fields must contain a value. A (C)hange record will have values in the fields that need to be changed; all other fields will be blank. A (D)elete record will contain only the customer number.

Write the logic needed to update the master file with records in the transaction file. Assume the master file uses the random file organization method with the customer number as the key field.

Flowchart Solution

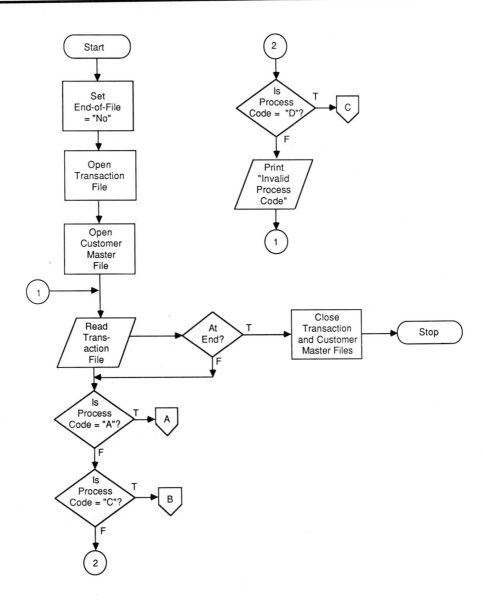

(continued)

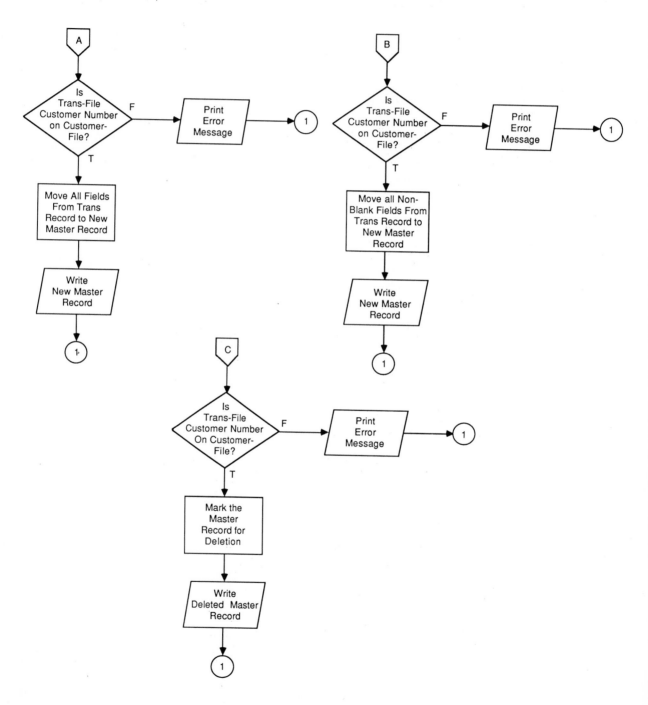

Pseudocode Solution

1. Perform initialization activities:
   - Set end-of-file indicator = "NO"
   - Open transaction file
   - Open master file
   - Read first transaction file record
   - If an end-of-file condition is encountered
       then
           close transaction file and master file
           stop processing.
2. If Process Code = "A"
       then
           check to see if transaction record customer number is already on the master file,
           if the customer number is already on the master file
               then
                   print error message—"customer number already exists"
           else
               move all fields from the transaction record to the master record
               write the new master record to the master file.
3. If Process Code = "C"
       then
           check to see if transaction record customer number is on the master file,
           if the customer number is not on the master file
               then
                   print error message—"customer number not on master file"
           else
               check each field on transaction record for blanks,
               move all non-blank transaction record fields to the corresponding master record fields,
               write changed master record to the master file.
4. If Process Code = "D"
       then
           check to see if transaction record customer number is on the master file,
           if the customer number is not on the master file
               then
                   print error message—"customer number not on master file"
           else
               mark the master record for deletion,
               write the deleted master record to the master file
5. Read the next transaction record.
   - If an end-of-file condition is encountered,
       set the end-of-file indicator = "YES."
6. Perform step 2 through step 5 until end-of-file indicator = "YES."
7. Close transaction file and master file.
8. Stop processing.

Hierarchy Chart Solution

FILE UPDATE DRIVER
1. Perform initialization activities.
2. Process requested transaction code.
3. Read next transaction record.
4. Perform step 2 and step 3 until end-of-file indicator = "YES."
5. Close transaction and customer master files.
6. Stop processing.

INITIALIZATION ACTIVITIES
1. Set end-of-file indicator (transaction file) = "NO."
2. Open transaction file.
3. Open master file.
4. Read first transaction file record.
5. If an end-of-file condition is encountered,
   then
       close transaction file and customer master file
       stop processing.

PROCESS REQUESTED TRANSACTION CODE
1. If Process Code = "A,"
   then
       perform ADDITION PROCESS.
2. If Process Code = "C,"
   then
       perform CHANGE PROCESS.
3. If Process Code = "D,"
   then
       perform DELETION PROCESS.

ADDITION PROCESS
1. Check to see if transaction record customer number is already on the master file.
2. If the customer number is already on the master file
   then
       print error message = "customer number already exists"
   else
       move all fields from the transaction record to the master record
       write the new master record to the master file.

CHANGE PROCESS
1. Check to see if transaction record customer number is on the master file.
2. If the customer number is not on the master file
   then
       print error message— "customer number not on master file"
   else
       check each field on transaction record for blanks,
       move all non-blank transaction record fields to the
           corresponding master record fields,
       write changed master record to the master file.

(continued)

(continued)

DELETION PROCESS
1. Check to see if transaction record customer number is on the master file.
2. If the customer number is not on the master file
   then
      print error message—"customer number not on master file"
   else
      mark the master record for deletion,
      write the deleted master record to the master file.

READ TRANSACTION FILE RECORD
1. Read transaction file.
2. If end-of-file condition is encountered
   then
      set end-of-file indicator = "YES."

This concludes the pseudocode for the hierarchy chart modules. The hierarchy chart for this problem follows.

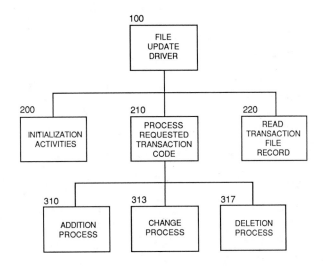

IPO Chart Solution

OUTPUT COLUMN

1. Updated customer master file.

INPUT COLUMN

1. Transaction file
   - Transaction (process) code
   - Customer number
   - Customer name
   - Customer address
   - Contact person
   - Phone number
   - Last order date
   - Number of labels ordered
   - Type of labels ordered
2. Customer master file
   - Transaction (process) code
   - Customer number
   - Customer name
   - Customer address
   - Contact person
   - Phone number
   - Last order date
   - Number of labels ordered
   - Type of labels ordered

PROCESS COLUMN

1. Perform initialization activities:
   - Set end-of-file indicator = "NO"
   - Open transaction file
   - Open customer master file
   - Read first transaction file record
   - If an end-of-file condition is encountered
       then
           close transaction file and customer master file,
           stop processing.

(continued)

(continued)

2. If Process Code = "A"
   then
       check to see if transaction record customer number is already on the master file,
       if the customer number is already on the master file
           then
               print error message—"customer number already exists"
           else
               move all fields from the transaction record to the master record
               write the new master record to the master file.
3. If Process Code = "C"
   then
       check to see if transaction record customer number is on the master file,
       if the customer number is not on the master file
           then
               print error message—"customer number not on master file"
       else
           check each field on transaction record for blanks,
           move all non-blank transaction record fields to the corresponding master record fields
           write changed master record record to the master file.
4. If Process Code = "D"
   then
       check to see if transaction file customer number is on the master file,
       if the customer number is not on the master file
           then
               print error message—"customer number not on master file"
       else
           mark the master record for deletion,
           write the deleted master record to the master file.
5. Read the next transaction record.
   - If an end-of-file condition is encountered,
     set the end-of-file indicator = "YES."
6. Perform step 2 through step 5 until end-of-file indicator = "YES."
7. Close transaction file and customer master file.
8. Stop processing.

Structure Chart Solution

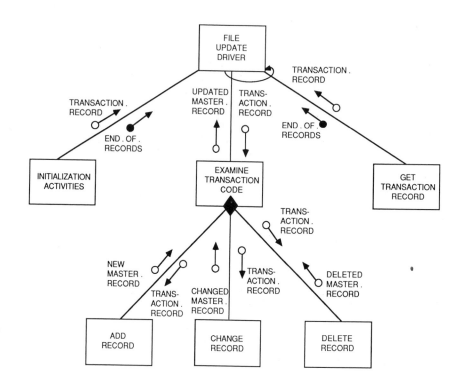

STRUCTURE CHART SOLUTION

<<DATA DICTIONARY>>

TRANSACTION.RECORD

TR.TRANSACTION.CODE	C
TR.CUSTOMER.NUMBER	NNNN
TR.CUSTOMER.NAME	C(20)
TR.CUSTOMER.ADDRESS	C(25)
TR.CONTACT.PERSON	C(20)
TR.PHONE.NUMBER	C(12)
TR.LAST.ORDER.DATE	C(6)
TR.NUMBER.OF.LABELS.ORDERED	N(5)
TR.TYPE.OF.LABELS.ORDERED	CC

MISCELLANEOUS.VARIABLES

END.OF.RECORDS	CCC
MASTER.FILE.SEARCH.VAR	NNNN

(continued)

(continued)

```
MASTER.RECORD
    MR.CUSTOMER.NUMBER              NNNN
    MR.CUSTOMER.NAME               C(20)
    MR.CUSTOMER.ADDRESS            C(25)
    MR.CONTACT.PERSON              C(20)
    MR.PHONE.NUMBER                C(12)
    MR.LAST.ORDER.DATE             C(6)
    MR.NUMBER.OF.LABELS.ORDERED    N(5)
    MR.TYPE.OF.LABELS.ORDERED      CC
```

```
<<MODULE PSEUDOCODE>>

FILE UPDATE DRIVER
    CALL INITIALIZATION ACTIVITIES
    WHILE END.OF.RECORDS = "NO"
        CALL EXAMINE TRANSACTION CODE
        CALL GET TRANSACTION RECORD
    END WHILE LOOP

INITIALIZATION ACTIVITIES
    END.OF.RECORDS = "NO"

    OPEN TRANSACTION FILE

    READ FIRST TRANSACTION FILE RECORD
    IF END OF FILE
        END.OF.RECORDS = "YES"


EXAMINE TRANSACTION CODE
    IF TR.TRANSACTION.CODE = "A"
        CALL ADD RECORD
    ELSE
        IF TR.TRANSACTION.CODE = "C"
            CALL CHANGE RECORD
        ELSE
            IF TR.TRANSACTION.CODE = "D"
                CALL DELETE RECORD
            ELSE
                ERROR - TRANSACTION CODE NOT = "A" OR "C" OR "D"
```

(continued)

(continued)

ADD RECORD
```
    MOVE TR.CUSTOMER.NUMBER TO MASTER.FILE.SEARCH.VAR
    READ (SEEK) RECORD ON MASTER FILE

    IF TR.CUSTOMER.NUMBER ON FILE
        ERROR -- CUSTOMER NUMBER ALREADY EXISTS
    ELSE
        BEGIN
            MOVE ALL FIELDS FROM TRANSACTION.RECORD TO MASTER.RECORD
            WRITE NEW MASTER.RECORD TO MASTER FILE
        END
```

CHANGE RECORD
```
    MOVE TR.CUSTOMER.NUMBER TO MASTER.FILE.SEARCH.VAR
    READ (SEEK) RECORD ON MASTER FILE

    IF TR.CUSTOMER.NUMBER NOT = MR.CUSTOMER.NUMBER
        ERROR --  CUSTOMER NUMBER MUST EXIST ON MASTER FILE
    ELSE
        BEGIN
            TEST EACH FIELD ON TRANSACTION RECORD FOR BLANKS
            IF FIELD NOT BLANK
                MOVE TRANSACTION.RECORD FIELD TO MASTER.RECORD FIELD
                WRITE CHANGED MASTER.RECORD TO MASTER FILE
        END
```

DELETE RECORD
```
    MOVE TR.CUSTOMER.NUMBER TO MASTER.FILE.SEARCH.VAR
    READ (SEEK) RECORD ON MASTER FILE

    IF TR.CUSTOMER.NUMBER NOT = MR.CUSTOMER.NUMBER
        ERROR --  CUSTOMER NUMBER MUST EXIST ON MASTER FILE
    ELSE
        BEGIN
            FLAG MASTER RECORD AS DELETED
            WRITE DELETED MASTER.RECORD TO MASTER FILE
        END
```

GET TRANSACTION RECORD
```
    READ TRANSACTION FILE
    IF END OF FILE
        MOVE "YES" TO END.OF.RECORDS
```

Nassi-Shneiderman Chart Solution

```
<<DATA DICTIONARY>>
```

```
TRANSACTION.RECORD
    TR.TRANSACTION.CODE            C
    TR.CUSTOMER.NUMBER            NNNN
    TR.CUSTOMER.NAME              C(20)
    TR.CUSTOMER.ADDRESS          C(25)
    TR.CONTACT.PERSON            C(20)
    TR.PHONE.NUMBER              C(12)
    TR.LAST.ORDER.DATE           C(6)
    TR.NUMBER.OF.LABELS.ORDERED  N(5)
    TR.TYPE.OF.LABELS.ORDERED     CC
```

```
MISCELLANEOUS.VARIABLES
    END.OF.RECORDS              CCC
    MASTER.FILE.SEARCH.VAR      NNNN
```

```
MASTER.RECORD
    MR.CUSTOMER.NUMBER            NNNN
    MR.CUSTOMER.NAME             C(20)
    MR.CUSTOMER.ADDRESS          C(25)
    MR.CONTACT.PERSON            C(20)
    MR.PHONE.NUMBER              C(12)
    MR.LAST.ORDER.DATE           C(6)
    MR.NUMBER.OF.LABELS.ORDERED  N(5)
    MR.TYPE.OF.LABELS.ORDERED     CC
```

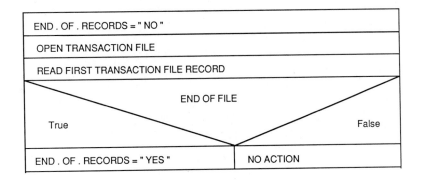

(continued)

(continued)

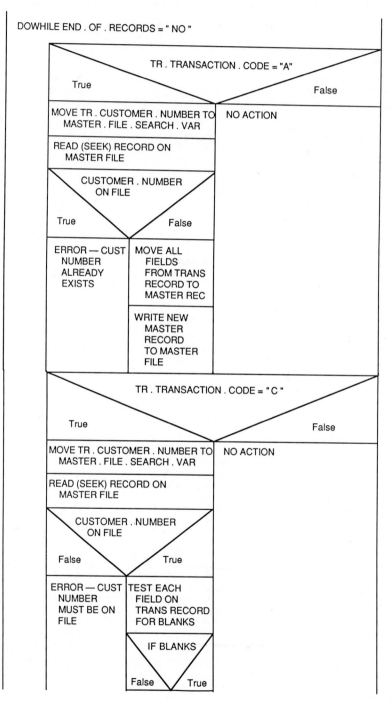

(continued)

(continued)

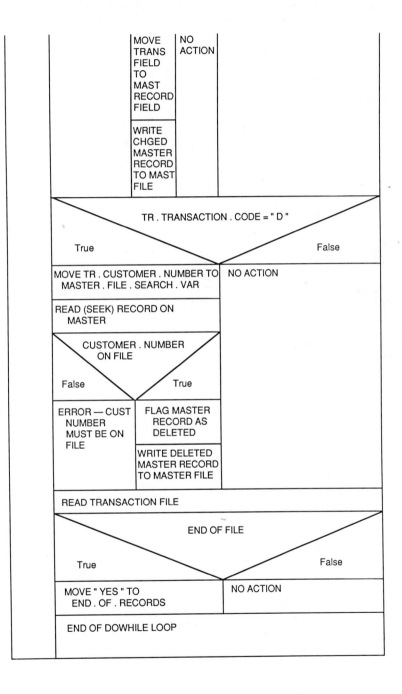

MOVE TRANS FIELD TO MAST RECORD FIELD	NO ACTION
WRITE CHGED MASTER RECORD TO MAST FILE	

TR . TRANSACTION . CODE = " D "

True — False

MOVE TR . CUSTOMER . NUMBER TO MASTER . FILE . SEARCH . VAR	NO ACTION
READ (SEEK) RECORD ON MASTER	

CUSTOMER . NUMBER ON FILE

False — True

ERROR — CUST NUMBER MUST BE ON FILE	FLAG MASTER RECORD AS DELETED
	WRITE DELETED MASTER RECORD TO MASTER FILE

READ TRANSACTION FILE

END OF FILE

True — False

MOVE " YES " TO END . OF . RECORDS	NO ACTION

END OF DOWHILE LOOP

Warnier-Orr Diagram Solution

<<DATA DICTIONARY>>

TRANSACTION.RECORD
```
    TR.TRANSACTION.CODE              C
    TR.CUSTOMER.NUMBER              NNNN
    TR.CUSTOMER.NAME                C(20)
    TR.CUSTOMER.ADDRESS             C(25)
    TR.CONTACT.PERSON               C(20)
    TR.PHONE.NUMBER                 C(12)
    TR.LAST.ORDER.DATE              C(6)
    TR.NUMBER.OF.LABELS.ORDERED     N(5)
    TR.TYPE.OF.LABELS.ORDERED       CC
```

MASTER.RECORD
```
    MR.CUSTOMER.NUMBER              NNNN
    MR.CUSTOMER.NAME                C(20)
    MR.CUSTOMER.ADDRESS             C(25)
    MR.CONTACT.PERSON               C(20)
    MR.PHONE.NUMBER                 C(12)
    MR.LAST.ORDER.DATE              C(6)
    MR.NUMBER.OF.LABELS.ORDERED     N(5)
    MR.TYPE.OF.LABELS.ORDERED       CC
```

MISCELLANEOUS.VARIABLES
```
    END.OF.RECORDS                  CCC
    MASTER.FILE.SEARCH.VAR          NNNN
```

(continued)

(continued)

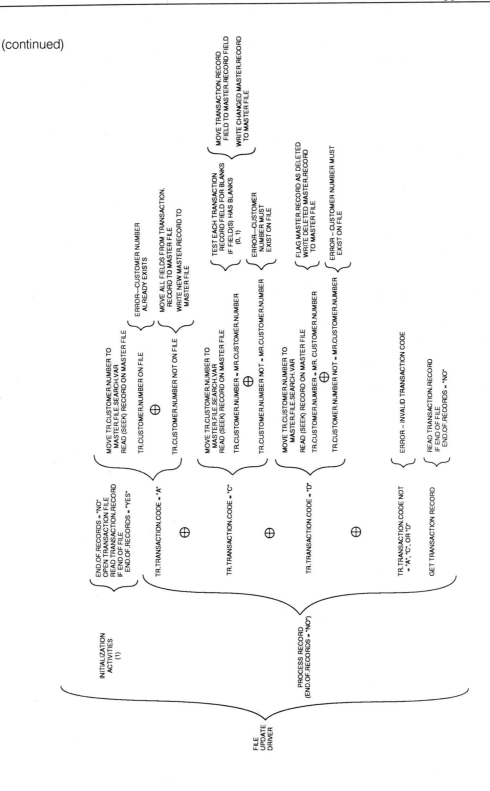

EXERCISES

1. Develop the logic required to update a Payroll Master File that has the following fields:
   a. Employee number (key field)
   b. Employee name
   c. Employee address
   d. Social security number
   e. Hourly pay rate
   f. Federal tax
   g. FICA tax
   h. Personal exemptions
   i. Health deduction
   j. Other deductions

   Assume that the Payroll Master File is a sequential file.

2. Develop the logic required to update the Company Inventory Master File that has the following fields:
   a. Part number (key field)
   b. Part name
   c. Department number
   d. Quantity on-hand
   e. Quantity on-order
   f. Safety stock level
   g. Substitute part number

   Assume that the Company Inventory Master File is an indexed file.

Sorting

Introduction

Once the data is initially captured in a file, data base, or within an array, a common problem occurs: the data may not be in the proper order or sequence. What is meant by order or sequence of data? Let's look at an example. Assume you have six numbers.

23

87

41

516

179

204

Currently, those numbers are not in any particular sequence. There are two types of sequence available when dealing with numbers: ascending and descending. Ascending sequence places a group of numbers in order, starting with the lowest value and proceeding to the highest value. Here are the same six numbers in ascending sequence:

23

41

87

179

204

516

Descending sequence places a group of numbers in order, starting with the highest value and proceeding to the lowest value. Here are the six numbers in descending sequence:

516

204

179

87

41

23

You may be asking yourself, "What if I want to sort characters?" Characters can be sorted in ascending or descending sequence. The tricky part involves the hardware utilized. The computer hardware involved has rules concerning the sequence of characters and numbers. These rules are referred to as *collating sequence*, and each hardware vendor chooses its own collating sequence. The kinds of questions answered by collating sequence can include the following: If you are placing numbers in ascending sequence, do characters come before numbers? What is the ascending sequence order for characters? What about special characters such as %, #, $, or !? For example, how would you place the following characters or numbers in ascending order:

C

*

67

b

B

?

198

e

The collating sequence establishes the order rules to follow and it's dependent on the computer hardware. Generally, for ascending sequence the collating sequence is:

1.   Special characters such as ! @ # * % ?

2.   Lower-case a through z

3.   Upper-case A through Z

4.   Numeric digits 0 through 9

Following these rules, ordering the previous characters or numbers in ascending sequence appears as:

*

?

b

e

B

C

67

198

Now let's get back to sorting. What exactly is sorting? Sorting takes a group of numbers or characters and places them in ascending or descending order following the collating sequence rules of the specific computer hardware used. The practical application of this concept can be taken a step further. In the data processing industry, most sorting involves the reordering of records based on a key field. This key field could be an employee's name, yearly salary, or state of residence. All of this information could be stored on one record, but several users may require reports with different types of information. The personnel department may want the name and address of each employee sorted in ascending sequence by last name key field. The payroll department may request a report showing the name and yearly salary of each employee sorted in descending sequence by the yearly salary key field.

As you have probably guessed, there is not just one method to follow when sorting data. There are many different sorting algorithms available. This appendix considers two sorting algorithms: the bubble sort and Shell sort. During the sort process, the data values sorted must be available for manipulation during the entire process. The main programming data structure allowing this constant manipulation is an array. (For more information about arrays, refer to Appendix A.) Sorting cannot be limited to the concept of processing one record at a time since the values read in by one record "wipes out" the previous record's values. The use of arrays overcomes this limitation.

Bubble Sort

The bubble sort is considered the simplest sorting algorithm. With this technique, you start with the first array item and compare it to the next adjacent array item. Depending on the sequence (ascending or descending), you may swap data item contents. This comparison is made with all elements in the array. Assume that the data has been loaded in array A as illustrated in Figure C.1.

The contents of the first element A(1) is compared to the next adjacent element A(2). A swap of array element contents occurs if they are not in the proper order (dependent on ascending or descending sequence). This process is repeated for each of the elements in the array. To illustrate, consider sorting array A in ascending order; A(1) is compared to A(2), if A(1) is less than or equal to A(2), no swap occurs. In the next steps, A(2) is compared to A(3), A(3) to A(4), and so on. Notice in Figure C.2 how the elements in array A have changed after this process.

Look closely at array A. All of the values are not in correct ascending sequence. Notice that the highest value is in the last element, position A(6). The process of array element comparison, starting with the first element and proceeding to the last element, is known as a

Array A

A (1)	23
A (2)	20
A (3)	100
A (4)	42
A (5)	55
A (6)	17

Figure C.1 Array A

pass. We have just completed the first pass. Array A appears as shown in Figure C.3 after the second pass. The only swap occurred with A(4) and A(5). Observe what happens after the third pass as shown in Figure C.4.

The only swap occurred between elements A(3) and A(4). Do you see a trend developing? View the array as shown in Figure C.5 after the fourth pass.

Elements A(2) and A(3) swapped data element contents. To place all elements in the array in ascending order requires a fifth pass as shown in Figure C.6.

Now all elements in the array are in ascending order. How many passes are required to ensure that the array is in the proper order? The maximum number of passes required to ensure that all elements in the array are in order is equal to the number of elements in the array minus 1. Since array A has six elements, the maximum number of passes needed to sort the array is five.

	BEFORE COMPARISON			AFTER COMPARISON
A (1)	23	A (1) <= A (2) – Swap	A (1)	20
A (2)	20	A (2) <= A (3) – No change	A (2)	23
A (3)	100	A (3) <= A (4) – Swap	A (3)	42
A (4)	42	A (4) <= A (5) – Swap	A (4)	55
A (5)	55	A (5) <= A (6) – Swap	A (5)	17
A (6)	17		A (6)	100

Figure C.2 Bubble Sort—First Pass

	AFTER FIRST PASS			AFTER SECOND PASS
A (1)	20	A (1) <= A (2) – No change	A (1)	20
A (2)	23	A (2) <= A (3) – No change	A (2)	23
A (3)	42	A (3) <= A (4) – No change	A (3)	42
A (4)	55	A (4) <= A (5) – Swap	A (4)	17
A (5)	17	A (5) <= A (6) – No change	A (5)	55
A (6)	100		A (6)	100

Figure C.3 Bubble Sort—Second Pass

AFTER
SECOND PASS

A (1)	20
A (2)	23
A (3)	42
A (4)	17
A (5)	55
A (6)	100

A (1) <= A (2) − No change
A (2) <= A (3) − No change
A (3) <= A (4) − Swap
A (4) <= A (5) − No change
A (5) <= A (6) − No change

AFTER
THIRD PASS

A (1)	20
A (2)	23
A (3)	17
A (4)	42
A (5)	55
A (6)	100

Figure C.4 Bubble Sort—Third Pass

AFTER
THIRD PASS

A (1)	20
A (2)	23
A (3)	17
A (4)	42
A (5)	55
A (6)	100

A (1) <= A (2) − No change
A (2) <= A (3) − Swap
A (3) <= A (4) − No change
A (4) <= A (5) − No change
A (5) <= A (6) − No change

AFTER
FOURTH PASS

A (1)	20
A (2)	17
A (3)	23
A (4)	42
A (5)	55
A (6)	100

Figure C.5 Bubble Sort—Fourth Pass

AFTER
FOURTH PASS

A (1)	20
A (2)	17
A (3)	23
A (4)	42
A (5)	55
A (6)	100

A (1) <= A (2) − No change
A (2) <= A (3) − Swap
A (3) <= A (4) − No change
A (4) <= A (5) − No change
A (5) <= A (6) − No change

AFTER
FIFTH PASS

A (1)	17
A (2)	20
A (3)	23
A (4)	42
A (5)	55
A (6)	100

Figure C.6 Bubble Sort—Fifth Pass

It is important to notice the activity that has occurred at the end of each pass. For an ascending sort, at the end of the first pass, the highest data value is stored in the highest data element location. At the end of the second pass, the second highest data value is stored in the second highest data element location. When the third pass is completed, the third highest data value is stored in the third highest data element location. This process repeats in each of the passes. For example, assume an array with seven elements. At the end of the first pass, the highest data value is stored in element 7. When the second pass is completed, the second highest data value is stored in element 6. After the third pass, the third highest data element is stored in element 5. This logic is repeated until the sixth pass ensures that the entire array is in the correct order. This is why the algorithm is called a bubble sort. For an ascending sort, the lower values begin to "bubble" to the top after each pass. For a descending sort, the higher values begin to "bubble" to the top after each pass.

Pseudocode Bubble Sort Solution

The bubble sort pseudocode solution to the example presented earlier with array A is shown in Figure C.7. Assume all data variables and array A are defined as numeric data types in the data dictionary.

The outer REPEAT loop ensures that the maximum number of passes are performed. The inner WHILE loop contains the element comparison logic necessary to complete one pass. The IF statement is set for an ascending sort. (To modify logic to descending sort, change $<=$ sign to $>=$.) The three statements after the ELSE clause perform the SWAP logic. SUBSCRIPT is incremented by one so the next two elements can be compared. Walk through this pseudocode solution with array A values used previously to confirm your understanding.

There is a problem with the bubble sort solution discussed to this point. What if array A contained the values shown in Figure C.8? After one pass, A(1) and A(2) would swap values

```
NUM.OF.ARRAY.ELEMENTS = 6
REPEAT NUM.OF.ARRAY.ELEMENTS − 1 TIMES
   SUBSCRIPT = 1
   WHILE SUBSCRIPT <= NUM.OF.ARRAY.ELEMENTS − 1
      IF A (SUBSCRIPT) <= A (SUBSCRIPT + 1) THEN
         NO ACTION
      ELSE
         TEMP.VARIABLE = A(SUBSCRIPT)
         A (SUBSCRIPT) = A(SUBSCRIPT + 1)
         A(SUBSCRIPT + 1) = TEMP.VARIABLE
      ENDIF
         SUBSCRIPT = SUBSCRIPT + 1
   END OF WHILE LOOP
END OF REPEAT LOOP
```

Figure C.7 Pseudocode Bubble Sort Solution

and all values in the array would be sorted in ascending sequence. However, the logic is structured to make five passes against the array and will complete all five passes. The last four passes are unnecessary since the array is already sorted so this solution is inefficient.

The answer involves a concept known as a switch or flag. A switch usually has two values representing an on and off situation. The switch is set before an activity occurs and some action in the activity could change the value of the switch. At the end of the activity, the switch is tested for a change. For the bubble sort example, if a pass is made and none of the values are swapped, the array is sorted. A switch is tested at the end of each pass to determine if the sort is finished before the maximum number of passes. Study the new pseudocode solution shown in Figure C.9 which includes the switch.

Array A

A (1)	29
A (2)	18
A (3)	56
A (4)	88
A (5)	149
A (6)	820

Figure C.8 Array A

```
NUM.OF.ARRAY.ELEMENTS = 6
ITEMS.SORTED.SWITCH = "NO"

WHILE ITEMS.SORTED.SWITCH = "NO"
   SUBSCRIPT = 1
   ITEMS.SORTED.SWITCH = "YES"
   WHILE SUBSCRIPT < = NUM.OF.ARRAY.ELEMENTS − 1
      IF A(SUBSCRIPT) < = A(SUBSCRIPT + 1) THEN
        NO ACTION
      ELSE
        TEMP.VARIABLE = A(SUBSCRIPT)
        A(SUBSCRIPT) = A(SUBSCRIPT + 1)
        A(SUBSCRIPT + 1) = TEMP. VARIABLE
        ITEMS.SORTED.SWITCH = "NO"
      ENDIF
      SUBSCRIPT = SUBSCRIPT + 1
   END OF WHILE LOOP
END OF WHILE LOOP
```

Figure C.9 New Pseudocode Solution

Initially ITEMS.SORTED.SWITCH is set to "NO," the outer WHILE loop continues to execute if the test is TRUE. Before the inner WHILE loop is executed, ITEMS.SORTED.SWITCH is assigned the value "YES." The inner WHILE loop performs one pass. If an element was swapped, ITEMS.SORTED.SWITCH is set equal to "NO," which would allow the outer WHILE loop to execute again. If the ITEMS.SORTED.SWITCH is not reset to "NO," then the array is sorted and the sort process ends at that point.

Shell Sort

The bubble sort is acceptable for a small number of items, but it can be very time consuming for arrays larger than 100 elements. The algorithm is slow because only adjacent items are being moved when the swap takes place. Donald Shell developed a sorting algorithm that is similar to the bubble sort but is more efficient when sorting a large number of data elements.

The Shell sort does not compare and swap adjacent elements (as does the bubble sort) but compares and swaps elements based on a gap value which starts at a value half the size of the array. The first element in the array is compared to the element residing at the current position plus the gap value. This gap value changes during the sort process. Observe the pseudocode Shell sort solution for array B which contains 11 elements as shown in Figure C.10.

```
NUM.OF.ARRAY.ELEMENTS = 11
GAP = NUM.OF.ARRAY.ELEMENTS / 2

WHILE GAP < > 0
ITEMS.SORTED.SWITCH = "NO"
  WHILE ITEMS.SORTED.SWITCH = "NO"
    SUBSCRIPT = 1
    ITEMS.SORTED.SWITCH = "YES"
    WHILE SUBSCRIPT < = NUM.OF.ARRAY.ELEMENTS − GAP
      IF B(SUBSCRIPT) < = B(SUBSCRIPT + GAP) THEN
        NO ACTION
      ELSE
        TEMP.VARIABLE = B(SUBSCRIPT)
        B(SUBSCRIPT) = B(SUBSCRIPT + GAP)
        B(SUBSCRIPT + GAP) = TEMP.VARIABLE
        ITEMS.SORTED.SWITCH = "NO"
      ENDIF
      SUBSCRIPT = SUBSCRIPT + 1
    END OF WHILE LOOP
  END OF WHILE LOOP
  GAP = GAP / 2
END OF WHILE LOOP
```

Figure C.10 Pseudocode Shell Sort Solution

This solution consists of a WHILE loop containing two nested WHILE loops. GAP is initially calculated by dividing the number of array elements by two. When implementing this solution in a program, define GAP as an integer variable to allow for odd-numbered GAP values. With integer variables, a fractional recalculation of GAP, such as 5.5, is truncated or rounded down to the next lowest integer value. ITEMS.SORTED.SWITCH is assigned the value "NO" to prepare for a pass. SUBSCRIPT is set to 1 and ITEMS.SORTED.SWITCH is set to "YES." The innermost WHILE loop makes the element comparisons in the same manner as the bubble sort except the comparison element is incremented by GAP instead of 1. ITEMS.SORTED.SWITCH keeps the loop repeating until no element values are swapped. When ITEMS.SORTED.SWITCH stays equal to "YES" after comparing elements within the innermost WHILE loop, the GAP value is divided by two and the next pass occurs unless GAP = 0, then the sort is complete.

To fully understand this sort technique, look at array B, as shown in Figure C.11, which consists of eleven elements. Walk through the ascending sequence Shell sort pseudocode algorithm. For the following illustrations, when comparing array element results, S represents swap and NC represents no change. The first gap value divides the number of array elements by two.

The comparisons are made one more time with no element values swapped. The definition of pass changes slightly for the Shell sort: one pass is completed when no more swaps occur for the gap value. The pass definition is different because the gap value does not compare adjacent elements until the final pass (GAP is one). Observe the activities that occur in the second pass as shown in Figure C.12.

$$GAP = 11 / 2 = 5$$

BEFORE
FIRST PASS

						AFTER FIRST PASS	
B (1)	6	B (1) <= B (6) − S	B (1)	1	B (1) <= B (6) − NC	B (1)	1
B (2)	7	B (2) <= B (7) − NC	B (2)	7	B (2) <= B (7) − NC	B (2)	7
B (3)	2	B (3) <= B (8) − NC	B (3)	2	B (3) <= B (8) − NC	B (3)	2
B (4)	8	B (4) <= B (9) − NC	B (4)	8	B (4) <= B (9) − NC	B (4)	8
B (5)	3	B (5) <= B (10) − NC	B (5)	3	B (5) <= B (10) − NC	B (5)	3
B (6)	1	B (6) <= B (11) − NC	B (6)	6	B (6) <= B (11) − S	B (6)	5
B (7)	12		B (7)	12		B (7)	12
B (8)	4		B (8)	4		B (8)	4
B (9)	8		B (9)	8		B (9)	8
B (10)	4		B (10)	4		B (10)	4
B (11)	5		B (11)	5		B (11)	6

Figure C.11 Shell Sort—First Pass

The comparison process during the second pass is repeated until there is no swap between the array elements. (Not shown. If needed, the reader can walk through the remainder of the second pass.) For the third pass (refer to Figure C.13), gap is divided by 2 and the result is one. At this time, adjacent elements are compared; the last pass of a Shell sort functions exactly the same as a bubble sort.

The array is finally sorted. The array elements are compared one more time in which no swap occurs. The gap value of one is divided by two with a result of 0.5. A fractional result stored in an integer variable is truncated into a final value of zero.

After walking through this solution, it is time to summarize the differences between the bubble sort and the Shell sort.

1. For arrays less than 100 elements, the bubble sort is generally faster than the Shell sort.

2. For larger arrays (greater than 100 elements), the Shell sort is significantly more efficient than the bubble sort.

3. The Shell sort forces a certain number of passes to be executed (until gap is one) even if the array is sorted as the result of an earlier pass.

4. If the values in the array are almost in sorted order initially, the bubble sort is more efficient than the Shell sort.

5. The Shell sort is generally faster than the bubble sort because fewer comparisons are made within the sort process.

GAP = 5/2 = 2

BEFORE SECOND PASS						AFTER SECOND PASS		
B (1)	1	B (1) <= B (3) – NC	B (1)	1	B (1) <= B (3) – NC	B (1)	1
B (2)	7	B (2) <= B (4) – NC	B (2)	7	B (2) <= B (4) – S	B (2)	5
B (3)	2	B (3) <= B (5) – NC	B (3)	2	B (3) <= B (5) – NC	B (3)	2
B (4)	8	B (4) <= B (6) – S	B (4)	5	B (4) <= B (6) – S	B (4)	4
B (5)	3	B (5) <= B (7) – NC	B (5)	3	B (5) <= B (7) – NC	B (5)	3
B (6)	5	B (6) <= B (8) – S	B (6)	4	B (6) <= B (8) – S	B (6)	4
B (7)	12	B (7) <= B (9) – NC	B (7)	8	B (7) <= B (9) – S	B (7)	6
B (8)	4	B (8) <= B (10) – S	B (8)	4	B (8) <= B (10) – NC	B (8)	7
B (9)	8	B (9) <= B (11) – S	B (9)	6	B (9) <= B (11) – NC	B (9)	8
B (10)	4		B (10)	8		B (10)	8
B (11)	6		B (11)	12		B (11)	12

Figure C.12 Shell Sort—Second Pass

GAP = 2/2 = 1

AFTER SECOND PASS   AFTER THIRD PASS

B (1)	1	B (1) <= B (2) – NC	B (1)	1	B (1) <= B (2) – NC	B (1)	1
B (2)	4	B (2) <= B (3) – S	B (2)	2	B (2) <= B (3) – NC	B (2)	2
B (3)	2	B (3) <= B (4) – NC	B (3)	4	B (3) <= B (4) – S	B (3)	3
B (4)	4	B (4) <= B (5) – S	B (4)	3	B (4) <= B (5) – NC	B (4)	4
B (5)	3	B (5) <= B (6) – NC	B (5)	4	B (5) <= B (6) – NC	B (5)	4
B (6)	5	B (6) <= B (7) – NC	B (6)	5	B (6) <= B (7) – NC	B (6)	5
B (7)	6	B (7) <= B (8) – NC	B (7)	6	B (7) <= B (8) – NC	B (7)	6
B (8)	7	B (8) <= B (9) – NC	B (8)	7	B (8) <= B (9) – NC	B (8)	7
B (9)	8	B (9) <= B (10) – NC	B (9)	8	B (9) <= B (10) – NC	B (9)	8
B (10)	8	B (10) <= B (11) – NC	B (10)	8	B (10) <= B (11) – NC	B (10)	8
B (11)	12		B (11)	12		B (11)	12

Figure C.13   Shell Sort—Third Pass

Sorting Problem

Moncrief's Military Manufacturer Corporation assembles tanks and other fighting vehicles for the Department of Defense. In manufacturing these vehicles Moncrief's must deal with over 4000 vendors. Moncrief's keeps information on each of these vendors in a Vendor Information System file. This file contains pertinent data which allows each vendor to be ranked based on satisfaction and performance relating to past business contracts and activities. For reporting purposes each record in the file is sorted on several different fields. Assume that you were asked to develop the logic to sort (use Shell sort techniques) this file in ascending sequence on the vendor name field in each record.

Flowchart Solution

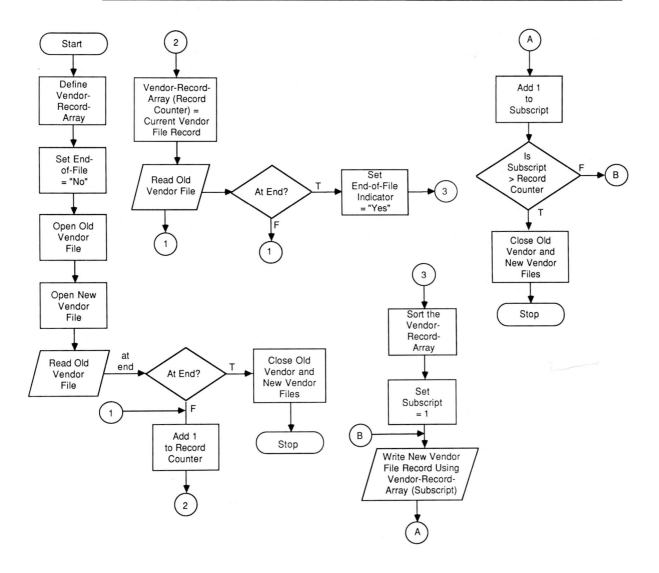

Pseudocode Solution

1. Perform initialization activities:
   -Define a 4500-cell array (VENDOR-RECORD-ARRAY).
   -Set end-of-file indicator = "NO."
   -Open old vendor file.
   -Open new vendor file.
   -Read first old vendor file record.
   -If an end-of-file condition is encountered
        then
             close old vendor file,
             close new vendor file,
             stop processing.
   -Set record counter = 0.
2. Increment record counter by 1.
3. Move the current vendor file record to VENDOR-RECORD-ARRAY (record counter).
4. Read the next vendor file record.
   -If an end-of-file condition is encountered,
        then
             set the end-of-file indicator = "YES."
5. Perform step 2 through step 4 until end-of-file indicator = "YES."
6. Sort the array using the Shell sort technique.
7. Set subscript to 1.
8. Write new vendor file record from VENDOR-RECORD-ARRAY (subscript).
9. Increment subscript by 1.
10. Perform step 8 and step 9 until subscript greater than record counter.
11. Close old vendor file and new vendor file.
12. Stop processing.

Hierarchy Chart Solution

SORT DRIVER
1. Perform initialization activities.
2. Load vendor records to array (VENDOR-RECORD-ARRAY).
3. Sort array on vendor name field.
4. Write new sorted vendor file.
5. Close old vendor file and new vendor file.
6. Stop processing.

INITIALIZATION ACTIVITIES
1. Define a 4500-cell array (VENDOR-RECORD ARRAY).
2. Set end-of-file indicator = "NO."
3. Open old vendor file.
4. Open new vendor file.
5. Read first old vendor file record.
6. If an end-of-file condition is encountered
    then
        close old vendor file,
        close new vendor file,
        stop processing.
7. Set record counter = 0.

LOAD VENDOR RECORDS TO ARRAY
1. Increment record counter by 1.
2. Move the current vendor file record to VENDOR-RECORD-ARRAY (record counter).

READ OLD VENDOR FILE
1. Read old vendor file record.
2. If end-of-file condition is encountered
    then
        set end-of-file indicator = "YES."

SORT ARRAY ON VENDOR NAME FIELD
1. Sort VENDOR-RECORD-ARRAY on the vendor name field using the Shell sort technique.

WRITE NEW SORTED VENDOR FILE
1. Write new vendor file record from VENDOR-RECORD-ARRAY (subscript) for the range subscript = 1 to record counter.

(continued)

(continued)

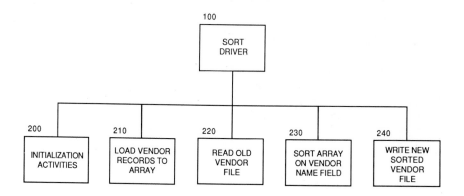

IPO Chart Solution

<u>OUTPUT COLUMN</u>

1. New (sorted) vendor file

<u>INPUT COLUMN</u>

1. Vendor file
    -Vendor number
    -Vendor name
    -Various vendor fields

<u>PROCESS COLUMN</u>

1. Perform initialization activities:
    -Define a 4500-cell array (VENDOR-RECORD-ARRAY).
    -Set end-of-file indicator = "NO."
    -Open old vendor file.
    -Open new vendor file.
    -Read first old vendor file record.
    -If an end-of-file condition is encountered
        then
            close old vendor file,
            close new vendor file,
            stop processing.
    -Set record counter = 0.
2. Increment record counter by 1.
3. Move the current vendor file record to VENDOR-RECORD-ARRAY (record counter).
4. Read the next vendor file record.
    -If an end-of-file condition is encountered,
        then
            set the end-of-file indicator = "YES."
5. Perform step 2 through step 4 until end-of-file indicator = "YES."
6. Sort the array using the Shell sort technique.
7. Set subscript to 1.
8. Write new vendor file record from VENDOR-RECORD-ARRAY (subscript).
9. Increment subscript by 1.
10. Perform step 8 and step 9 until subscript greater than record counter.
11. Close old vendor file and new vendor file.
12. Stop processing.

Structure Chart Solution

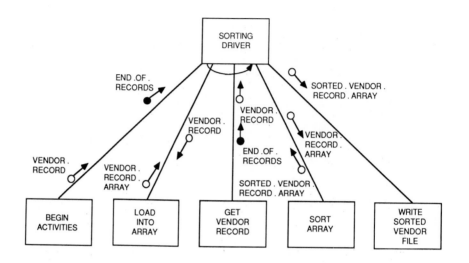

```
<<DATA DICTIONARY>>
```

```
VENDOR.RECORD
     VENDOR.NUMBER               NNNN
     VENDOR.NAME                 C(30)
     VARIOUS VENDOR FIELDS       C(?)
```

```
MISCELLANEOUS.VARIABLES
     END.OF.RECORDS                  CCC
     SUB                             NNNN
     GAP                             NNNN
     RECORD.CTR                      NNNN
     NUM.OF.ARRAY.ELEMENTS           NNNN
     ITEMS.SORTED.SWITCH             CCC
```

```
VENDOR.RECORD.ARRAY OCCURS 4500 TIMES
     VRA.VENDOR.NUMBER           NNNN
     VRA.VENDOR.NAME             C(30)
     VARIOUS VENDOR FIELDS       C(?)
```

```
TEMP.RECORD
     TR.VENDOR.NUMBER            NNNN
     TR.VENDOR.NAME              C(30)
     VARIOUS VENDOR FIELDS       C(?)
```

```
<<MODULE PSEUDOCODE>>

SORTING DRIVER
   CALL BEGIN ACTIVITIES
   WHILE END.OF.RECORDS = "NO"
     CALL LOAD INTO ARRAY
     CALL GET VENDOR RECORD
   END OF WHILE LOOP
   CALL SORT ARRAY
   CALL WRITE SORTED VENDOR FILE


BEGIN ACTIVITIES
   END.OF.RECORDS = "NO"

   OPEN VENDOR FILE

   READ FIRST VENDOR FILE RECORD
   IF END OF FILE THEN
      END.OF.RECORDS = "YES"

   RECORD.CTR = 0


LOAD INTO ARRAY
   RECORD.CTR = RECORD.CTR + 1
   VENDOR.RECORD.ARRAY [RECORD.CTR] = VENDOR.RECORD


GET VENDOR RECORD
   READ VENDOR FILE RECORD
   IF END OF FILE THEN
      END.OF.RECORDS = "YES"
```

(continued)

```
SORT ARRAY
NUM.OF.ARRAY.ELEMENTS = RECORD.CTR
GAP = NUM.OF.ARRAY.ELEMENTS / 2

WHILE GAP <> 0
    ITEMS.SORTED.SWITCH = "NO"
    WHILE ITEMS.SORTED.SWITCH = "NO"
        SUB = 1
        ITEMS.SORTED.SWITCH = "YES"
        WHILE SUB <= NUM.OF.ARRAY.ELEMENTS - GAP
            IF VRA.VENDOR.NAME [SUB] <= VRA.VENDOR.NAME [SUB + GAP] THEN
                NO ACTION
            ELSE
                TEMP.RECORD = VENDOR.RECORD.ARRAY [SUB]
                VENDOR.RECORD.ARRAY [SUB] = VENDOR.RECORD.ARRAY [SUB + GAP]
                VENDOR.RECORD.ARRAY [SUB + GAP] = TEMP.RECORD
                ITEMS.SORTED.SWITCH = "NO"
            ENDIF
            SUB = SUB + 1
        END OF WHILE LOOP
    END OF WHILE LOOP
    GAP = GAP / 2
END OF WHILE LOOP


WRITE SORTED VENDOR FILE
    OPEN NEW VENDOR RECORD FILE

    FOR SUB = 1 TO RECORD.CTR
        VENDOR.RECORD = VENDOR.RECORD.ARRAY [SUB]
        WRITE NEW VENDOR.RECORD
    END OF FOR LOOP
```

Nassi-Shneiderman Chart Solution

<<DATA DICTIONARY>>

VENDOR.RECORD
    VENDOR.NUMBER   NNNN
    VENDOR.NAME   C(30)
    VARIOUS VENDOR FIELDS   C(?)

VENDOR.RECORD.ARRAY OCCURS 4500 TIMES
    VRA.VENDOR.NUMBER   NNNN
    VRA.VENDOR.NAME   C(30)
    VARIOUS VENDOR FIELDS   C(?)

TEMP.RECORD
    TR.VENDOR.NUMBER   NNNN
    TR.VENDOR.NAME   C(30)
    VARIOUS VENDOR FIELDS   C(?)

MISCELLANEOUS.VARIABLES
    END.OF.RECORDS   CCC
    SUB   NNNN
    GAP   NNNN
    RECORD.CTR   NNNN
    NUM.OF.ARRAY.ELEMENTS   NNNN
    ITEMS.SORTED.SWITCH   CCC

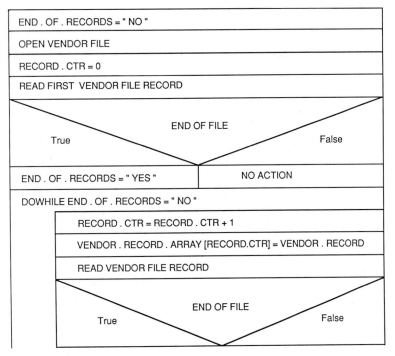

(continued)

(continued)

	END . OF . RECORDS = " YES "	NO ACTION
	END OF DOWHILE LOOP	

NUM . OF . ARRAY . ELEMENTS = RECORD . CTR

GAP = NUM . OF . ARRAY . ELEMENTS / 2

WHILE GAP < > 0

    ITEMS . SORTED . SWITCH = " NO "

    WHILE ITEMS . SORTED . SWITCH = " NO "

        SUB = 1

        ITEMS . SORTED . SWITCH = " YES "

        WHILE SUB < = NUM . OF . ARRAY . ELEMENTS – GAP

VRA . VENDOR . NAME [SUB] < = VRA . VENDOR . NAME [SUB + GAP]	
True	False
NO ACTION	TEMP . RECORD = VENDOR. RECORD . ARRAY [SUB]
	VENDOR . RECORD . ARRAY [SUB] = VENDOR . RECORD . ARRAY [SUB + GAP]
	VENDOR . RECORD . ARRAY [SUB + GAP] = TEMP . RECORD
	ITEMS . SORTED . SWITCH = " NO "

        SUB = SUB + 1

        END OF WHILE LOOP

    END OF WHILE LOOP

GAP = GAP / 2

END OF WHILE LOOP

(continued)

(continued)

OPEN NEW VENDOR RECORD FILE		
FOR SUB = 1 TO RECORD . CTR		
	VENDOR . RECORD = VENDOR . RECORD . ARRAY [SUB]	
	WRITE NEW VENDOR . RECORD	
	END OF FOR LOOP	

Warnier-Orr Diagram Solution

```
<<DATA DICTIONARY>>
```

VENDOR.RECORD
    VENDOR.NUMBER   NNNN
    VENDOR.NAME   C(30)
    VARIOUS VENDOR FIELDS   C(?)

VENDOR.RECORD.ARRAY OCCURS 4500 TIMES
    VRA.VENDOR.NUMBER   NNNN
    VRA.VENDOR.NAME   C(30)
    VARIOUS VENDOR FIELDS   C(?)

TEMP.RECORD
    TR.VENDOR.NUMBER   NNNN
    TR.VENDOR.NAME   C(30)
    VARIOUS VENDOR FIELDS   C(?)

MISCELLANEOUS.VARIABLES
    END.OF.RECORDS   CCC
    SUB   NNNN
    GAP   NNNN
    RECORD.CTR   NNNN
    NUM.OF.ARRAY.ELEMENTS   NNNN
    ITEMS.SORTED.SWITCH   CCC

(continued)

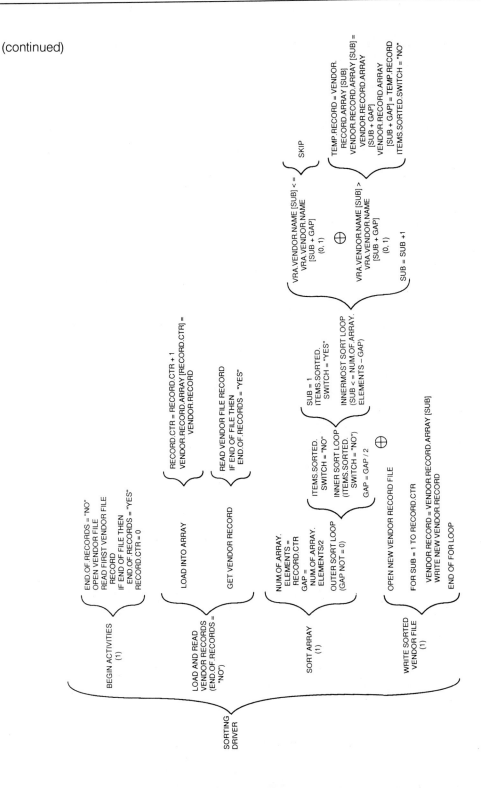

EXERCISES

1. Write the logic to load a 20-element array with integer values and sort the array in ascending order using the bubble sort technique.

2. Perform the same functions as in problem 1 but change the order to descending using the Shell sort algorithm.

3. Using the Shell sort technique, sort a 200-element array consisting of numbers in ascending order and print the highest number and lowest number.

4. Sort a 50-element character array consisting of employee last names in ascending order. Print all employees whose last name begins with the letter M.

5. Write the logic needed to sort Harry and Larry's file as specified by the instructions in problem 6–5.

6. Refer to problem 7–1. Write the logic to sort Vic's file in descending order by date rented. Date rented is stored in YYMMDD format where YY is year, MM is month, and DD is day.

7. Write the logic to sort the file in problem 8–3 by team name and player name.

Index